Bible-based resources for youth groups

# YOU'D BETTER BELIEVE IT!

**Ten sessions on Doctrine for 13-18 year olds**

Written by Alan Hewerdine, Phil Moon and Steve Tilley

Edited by Mark Tomlinson

# YOU'D BETTER BELIEVE IT!

## WHAT'S IT ALL ABOUT

As Christians it is vital that we make every effort to understand the Bible. This requires us to identify the main doctrines and do as much as we can to understand them. Christian Doctrine, like a precious stone such as a diamond, has many facets. But it should also be seen as a whole to be fully appreciated.

'YOU'D BETTER BELIEVE IT!', aims to help you to understand and teach some of these doctrines.

Although the book can be taught as individual sessions, it is also important to see how they fit together as part of the whole picture.

In a book such as this we are only able to scratch the surface. You will need to supplement the material here with further reading. There are many very good books on doctrine available, so check out your local Christian book shop.

## WHAT'S IN IT?

# NOTES FOR YOUTH LEADERS

## How you might use this book

'YOU'D BETTER BELIEVE IT!' has been written in ten individual sessions, each looking at a different element of Christian doctrine. Although it is possible to teach each one of these as a totally separate and individual session, your group members will benefit more from studying a specific session over consecutive weeks together with the other sessions that complement it.

For this reason we have arranged the book into four Modules and we suggest that you teach the sessions within a Module on consecutive weeks and then take a break for a week or two before returning to do another Module, rather then doing all ten sessions consecutively.

This will give you the opportunity to use other resources such as 'Pressure Points', and 'Harping On', both published by CPAS and COVENANTERS, during the weeks in-between.

## Running Individual Sessions

Each session is laid out in a standard way as if eating a special meal.

### PREPARATION

A lot of work goes on before the guests receive the menu. There is cutlery and crockery to select, the table to lay and cooking to do. All these things represent leader's preparation time. Badly prepared meals can do harm rather than good. So can badly prepared Bible teaching sessions. Take time to prepare by using the 'Laying The Table', 'Equipment' and 'Cooking' sections of each session.

### SELECT AND ADAPT

Towards the beginning of each session is a menu which tells you all the things available in the session. Most of us don't eat everything on the menu when we go into a restaurant; we make choices. A balanced meal includes things to enjoy and things that are good for us. Take the same selective approach as you plan your Bible teaching from this book. Choose what will be good for your group; adapt things that won't be exactly to your group's taste. And be as sensible as you would in a restaurant. Once in a lifetime you may skip the main course and have three puddings, but don't make a habit of it. Please also note that our timings in the menu are only approximate for guidance when preparing.

### PRAYER AND WORSHIP

Each session also includes 'Grace' and 'Music' - some creative ideas for praying in your group and suggestions for music to use in worship.

### TAKEAWAYS

The 'Takeaways' sheets are for you to photocopy and give out. They will help your group to remember the session by joining in the activities and having something to take home and keep.

### RELATIONSHIPS

This resource should help you with part of your work. It won't help you in the harder task of spending time with your group members outside the meeting. The best youth work is relationship based. If what you teach and the way you behave outside meetings are consistent then your youth group will listen to you and remember you. In fact they will remember you long after they forget everything you ever said to them. As you share the Gospel with young people share your life with them as well.

# Who Am I?

## TEACHING POINT

**To teach that human beings are a unique part of God's creation.**

## GROUP ACTION

**For members to understand that every individual is equally valued in God's sight.**

MENU

**GRACE**

**Chaos** 8 minutes.

**STARTERS**

**Bits and Pieces** 5 minutes

**Feet First** 5 minutes

**MAIN COURSE**

**Images** 7 minutes

**Responsibility** 7 minutes

**What Makes Me Tick** 5 minutes

**Nature** 8 minutes

**PUDDING**

**Lifelines** 10 minutes

**CHEESE AND BISCUITS**

**Scruples** 10 minutes – one hour plus

**I Woke Up This Morning** 4 minutes

**Who am I** 8 minutes

**THE BILL**

**Playing God** 5 minutes

## LAYING THE TABLE

This teaching session has a number of short activities. Why not emphasise that the whole session will be done with short items. It might make a change from the usual format, especially if your group is used to a talk every week. God created us all different so why not have a lot of different items to make the point.

## EQUIPMENT

- ✔ Bibles for everyone
- ✔ Music for 'Chaos' and 'I Woke Up This Morning'
- ✔ Measuring Tape for 'Bits and Pieces'
- ✔ Blanket for 'Feet First'
- ✔ Pictures, photos etc. for 'Images'
- ✔ OHP or large sheets of paper and appropriate pens
- ✔ Copies of 'Takeaways' sheet and pencils for 'What Makes Me Tick?'
- ✔ Pencils, paper and Polaroid camera for 'Lifelines'
- ✔ Scruples game for 'Scruples'

## MUSIC

The Earth Is The Lords And Everything In It

Ah Lord God

Jesus Is Lord, Creation's Voice .....

I Am A New Creation

Such Love, Pure As The .....

## COOKING

People are very quick to do themselves down. The world seems so big that we can't believe we have any part to play in it. More weight is given to this pessimistic view of humanity if we see ourselves as no more than clever monkeys. But Christians believe that every human being is unique and special. Christians believe that God made us in his own image and gave us a unique responsibility to look after his world. That is what this session will explore.

If you want to do some good background reading on the doctrine of humanity why not try the section in John Balchin's, 'What Christians Believe', or John Allan's excellent book, 'The Human Difference'. For a longer Bible study the New International Version 'Disciple's Study Bible' follows through key doctrines with study notes on each one. To go into the subject in a different way look at the section on Psalm 8 in 'Harping On?', also from CPAS and Covenanters.

## GRACE

**CHAOS**

Read **Genesis 1:1-31** whilst some music is playing. Choose a piece of music that seems discordant at the beginning but resolves into harmony. If you have a good musician who could do this live it would be even better.

## STARTERS

### BITS AND PIECES

Stress the difference between people by measuring each other. Who has the biggest smile? Who has the smallest hands? The longest nails? Look for tricks members can do with their bodies. Is anyone double-jointed? Who has the most unusual hair colour? (Beware of making fun of anyone who is sensitive about their appearance. It's probably best not to have a 'Who has the most spots' or a 'best/worst dressed member' competition)

### FEET FIRST

Get four volunteers to hide behind a large blanket exposing just one foot. Have a competition to identify the owners.

**After either of these games make the point that we are all individuals.**

## MAIN COURSE

### IMAGES

People are the final point of God's creative activity in Genesis. God's first six days of creation were:

| | |
|---|---|
| **Day 1** | Light |
| **Day 2** | Sky |
| **Day 3** | Land and plants |
| **Day 4** | Sun, moon and stars |
| **Day 5** | Sea creatures and birds |
| **Day 6** | Land animals |

**But at the end of day six God created human beings in his own image.**

Have a variety of images of well-known people available. Use newspaper photos, cartoons, paintings, your own photos, posters or video. See who can recognise the most. Summarise by stressing that you have only been dealing with images, the real people were not in the room.

Make the point that we are all images; images of God. Read **Genesis 1:27**. Then read **Genesis 2:7** which balances this by reminding us that we are created out of dust. (**Psalm 103:14-16** also makes this point).

Although we will see in subsequent sessions that the image is spoiled by sin, stress the positive aspects in this session. Perhaps look at **Colossians 3:9-11** which reminds us that Christians are people in the process of having their images restored.

### RESPONSIBILITY

God gave humans responsibility to go with our position in creation. Brainstorm things that your group members think are their responsibilities, then compare their list with the specific responsibilities in **Genesis 1 and 2**. See if your group can find them:

1. Be fruitful and increase in number. (Yes, sex was the first thing God talked about, see **1:28a**).
2. Rule over the other creatures (But at this stage no mention is made of eating them, see **1:28b**)
3. Work and take care of the garden (**2:15**)
4. Don't eat from the tree of knowledge (**2:17**)

We are responsible for God's world. We are to look after the land and rule over the other creatures, keep the population going and not cross the boundaries God has set.

### WHAT MAKES ME TICK?

If you have a Polaroid camera take photos of each member of the group while they are filling out the 'Takeaways' sheet. Then display the sheets on the wall or board for everyone to see, sticking the photos next to the cartoons that have been drawn. (If anyone in your group is good at cartoons then they could do a drawing of each member, either during this section, or before the meeting and bring them along as a surprise). Discuss the interesting answers.

### NATURE

Prepare a short talk, or be prepared to lead a Bible search, on the following four points about the nature of God's human creation:

**1. Physical nature.**

The body is God's gift. It will die (**2 Peter 1:13-15**). Resurrected humans will receive a resurrected body (**1 Corinthians 15:42-44**).

**2. Spiritual nature.**

There is in human nature an inbuilt desire to respond to God. Look at some of the passages in Job (try **Job 1:20,21** or **Job 23:13-17**) where Job tries to come to terms with the suffering he has to endure. This might also be an opportunity to read some of the more obscure passages about the construction of the Temple in **1 Chronicles 28 - 2 Chronicles 4**. This desire to please God by building such a Temple is because of the spiritual human nature. We want to respond to God.

**3. Intellectual nature.**

Read **Proverbs 1:1-7**. Humans have been given minds and are expected to use them, in God's service. However God's word is wiser than any human wisdom and any attempt to do things by human wisdom alone will fail (See **Ecclesiastes 1:12-14**).

**4. Psychological nature.**

Humans also have feelings and emotions. We are more than just physical. (A random selection from the Psalms should illustrate this clearly).We can enter into relationships. We can share joys and sorrows. We can develop commitments (e.g. marriage, working relationships). Indeed a commitment to a partner is God's clear intention (**Genesis 2:21-25**).

---

## PUDDING

### LIFELINES

Encourage your group to think about their future by charting the key moments of their lives so far on a large piece of paper and then anticipating what will come next. Make sure each chart includes references to birth, childhood, relationships, work and death. If your group are not so good at written work then you could do the charting, or break into smaller groups and have one person in each group responsible for the charting.

Emphasise that we can all have exciting plans for our lives, but only God knows the right time for things to happen (**Ecclesiastes 3:1-8**). It is more important for us to use each God given opportunity as it comes along than it is to worry about the length of our lives (**Matthew 6:25-27**).

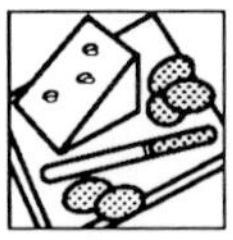

CHEESE & BISCUITS

### SCRUPLES

This game is available in good toy shops and games shops. It is quite expensive but one of your members may have it. The idea is to discuss your reaction to various dilemmas and for others to vote on whether they think you are being honest or not. Good as an introduction to the section on responsibility.

### I WOKE UP THIS MORNING

Get all the group members to squash into a huge pile of bodies on the floor. Say that you will give a command for them to live and they must animate. Let them role-play their own creation, discovering their bodies and then discovering each other. Good for the more dramatically inclined groups. Do this to music if you want. Don't let it go on too long, and remember to debrief. What did it feel like? Did anything surprise people?

### WHO AM I

This game is ideal for introducing the title of this session and requires no equipment.

The idea of the game is for you to choose a famous person, but keep his/her identity secret. Your group members should then be divided into two teams and they have ten questions each to ask you, to which you can only answer 'yes' or 'no', and they must identify who you are thinking of before their questions run out.

Play two or three rounds before getting into the meeting.

---

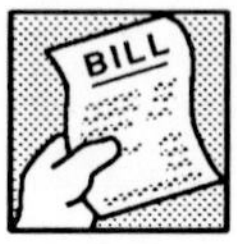


THE BILL

### PLAYING GOD

Over the years many people have tried to play God, predict God, outwit God. But God knows us better than we know ourselves. There won't have been many moments of quiet if you have tried a lot of this session's activities, so end with a challenge to members to look at areas of their lives where they try to play God, or fail to give God the glory.

# Takeaways

**Draw yourself here, firstly as you see yourself, then as you would like others to see you.**

**1.**

**2.**

**3.** (space for your own photo)

**Fill in this 'What Makes Me Tick?' questionnaire:**

Who knows me best? ..........................................................................................................

What are my 'distinguishing features'? ..................................................................................

What is my most treasured possession? ..................................................................................

What personal quality am I glad to have? ...............................................................................

What is my aim in life? .........................................................................................................

What is the best thing I ever did? .........................................................................................

Who would I most like to meet? ............................................................................................

What year do I expect to die? ...............................................................................................

# God - Holy, Sovereign, Creator

## TEACHING POINT

**To show that the only credible explanation of our very existence is to believe in a holy God who created us and rules over us.**

## GROUP ACTION

**Members should have a greater realisation of who God is and of their value to him.For the group to understand that the appropriate response to such a holy God is to worship him.**

MENU

**GRACE**
- **Map Prayers** 7 minutes
- **Atlas Prayers** 7 minutes

**STARTERS**
- **Creativity** 12 minutes
- **Holiness** 6 minutes
- **The Perfect Leader** 5 minutes

**MAIN COURSE**
- **Woe To Me** 5 minutes
- **Mirror Moves** 5 minutes
- **Queen For The Day** 10 minutes

**PUDDING**
- **Props** 10—30 minutes

**CHEESE & BISCUITS**
- **Lord's Prayer** 2 minutes
- **Doodles** 3 minutes

**THE BILL**
- **Be Still** 5 minutes

## LAYING THE TABLE

There will be two sessions on the doctrine of God, but they are not consecutive. Module three, session one will look at God as loving, caring and acting as it fits better into the structure if you look at it when covering the cross and the resurrection. This session looks again at creation, but looking out towards God rather than in towards ourselves.

This session will point towards worship. If your meetings normally include a time of prayer, praise and singing then it is suggested that this happens at the end of the session.

## EQUIPMENT

- ✔ An old map and/or atlas for 'Grace'
- ✔ Various materials for 'Creativity'
- ✔ OHP and pens, or large sheets of paper and markers
- ✔ Card and marker pens for 'The Perfect Leader'
- ✔ Copies of 'Takeaways' sheet for 'Mirror Moves'
- ✔ Red and yellow cards, plus props for 'Props'
- ✔ Music and soft lights for 'Props'
- ✔ A whistle for 'Lord's Prayer'
- ✔ Pencils and a prize for 'Doodles'

## MUSIC

Father We Adore You
Holy, Holy, Holy Is The Lord
Lord, The Light Of Your Love Is Shining
I Will Sing Unto The Lord
Jesus, We Enthrone You

## COOKING

We are not embarking on a session of 'worm' theology; thinking of ourselves as worms is to devalue the pinnacle of God's creation — human beings. However, when we concentrate on the holiness, sovereignty and creativity of God we will inevitably feel rather small. If this session follows on from one where you have looked carefully at the doctrine of humanity then it will serve as a good balance. If you are doing this session as a one-off beware of putting people down without building them up again.

We are unworthy to stand before God in our own right, but Jesus has broken that barrier down. We should still be aware of God's justice — one day he will judge us, but also be aware that he wants a personal relationship with each one of us through the death and resurrection of Jesus.

## GRACE

Prayers and singing will fit best at the end of the session. Prepare some songs that focus on God as creator, or as the Holy One. Ask members to think of one sentence prayers thanking God for some aspect of his creation.

### MAP PRAYERS

If you have an old map or atlas of Britain then tear it up and give it to your group, perhaps working in small groups of three if necessary.

Ask them to think of things to thank God for, or ask him for, as prompted by that map page, e.g. people who live in remote areas; people who drive long distances; thank God for areas of beauty like the Lake District, the Scottish Highlands or the Cornish Coast.

### ATLAS PRAYERS

Do the same as in 'Map Prayers' but use an atlas instead. In small groups, pray for those countries you come across.

For specific information on individual countries, use OM's book, 'Operation World'. This might help with items for prayer.

## STARTERS

### CREATIVITY

Bring something into existence that didn't exist at the start of the meeting. Maybe some people could spend a few moments composing a short tune on guitar or keyboard; others could do a quick painting or drawing, a poem or some sculpture with plasticine or fimo. Most popular of all would be if someone could quickly knock up some chocolate cake or biscuits using one of the no-cook recipes available.

Discuss the difference between our creativity and God's. We do the best we can with pre-existing ingredients (notes, words, plasticine, chocolate whereas God creates 'ex nihilo' (out of nothing). (Read **Genesis 1:1,2**)

### HOLINESS

Talk about people the group know, or have met, who seem to be holy. What are their attributes? List them on the OHP or a large sheet of paper. Compare these people with the sort of holiness God demonstrates.

### THE PERFECT LEADER

What would be the attributes of the perfect youth group leader?

Do a large drawing of a person on card. Get the group to add features necessary for perfection; an inexhaustible supply of jokes, stories and illustrations; no ears to hear abuse; lots of pockets to hold keys, lost property, games, Bible, notes etc. Go on! Be daft. It's only an ice-breaker.

Contrast the allegedly perfect leader with the holiness and sovereignty of God.

## MAIN COURSE

### WOE TO ME

There are several illustrations in the Bible of places where sinful humans met with God. Look up these examples:

- Moses: required to remove his sandals because he was standing on holy ground (**Exodus 3:5**)
- Isaiah: felt he was 'ruined' because he saw the holy God (**Isaiah 6:1-5**)
- John (the Divine): his vision of heaven included living creatures who never stopped saying 'Holy, holy, holy is the Lord...' day and night (**Revelation 4:8**).

The difference between us and God is that he is holy and we are not. It is, 'the unique quality of God's existence that marks him off as separate from all else.' (J. Terry Young, 'N.I.V. Disciples Study Bible'). The only way we can talk about human beings as holy is in their relationship to God.

**MIRROR MOVES**

Get the group to work with a partner. It should be someone they can trust. Stand facing each other and as one person moves the other mirrors their actions. These actions should be smooth and gentle; the exercise is hard enough without jerks. After a couple of minutes swap roles so the other person leads.

Partners then sit down and share how the exercise felt to do. Ask the two's to go on to talk about what this has to do with holiness. Hopefully some will cotton on to the idea of copying God; looking to him for a model of behaviour.

Fill in the check sheet on the 'Takeaways' sheet and use it to talk through the ideas of God members have. Be prepared to correct, gently, any that are inappropriate. Also be ready to stress good things that have come out of this exercise. Look particularly for good contributions from members who are shy or quiet, to encourage them.

**QUEEN FOR THE DAY**

Work in fours. If you were Queen for the Day what would you do? You can pass one new law and require two further things to be done for you. Spend five minutes making the decisions and then share results if there is more than one group.

God is sovereign over his creation, but he respects free will. He works in history, although not necessarily in the way we want. Read **Isaiah 60:21**. God wants his people to reflect his glory. His purpose will be carried out but we must remember God can work either in light years or split seconds. He can change the landscape with an earthquake or a snowflake.

In 'Shine Jesus, Shine', Graham Kendrick wrote:

> 'As we gaze on your kingly brightness
> So our faces display your likeness
> Ever changing from glory to glory
> Mirrored here may our lives tell your story
> Shine on me...'

So draw out the point that God's sovereignty is very different to the way we would act if we were in charge. We see the sovereignty of God only fleetingly. For everyone who thanks God for the wonder of his kingship there is another who wonders why God does not intervene. We can only understand God from our human perspective. It is like seeing a reflection in a mirror (make the connection with the mirroring exercise if you did it earlier in the session). One day we will see clearly (Read **1 Corinthians 13:12**)

---

PUDDING

**PROPS**

The popular TV improvisation game 'Whose Line Is It Anyway?' includes a game called 'Props'. Pairs are given an unusual prop (Large pieces of kitchen apparatus are particularly useful for this and may be available in your church hall). They then have to think of as many new uses for this prop as possible. Score a point for each new use in one minute. Make referees' yellow and red cards to show for any rude suggestions. Pairs lose a point for a yellow card and their turn ends if they get a red.

After the game read some of **Job 38-41**, quietly. Allow people to be amazed by the variety of God's creativity compared to their struggle in the game. If your group can cope with a long reading then why not read it all with some atmospheric music and dimmed lights. It would make a good start to your special time of worship.

## CHEESE & BISCUITS

**LORD'S PRAYER**

Use the Lord's prayer during the 'Main Course' section on God's holiness. When you get to the second line, 'hallowed be your name' blow a whistle very loud and refuse to continue until someone tells you what it means. Be prepared to tell them yourself if they don't know.

To hallow something is to set something apart for holy use (from the Greek word 'hagiazo'). When we hallow God's name we give him the recognition he deserves and acknowledge his superiority.

**DOODLES**

When you photocopy the 'Takeaways' sheet put a small, identical doodle on each sheet. Award a silly prize for the most creative picture using the doodle as an integral part. A packet of wax crayons would be a suitable prize, or a postcard of some famous painting. Use this to lead into any discussion on creativity, or to emphasise the points made earlier.

## THE BILL

**BE STILL**

God is knowable, because he has revealed himself uniquely in Jesus. We can know Jesus because he is alive and because he speaks to us from the pages of the Bible.

To avoid focusing on our own inadequacy we should spend time in quiet prayer thinking about some aspect of God we have looked at in the session, then lead into open prayer and music as suggested in 'Grace'.

# Takeaways

| When I think of God I imagine... |
| --- |
| The three words I am most likely to use to describe God are... |
| The part of God's creation I am most impressed by is... |
| The part of God's creation I find hardest to understand is... |
| When I get to heaven I will ask  God... |
| The Bible verse that most encourages me when I think of God is... |

# Sin
# - The Heart of the Matter

## TEACHING POINT

**To teach that every part of everyone rebels against God and that this damages all relationships.**

## GROUP ACTION

**For group members to come to terms with their own sinfulness and their need to repent.**

MENU

**GRACE**
**Confession** 5 minutes

**STARTERS**
**Graffiti Board** 5 minutes or as people enter
**Black Evening** Preparation time

**MAIN COURSE**
**Sin Search** 20 minutes
**The Extent of Sin** 5 minutes

**PUDDING**
**The Effects of Sin** 15 minutes

**CHEESE & BISCUITS**
**Tear Out** 5/7 minutes
**Whopper** 10 minutes
**Memory Verses** 1 minute

**THE BILL**
**Sin Chart** 3 minutes

## LAYING THE TABLE

This is the first of two sessions on sin. Although it is possible to do just one of the sessions on its own, you will find it far more helpful to do both of them, as they form an integrated whole and are intended to complement each other.

This session looks at the nature, extent and effects of sin and contains a lot of material, so prune what is available and keep it moving. The subject matter is also fairly heavy so don't make the session any heavier than it needs to be by being over long.

The second session, 'Sin - Truth Decay', focusses on the Fall in **Genesis 3**.

## EQUIPMENT

- ✔ Bibles
- ✔ Copies of past newspapers, including some tabloids
- ✔ Graffiti board and pens
- ✔ Black edged handouts, clothes etc. for a 'Black Evening'
- ✔ Bin liners for newspaper rubbish
- ✔ A cake or some other foodstuff with salt in it
- ✔ OHP/screen or cards for Bible verses
- ✔ If no OHP, large sheet of paper for brainstorming

## MUSIC

God Forgave My Sin In Jesus Name

There Is A Redeamer

For This Purpose Christ Was Revealed

Give Thanks With A Grateful Heart

O Lord, The Clouds Are Gathering

## COOKING

The biblical teaching on sin is the most satisfactory way of explaining the state of the world today. We are not just a product of our environment and our upbringing. Not everyone from bad housing becomes an equally bad person. Not everyone with bad experiences of parenthood becomes a bad parent. There is more to it than that. Sin is complex. There is a connection between sin and illness, but it is not straightforward. It is not a case of 'what did I do to deserve this?'

## GRACE

**CONFESSION**

Lead your group in a short time of prayer, asking forgiveness for their sins, and thanking Jesus for his death. Ask group members to screw up their 'sins', and throw them in a bin. Or best of all if your group meet in a home with an open fire, throw them on the fire.

## STARTERS

**GRAFFITI BOARD**

As your members arrive, have a 'Graffiti Board' titled 'What's wrong with the World?' up in a prominent place. Have some suitable pens available, and ask for contributions. You may like to start the ball rolling yourself with some witty and humorous comment. Near the start of the meeting make reference to this, and make sure you defuse any of the more unpleasant contributions that name other group members!

**BLACK EVENING**

Another possibility is to have a 'Black Evening'. Whilst the Bible uses images of light and darkness to contrast good and evil and we can, therefore, legitimately do the same, be VERY CAREFUL NOT to convey the impression that black people should be associated with evil. If in doubt leave it out! As one of the effects of sin is death, have as many black things as possible in the meeting. Ask group members to wear as much black as possible, and do so yourself. Maybe have black edged invitations to the meeting. Have a black border on the OHP and any handouts you use. Only have black tea and coffee and decorate the room with black pieces of paper.

---

## MAIN COURSE

**SIN SEARCH**

Tell your members that this evening is even more serious than usual. It's relevant for everyone and there are serious consequences for everyone. You may want to draw attention to the 'Graffiti Board' and point out that no-one suggested that there wasn't anything wrong with the world. This session reveals what the Bible (and therefore God) says is wrong with the world.

In essence, sin is a rejection of God's authority over us and trying to put ourselves in God's place. The Bible uses a number of different words to describe what sin is. The list below translates different words in the original Bible language (Hebrew or Greek) and all of them help to explain what sin is.

Ask your members to look up the following references, and see what they have to tell us about sin, or divide up into smaller groups and give each group a couple of verses to look up, or give a short talk outlining the main points below.

**Psalm 51.9, Exodus 32:30** (chatatth, or chett)
The commonest word for sin in the Old Testament, meaning missing the mark or erring.

**Proverbs 28:13** (pesha)
Active rebellion, trespass of God's will.

**Leviticus 4:13** (shagah)
Going astray.

**1 Kings 17:18** (awon)
To twist or distort giving the idea of guilt which sin produces

**Matthew 1:21** (hamartia)
Missing the mark, failure, fault, concrete wrongdoing.

**Romans 4:15** (parabasis)
Breaking the law.

**1 Corinthians 6:8** (adikia)
Unrighteousness or injustice.

**Titus 2:12** (asebia)
Godlessness.

**James 2:10** (ptaio)
Moral stumble.

**1 John 3:4** (anomia)
Lawlessness.

If you use group work here make sure everyone has a chance to learn from the other groups, and that you are clear what you want them to be finding out, so that when they feedback, no important points are missed out.

Complete this section by highlighting one other very important verse - **Psalm 51:4** points to the fact that sin is something we do first and foremost against God. This is very important for our groups to understand. Make sure they have grasped this point.

**THE EXTENT OF SIN**

In this shorter teaching segment we want to show our groups that sin is universal. It affects every part of everyone.

To illustrate this point before turning to the Bible, have a baked cake prepared beforehand but with a good deal of salt or food colouring used in it. At this point in the session cut it up and give each member a piece, instructing them not to eat it until you say. On your permission, they all eat and hopefully are all disgusted. Explain that this is a picture of sin. Every piece of cake was infected, and every part of the human personality is infected with sin.

Using the key verses below, either give a short talk (no more than four minutes), or simply start a group discussion by asking what they reveal about the extent of sin.

**Psalm 14:1-3 Romans 3:10 Isaiah 64:6 Romans 3:23**

Sin affects every part of us, 'total depravity' - this doesn't mean that we are as bad as we can be, but that every part of us is affected.

Sin affects our:

- Will - **John 8:34** (Also **Romans 7:14-24**)
- Mind - **Ephesians 4:17, 18**
- Affections/Emotions - **2 Timothy 3:4** (Also **Romans 1:24-27**)
- Speech/Behaviour - **Galatians 5:19-21** (also **Mark 7:21-23**).
- Personality - **Jeremiah 17:9** (Also **Romans 7:23**).

---

PUDDING

**THE EFFECTS OF SIN**

Start this teaching segment by brainstorming the effects of sin. By this stage in the meeting your young people should know enough of the subject to be able to come up with a reasonable list.

Begin by asking them to jot down their own list of the effects of sin, then brainstorm these onto an OHP/sheet of paper. Now tell them that the Bible tells us that the effects of sin are actually far wider than they imagine.

The structure which follows is from Bruce Milne's 'Know the Truth' (IVP 1982). Ask your group either individually or in small groups to match the Bible verses with each relationship sin destroys. Use the 'Takeaways' sheet for this.

**1. With God**

- Unfit for God's presence (**Genesis 3:23, Romans 1:18**).
- Unable to do God's will (**John 8:34, Romans 7:15 -21**).
- Unrighteous before God's law (**Galatians 3:10, Ephesians 2:1-3**).
- Insensitive to God's Word (**2 Corinthians 4:4**).

**2. With Others**

- Sin produces conflict, division, prejudice, exploitation, fear, weakness, misunderstanding (**Genesis 3:12, Genesis 4:1-16**).

**3. With Myself**

- Sin results in inner conflict, and people cannot accept themselves (**Romans 7:23, Genesis 3:7-8**).

**4. With the World**

- The world is affected directly by sin, and people now exploit the world, selfishly. (**Genesis 3:14, 17, Romans 8:21-23**).

**5. With Time**

- People no longer live for ever, and now face anxiety in the face of death (**Genesis 2:17, Genesis 3:19, Romans 6:23**).

Make sure when you go through this that you have some remarks, illustrations or underlining which you want to make. Make this your own rather than just following this published resource.

## CHEESE & BISCUITS

### TEAR OUT

Hand out copies of old newspapers and ask group members working in teams of two or three to tear out anything which has anything to do with sin. Be ruthless. Ask groups to show the whole group what little they have left over. In many cases this will amount to very little especially if you are uncompromising in your comments about certain news stories.

### WHOPPER

Or you could play 'Whopper'. Each group member thinks up four pieces of information either about themselves, or some item which they know about but the rest of the group don't (e.g. a specialist hobby). Three of these pieces of information must be true and one false. The other group members write down the names of the other participants in the order they will give their information, and everyone has to guess and write down which piece of information was the whopper for each person. Score the results.

### MEMORY VERSES

If your group like to learn verses then use either, or both, of these:

**Jeremiah 17:9**

'The heart is deceitful above all things and beyond cure. Who can understand it?'

**Romans 3:23**

'There is no difference, for all have sinned and fall short of the glory of God'

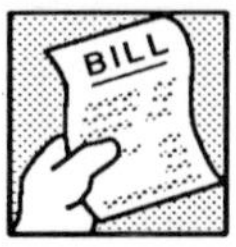

## THE BILL

It is possible that your members won't have seen how it all applies to them, so try this:

Stress that this is a PRIVATE EXERCISE, and ask each member to jot down some of their own sins from the last 24 hours. Suggest areas they may like to think about - at school, at home, with friends, at work etc. They should consider:

- things they have done
- things they have failed to do
- things they have said
- things they have thought

Use this to recap anything in the session which needs re-emphasising.

Explain that Jesus died to bear the punishment that our sins deserve, as our **SUBSTITUTE**, so that we might be forgiven.

# Takeaways

## Sin Destroys Relationships

**The following are the five main effects of sin. Match up the Bible verses with these headings and add your own further comments as necessary.**

| Effects of Sin | Bible Verses | My Comments |
|---|---|---|
| • **With God –**<br>unfit for God's presence<br>unable to do God's will<br>unrighteous before God's law<br>insensitive to God's Word. | | |
| • **With Others –**<br>Sin produces conflict,<br>division, prejudice,<br>exploitation, weakness,<br>fear, misunderstanding. | | |
| • **With Myself –**<br>Sin results in inner conflict<br>and people cannot<br>accept themselves. | | |
| • **With the World –**<br>The world is affected<br>directly by sin, and<br>people now exploit<br>the world selfishly | | |
| • **With Time –**<br>People no longer live<br>forever, and now face<br>anxiety in the face of death | | |

**Verses –**

Genesis 2:17
Genesis 3:12
Genesis 3:14 & 17
Genesis 3:19
Genesis 3:23
Genesis 4:1-16
John 8:34
Romans 1:18
Romans 6:23
Romans 7:15 & 21
Romans 8:21-23
2 Corinthians 4:4
Galatians 3:10
Ephesians 2:1-3

# Sin - Truth Decay

## TEACHING POINT

To teach that sin is a desire to become like God.

## GROUP ACTION

For members to discover any areas of their lives where God is excluded.

MENU

**GRACE**
**Confession** 5 minutes

**STARTERS**
**Back to Front** Preparation time
**Killer** 6 minutes
**Cheat** 10 minutes
**Balloon Stomp** 3 minutes

**MAIN COURSE**
**Getting Going** 5 minutes
**Right or Wrong** 15 minutes

**PUDDING**
**Curses** 15 minutes

**CHEESE & BISCUITS**
**Call My Bluff** 8 minutes
**Memory Verse** 1 minute

**THE BILL**
**Jigsaw** 5 minutes

## LAYING THE TABLE

This is the second of two sessions on sin. Although this one is self-contained, it does follow on from the one immediately preceding ('Sin - The Heart of the Matter'). It would be best to do that one first.

Be aware, when covering this subject, that it can touch sensitive areas and there may be individuals to follow up personally at the end of the meeting or soon afterwards.

## EQUIPMENT

- ✔ Copies of 'Takeaway' sheets
- ✔ Bibles or copies of **Genesis 3**
- ✔ Playing cards for 'Killer'
- ✔ Cassette recorder and microphone, or Camcorder/TV
- ✔ OHP/screen and pens
- ✔ Cardboard/acetate cut into jigsaw shaped pieces
- ✔ Balloons and string for 'Balloon Stomp'

## MUSIC

In My Life Lord, Be Glorified

Jesus Take Me As I Am

Just As I Am, Without One Plea

Soften My Heart Lord, Soften My Heart

Spirit Of The Living God

Take My Life, And Let It Be

## COOKING

Although this is a doctrinal study, we will be focusing on one particular passage, **Genesis 3**, as this is so central to our understanding of sin.

If you want to dip into other passages then look at:

**Romans 1:18-32**, or **Romans 6**.

In this session we are trying to be positive; to welcome God into areas of our lives previously closed to Him. Try and do it this way round rather than going sin-hunting. The tabloid newspapers tend to do this very well, but all sin is about falling short of God's standards, not just sexual or violent sin. Who is to say that a greedy person is any better than an adulterer? So particularly when studying examples of sin in the world today try and be more imaginative than the newspapers are. Look for original sins (yes, that was meant to be funny).

## GRACE

**CONFESSION**

Explain the death of Jesus, dying in our place for our sin, and therefore pray together asking for God's forgiveness and thanking him for his Son. Why not pray in silence, prayers of confession, whilst listening to a suitable piece of instrumental music.

## STARTERS

**BACK TO FRONT**

As the essence of this session is to teach how sin reverses the God ordained order in the world you may like to have a 'Back to Front' evening. This starts with you saying good-bye, ends with you saying hello, and you turn as much as you can get away with back to front.

So reverse the normal running order (perhaps have it before church rather than after it if you meet on Sunday), read the notices backwards, do the reading backwards (and then forwards!), or at least announce it after you've read it, etc.

**KILLER**

In 'Killer' the group sit in a circle (in a slightly darkened room ideally), and one is nominated as the killer by being dealt a joker when everyone is dealt a playing card. The killer kills others by winking at them, whereupon the more theatrical come into their own! If the killer is seen in the act, he may be challenged and the game starts again.

**CHEAT**

'Cheat' is the well-known card game with a variety of different rules, the aim of which is to get rid of your cards. If you are not sure of the rules, take out a card game book from your local library.

**BALLOON STOMP**

Give each member a balloon and a length of string. Ask them to blow up the balloon and tie it to one of their ankles with the string. On the word go, they must stomp on everyone else's balloon whilst protecting their own. When theirs is stomped, they drop out. At the end, ask what this tells us about the winner!

This is actually a very selfish game, and you could draw a parallel with human sin.

**All these games draw attention to our sin, so move on from here to introduce this session.**

## MAIN COURSE

**GETTING GOING**

Begin by reviewing last week. Ask people what they remembered, and re-make the important points if they've forgotten.

Remind your group that this week is on sin too, if continuing on from last week and introduce them to **Genesis 3**. The controversy of whether Adam and Eve actually existed as two individuals or whether this is a picture of the state of the world now is something of a red herring which you could easily get diverted by. Be prepared to answer it if it comes up, but make sure that you spend the majority of time in this session teaching what **Genesis 3** has to say about the state of the world.

**RIGHT OR WRONG**

This first segment concentrates on **vv 1-15** and the 'events' of the Fall. 'Curses' (in 'Pudding') covers the rest of the chapter and the 'implications' of the Fall. Begin by reading **Genesis 3:1-13**.

To put it in context, it would be ideal to read **Genesis chapters 1 and 2** as well. This is a large chunk, but if your group are up to it it's well worth the effort. Maybe ask someone with a good reading voice to make a tape of **Genesis 1 and 2** and play this at the meeting if this would make a change.

Give your group copies of the 'Takeaways' sheet. Ask them to complete these either individually or in pairs. Then have an all together session when you go through the sheets and discuss the answers. You may think this is a little difficult for your group, but some of the questions are easier than others, so you could give it a try and be prepared to help with the difficulties. This forms the basis of your teaching, so make sure you are properly prepared and know what the correct answers are! The following comments should help:

**1 -** The serpent questions the truth of God's word, he misquotes God (**v 1**), and suggests that God is selfish, making petty rules which he demands we keep.

**2 -** If we compare **v 3** with **Genesis 2:16,17**, there is no mention here of 'touching'. Also note that in **chapter 2** the command is given to Adam before Eve is formed, and she is quoting what Adam has presumably told her here.

**3 -** The serpent's promise to Eve is that she will be like God (**v 5**), which is more than just right from wrong which she knows anyway.

**4 -** Temptation does not equal sin. The serpent does not command.

**5 -** There is no mention of an apple.

**6 -** **V 7** reveals Adam and Eve's naivety.

**7 -** In **Genesis 1 and 2** the order of authority in creation is God - humanity - animals. In seeking to become like God the Fall reverses this order.

**8 -** **Vv 9-11** don't reveal an ignorant God, rather, he is trying to get Adam and Eve to admit their sin.

**9 -** The essence of sin is trying to take God's place.

**10 -** Both Adam and Eve try to blame each other.

As an alternative, you could use these points as a basis for a short talk. Whether you give a talk or involve the group more, make sure that they grasp that sin is, in essence, a desire to become like God.

---

PUDDING

**CURSES**

In this teaching segment we will look at **Genesis 3:14-24**. Ask one of your group members to read this out. Number your group off, 1,2,3,1,2,3, etc. (In the light of what follows try to make sure, as far as possible, that 2s are male and 3s are female).

Ask the relevant groups to do the following:

- the 1's to investigate the 'curse on the serpent' (**vv 14-15**),
- the 2's to investigate the 'curse on the woman' (**v 16**),
- the 3's to investigate the 'curse on the man' (**vv 17-19**).

Say that you will come as a radio reporter and, in a short interview, ask group members for their report on what has happened.

Do the interviews using a tape recorder and microphone - most ghetto blasters have a built in microphone so ask one of your group members to bring theirs and help you out if you need them to. It would be even better to use a Camcorder and play it back on the TV. Maybe someone in your church has got one that you could borrow.

Give your group four minutes to work out, from the passage, what difference the Fall has made to them as a serpent, man or woman. Then, with the tape recorder or video, record a brief introduction from you, giving the outline of **vv 1-13** ('Right or Wrong') stressing that sin is in essence a desire to become like God. Then interview a small selection of serpents, men and women. Play back the results.

Be prepared to emphasise certain of the points made. Maybe have another leader ready to do this, who can make brief notes while you are handling the radio or TV report.

Complete the teaching by describing this new human government. This is a government of:

- **Deceit -** It started and continues with lies.
- **Darkness -** We have placed ourselves under the rule of Satan. This is not just a one-off act but a continuing rebellion involving everyone today. (See **Romans 5:12**).
- **Death - Genesis 3:22-24**. People are banished from God's presence. God is the source of life and so people reject life.
- **Decay -** The whole physical world is involved in decay because of the fall. But this decay is not total. God still cares for fallen humans (**Genesis 3:21**) and his hand is still at work in creation (e.g. rain, growth of crops etc.).

---

CHEESE & BISCUITS

### CALL MY BLUFF

Play 'Call my Bluff' from the TV panel game. Do some research beforehand and find out some really obscure words (the best place to find these is in the Oxford English Dictionary), and write these out on card together with true and false definitions. If you're really organised, let the participants have the cards beforehand so they have the opportunity of preparing something in advance. Play the game as it happens on TV. (i.e. two teams, three in a team, and each team takes it in turns to define a word, two of the definitions being bluff, and one is true. The other team then have to decide which is true and which is bluff).

What happens in Call my Bluff is that two-thirds of the people lie. Bring this point out carefully as you explain why you have played this game.

### MEMORY VERSE

**Genesis 3:5**

'For God knows that when you eat of it your eyes will be opened, and you will be like God, knowing good and evil'.

---

THE BILL

### JIGSAW

Cut up an OHP acetate or large piece of card into jigsaw shaped pieces, one for each member. Give each group member one piece of card or acetate and an appropriate pen (or divide into small groups if your group is too large for this).

Make sure they know which side of the acetates/card they are required to write on (write a number or word on this yourself before you give them out), and then ask group members to write on their acetate evidence from today's world that **Genesis 3** is right. They should give examples of sin in the world today, and be specific. Construct the jigsaw and make suitable comments.

Ask group members, privately and individually, to note down areas where they are easily tempted to believe (and then to act upon), the lie that God doesn't know best, and/or the lie that God has been unfair to me.

Most important, ask group members to note down where they have tried to take the place of God, shutting him out, and trying to rule their own lives.

# Takeaways

**Genesis 3:1-13**

## Right or Wrong?

(Give each statement a tick or a cross)

✓ OR ✗

☐ **1.** The serpent's strategy is to cast doubt on the truth of God's words and motives.

☐ **2.** In verse 3, Eve exaggerates God's command.

☐ **3.** The serpent promises Eve that if she eats the fruit she'll be able to tell right from wrong.

☐ **4.** The serpent commands Eve to eat the forbidden fruit.

☐ **5.** Eve ate the apple first, then Adam.

☐ **6.** Adam and Eve's naivety was destroyed by eating from the tree.

☐ **7.** Sin reverses the order of creation: God - People - Animals to become Animals - People - God.

☐ **8.** In verse 9 God doesn't know where Adam and Eve are, and in verse 11 God doesn't know whether Adam and Eve have eaten the forbidden fruit.

☐ **9.** The essence of Adam and Eve's sin is to try and take God's place, becoming like him.

☐ **10.** Both Adam and Eve deny responsibility for their sin.

# God - Loving, Caring, Acting

## TEACHING POINT

To teach that God's nature is love and it is out of love that God acts on our behalf.

## GROUP ACTION

For members to have a deeper appreciation that God's love led to action on our behalf and that true love for God will result in practical demonstrations of love for others.

MENU

**GRACE**
- **Starter** 2 minutes
- **Afters** 3 minutes

**STARTERS**
- **Love Is** 8 minutes
- **Party Guests** 12 minutes

**MAIN COURSE**
- **God Rescues His People** 15-30 minutes

**PUDDING**
- **God Restores His People** 15-30 minutes
- **Symbolic Actions** 5 minutes
- **What's In a Name?** 5 minutes

**CHEESE & BISCUITS**
- **If You Love Me** 6 minutes

**THE BILL**
- **God Redeems His People** 6 minutes
- **Love Is - Reprise** 10 minutes

## LAYING THE TABLE

In the first module, second session of this book we looked at 'God - Holy, Sovereign, Creator'. In this session we will concentrate on some more aspects of his person - loving, caring, acting. This also links back to module two on Sin and forms a bridge to the next session on God's solution for Sin: the Cross. But it is not just about God's love shown in salvation.

## EQUIPMENT

- ✔ Paper plates
- ✔ Spare Bibles
- ✔ OHP, acetates and pens or flip chart and markers
- ✔ Love is.. cartoons for 'Love Is'
- ✔ Lists of captions for 'Love Is'
- ✔ Character cards for 'Party Guests'
- ✔ Display of symbols for 'Symbolic Actions'
- ✔ List of names for 'What's In a Name?'
- ✔ Paper and pens/pencils

## MUSIC

Such Love

So Freely

A New Commandment

The King Is Among Us

Let There Be Love Shared Among Us

## COOKING

God's love in action is a vast subject. Indeed, it could be argued that this is the theme of the entire Bible. We do not propose to cover the entire Bible in this session but to select a few passages which clearly illustrate the truth that 'God is love' (**1 John 4:8b**), and highlight different aspects of it.

If your group have only a limited Bible knowledge and/or you have a majority of non-Christians, you will probably find it best to work on Moses and the Exodus as this provides a strong picture of redemption and is good preparation for the next session on the Cross. If members are likely to be reasonably familiar with the Exodus story, the material provides opportunity to explore some lesser-known passages as well.

## GRACE

It is the custom in some countries to say grace after the meal rather than before it. Some people do both. This session we will do both.

### STARTER

To emphasise our meal theme, set out the room with tables and a plate (paper?) at each place. Get members to put their Bibles on the plates and have spares for any without one. Ask someone to thank God for the 'food' they are going to receive from God's Word.

### AFTERS

At the end of the meeting get members to put their Bibles back on the plates. Ask someone to thank God for the 'food' they have eaten, for his love and to ask for a willingness to share it with others.

STARTERS

## LOVE IS

Display a series of 'Love is...' cartoons, from which the captions have been removed, around the room. These can be cut out of the Daily Mail or copied from books and enlarged. Try to choose cartoons where love is demonstrated in action rather than those which emphasise feelings. Give each person a list of the missing captions and get them to match the captions to the cartoons.

Give the correct answers. Make the point that the cartoons illustrate that love is not just a feeling or an emotion but shows itself through action. We can recognise love by the way people behave.

## PARTY GUESTS

Prepare a series of cards each naming a character trait e.g extrovert, shy, talkative, shifty etc. Ask for several volunteers and select one to act as party host(ess). Give each of the remaining volunteers a card, the contents of which they must keep a secret. One at a time they arrive at the party to be greeted by the host(ess), and proceed to act 'in character'. Dialogue is permitted and probably essential. Remaining group members try to guess the word on the card. It is not essential to wait for one guest's character trait to be identified before another party guest arrives. This can add to the fun (and confusion!).

Make the connection between our characters and the way we act. The kind of person we are inside will influence the way we behave and the things we do indicate the kind of person we are - though it is not <u>always</u> immediately obvious.

It is the same with God.

> Who God is DETERMINES how God acts.
> How God acts DEMONSTRATES who God is....
> though it is not <u>always</u> immediately obvious.

---

MAIN COURSE

## GOD RESCUES HIS PEOPLE

**(Exodus 1:1-14 & 3:1-10)**

This section has been presented as a straight talk, but it is important to involve members in digging into the Bible by question and answer. Use a flip chart or OHP to display the main headings as you proceed.

- **Scene 1 Into Egypt (Ex.1:1-5)**

  Draw a sketch map of Canaan and Egypt with the words 'FAMINE' written across Canaan and 'FOOD' across Egypt.

  Explain very briefly the problem facing Jacob (Israel) and his family i.e. there was famine in Canaan (where they lived) and food in Egypt (where Joseph now was), so the whole family (70 people) moved to Egypt and enjoyed a privileged position because of Joseph's standing with Pharaoh.

- **Scene 2 Into Slavery (Ex 1:6-10)**

  Joseph and all his generation died but their descendants continued to grow in number (**v7**). The new king (probably Sethos I) was of genuine Egyptian descent, whereas the pharaoh of Joseph's time was of the Hyksos dynasty, who were of Semitic descent and hence related to the Israelites. Not surprisingly, Sethos I felt threatened by the presence of a large concentration of foreigners and feared a takeover like the one which had brought the Hyksos to power. To prevent history repeating itself, the king enslaved the Israelites.

- **Scene 3 Into Action (Ex.3:1-10)**

  Moved by the plight of his people, God begins to act. Note the following sequence from **vv 7-10**:

I have seen.......(**v7a**)
I have heard......(**v7b**) } GOD KNOWS

I am concerned....(**v7c**) GOD CARES

I have come down..(**v8a**)
I am sending......(**v10**) } GOD ACTS

Display this sequence above on a chart/OHP acetate. The rest, as they say, is history, or as someone once put it 'history is his-story'.

If the group don't know the rest of the story, you could complete it by using the light-hearted script in 'Takeaways'.

The approach in this section is not an in-depth telling of the story of the Exodus, rather a brief overview from which the group will grasp the central fact that God cared enough to act.

Conclude this section, by referring back to the sequence of steps in God's rescue plan, 'I have seen...I have heard...' etc. Ask the question, 'How did God intend to act?' God's rescue plan involved sending a man. DON'T EXPAND ON THIS STATEMENT YET. We will pick up on it later and deal with it fully in the next session.

---

PUDDING

### SYMBOLIC ACTIONS

Display a series of symbols on an OHP, chart or sheets of paper e.g. road signs, scientific symbols, company logos etc. Get members to identify them. Next act out and/or discuss a series of symbolic actions e.g. exchanging rings in a marriage ceremony, a baptism, the breaking of bread and pouring of wine at Communion.

### WHAT'S IN A NAME?

Prepare in advance a list of your group members names and look up their meanings in a dictionary of names. You can use Christian names, surnames or both. Ask people if they know what their names mean and reveal the answers.

### GOD RESTORES HIS PEOPLE

(**Hosea 1, 3, 11, 14**)

The Exodus passages show God responding to the plight of his people in slavery in Egypt. Because of his love God acts on their behalf to rescue them from slavery and bring them into Canaan, the Promised Land.

The book of Hosea is a powerful enactment, in the life and marriage experience of the prophet, of God's relationship with his **already redeemed** people. It is worth noting that Hosea is another form of Joshua or Jesus, meaning 'Saviour' or 'God is Salvation'. The gist of the story is:

**1)** Hosea marries Gomer despite her probable previous history of prostitution;
**2)** 3 children are born and given symbolic names:
**3)** Gomer leaves Hosea and goes back to prostitution.
**4)** Hosea goes in search of his unfaithful wife and finds her in slavery.
**5)** Hosea buys Gomer out of slavery and takes her back home. He promises to be her husband again if she will give up her prostitution.

The remainder of the book is a poetic explanation of how Hosea's experience graphically portrays God's relationship with his people:

**1)** God had 'married' them when he entered into a Covenant relationship with them at Sinai.

2) Despite this demonstration of God's love, the people had 'prostituted themselves' by following other gods.
3) As a result God had allowed them to suffer the consequences by becoming 'enslaved' by the Assyrians.
4) Because of his love, God could not completely abandon them.
5) If they will repent and return, he will again be their God and bless them.

This story is particularly relevant to those who are already Christians. It presents the challenge of continuing to live in obedience to God if we are not to suffer the consequences of disobedience. Draw out the symbolic names/actions and their spiritual parallels on a chart/OHP acetate:

| SYMBOL | MEANING |
|---|---|
| Hosea marries Gomer | God chose Israel as His people |
| Gomer turns to prostitution | Israel turns to other gods |
| Gomer becomes a slave | God allows Israel to go into exile |
| Hosea buys back Gomer | God will restore His people |

CHEESE & BISCUITS

**GOD DISCIPLINES HIS PEOPLE - IF YOU LOVE ME**

On a chart/OHP acetate, display the words, 'If you love me you will...'. Get members to suggest ways to complete the sentence.

Re-emphasise the point made under 'Starters':

Who God is DETERMINES how God acts.
How God acts DEMONSTRATES who God is....
though it is not <u>always</u> immediately obvious.

Discuss the suggestions given above. If we were to be given everything we wanted would this always be the best way to demonstrate love? Does a refusal to give us what we want mean that love is absent?

The Israelites couldn't understand how God could love them and yet allow them to be defeated and be taken into exile. The message of Hosea was that God still loved them and would restore them. In Hebrews, the writer takes this one stage further by showing that even suffering itself can be a sign of God's love.

God acts out of love **at all times**, but sometimes this means allowing us to undergo suffering in order to discipline us. Read **Hebrews 12:4-11**.

THE BILL

**GOD REDEEMS HIS PEOPLE**

Redemption is about setting us free, not just from the consequences of sin but from its power. In other words, being redeemed should affect the way we now live. God has saved us to be different. Point this out to your group and allow them a few minutes to quietly consider the way they are living.

**LOVE IS...REPRISE**

Look together or in small groups at **1 John 4:7-21**. Focus on the statement in **vv8 & 16**, 'God is love'. This is who God is. How does he act as a result? Answer: **vv9-10**, he sent his Son.

How does God want us to respond? See **vv11-12 & 20-21**. Remind the group of the cartoons in 'Starters'. Love for others is not a gooey feeling; it must result in action. See **1 John 3:16-18**.

Have a few minutes of quiet, during which group members can think and write down specific practical ways in which they show love for one another.

# Takeaways

| | |
|---|---|
| **Narr. 1** | So Moses went to Egypt and said to Pharaoh |
| **Moses** | God says 'Let the Israelites go!' |
| **Narr. 2** | And Pharaoh said |
| **Pharaoh** | No! |
| **N1** | And Moses said |
| **Moses** | There's going to be a plague |
| **N2** | And the river turned to blood |
| **N1** | And Moses said |
| **Moses** | Can we go now? |
| **N2** | And Pharaoh said |
| **Pharaoh** | No! |
| **N1** | And Moses said |
| **Moses** | There's going to be another plague |
| **N2** | And the land was filled with frogs |
| **N1** | And Moses said |
| **Moses** | Can we go now? |
| **N2** | And Pharaoh said |
| **Pharaoh** | Call off the frogs and then you can go |
| **N1** | So Moses prayed and God removed the frogs |
| **N2** | And Pharaoh said |
| **Pharaoh** | I've changed my mind |
| **N1** | And Moses said |
| **Moses** | There's going to be a third plague |
| **N2** | And the land was filled with gnats |
| **N1** | And Moses said |
| **Moses** | Can we go now? |
| **N2** | And Pharaoh said |
| **Pharaoh** | No! |
| **N1** | And Moses said |
| **Moses** | There's going to be a fourth plague |
| **N2** | And the land was filled with flies |
| **N1** | And Moses said |
| **Moses** | Can we go now? |
| **N2** | And Pharaoh said |
| **Pharaoh** | Call off the flies and then you can go |
| **N1** | So Moses prayed and God removed the flies |
| **N2** | And Pharaoh said |
| **Pharaoh** | I've changed my mind |
| **N1** | And Moses said |
| **Moses** | There's going to be a fifth plague |
| **N2** | And the Egyptians' livestock died |
| **N1** | And Moses said |
| **Moses** | Can we go now? |
| **N2** | And Pharaoh said |
| **Pharaoh** | No! |
| **N1** | And Moses said |
| **Moses** | There's going to be a sixth plague |
| **N2** | And everyone was covered in boils |
| **N1** | And Moses said |
| **Moses** | Can we go now? |
| **N2** | And Pharaoh said |
| **Pharaoh** | No! |
| **N1** | And Moses said |
| **Moses** | There's going to be a seventh plague |
| **N2** | And the land was hit by a dreadful hailstorm |
| **N1** | And Moses said |
| **Moses** | Can we go now? |
| **N2** | And Pharaoh said |
| **Pharaoh** | Call off the storm and then you can go |
| **N1** | So Moses prayed and God stopped the storm |
| **N2** | And Pharaoh said |
| **Pharaoh** | I've changed my mind |
| **N1** | And Moses said |
| **Moses** | There's going to be an eighth plague |
| **N2** | And the land was filled with locusts |
| **N1** | And Moses said |
| **Moses** | Can we go now? |
| **N2** | And Pharaoh said |
| **Pharaoh** | Call off the locusts and then you can go |
| **N1** | So Moses prayed and God removed the locusts |
| **N2** | And Pharaoh said |
| **Pharaoh** | I've changed my mind |
| **N1** | And Moses said |
| **Moses** | There's going to be a ninth plague |
| **N2** | And the whole land was covered in darkness |
| **N1** | And Moses said |
| **Moses** | Can we go now? |
| **N2** | And Pharaoh said |
| **Pharaoh** | No! Get out of my sight. If I see you again you will die! |
| **N1** | And Moses said |
| **Moses** | You will not see me again! |
| **N2** | And God said |
| **God** | Let every Israelite family kill a lamb and mark the lintel and the doorposts of the house with its blood |
| **N1** | And the LORD sent a tenth plague |
| **N2** | And the firstborn in every house in Egypt died |
| **N1** | But death passed over every house where the entrance was marked with blood |
| **N2** | And God brought His people out of slavery in Egypt - because He loved them. |

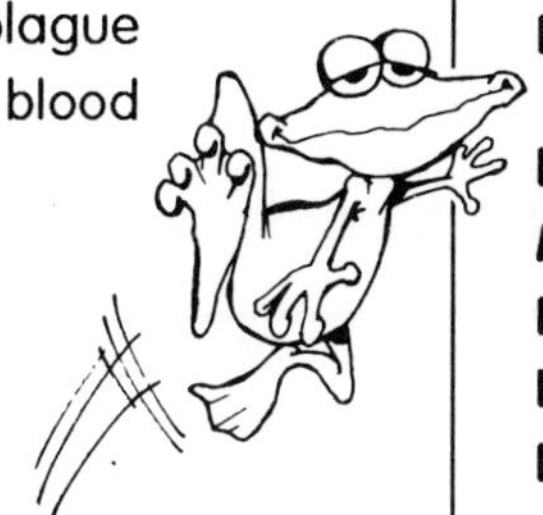

# The Cross - Cross-Words

## TEACHING POINT

**To teach that the Cross is God's complete solution to the problem of sin. Through the Cross, sinful people are reconciled to a Holy God.**

## GROUP ACTION

**For non-Christian members to be reconciled to God through the Cross and for Christians to become representatives for God in that process of reconciling others to him.**

MENU

**GRACE**
- **Cross-Words** 6 minutes

**STARTERS**
- **Review** 8 minutes
- **Clueless** 8 minutes

**MAIN COURSE**
- **Picture It** 15-20 minutes

**PUDDING**
- **Match Up 1** 10 minutes
- **Match Up 2** 15 minutes

**CHEESE & BISCUITS**
- **The Complete Solution** 10 minutes

**THE BILL**
- **In Christ** 10 minutes

## LAYING THE TABLE

There is no doubt that doctrine is a huge subject and to cover the specific elements of doctrine, in depth, in a comparatively short book, like this one, is impossible. Our main aim is to provide you with enough material to study the subject, or an element of the subject, in a one week session.

This session on the Cross is a prime example of this. Although the doctrine of the Cross is about Christ taking all our Sin on himself, taking our punishment, conquering death and reconciling us to God, we are not able to deal with all of these, in depth, in a one week session.

Therefore, you may want to look at the Cross over several weeks. We would recommend you obtain a copy of John Stott's book, 'The Cross Of Christ' (IVP) as it will help provide extra information and material, to enable you to do this as well as giving you more background help.

However little people know about the Christian gospel, most will at least be aware that Jesus died on a cross and that the Cross is a popular Christian symbol. Why Christians have chosen that particular symbol and what its significance is will probably be less familiar.

Whether your group are coming from a church background or not, this session is crucial (literally!). Unless we understand the Cross, our understanding of Christianity is defective.

## EQUIPMENT

- ✔ Cross-shaped cards with prayers/Bible verses on for 'Grace'
- ✔ OHP, acetates and pens or flip chart and markers
- ✔ Large Cross-word puzzle and smaller copies
- ✔ Enlarged copies of picture clues with references
- ✔ Labels for 'Match Up 1'
- ✔ Sets(s) of jigsaw-clues for 'Match Up 2'
- ✔ Bibles
- ✔ Paper & pens/pencils

## MUSIC

There Is A Redeemer

From Heaven You Came

You Laid Aside Your Majesty

When I Survey The Wondrous Cross

For This Purpose

Broken For Me, Broken For You

## COOKING

Clearly, Paul saw the Cross as absolutely central to the Christian gospel, describing it as 'the power of God for the salvation of everyone who believes..' (**Rom.1:16**) and '..the power of God and the wisdom of God' (**1 Cor.1:23-24**).

The whole of this session is linked to the central visual concept of a Cross-shaped puzzle (see the 'Takeaways' sheet). Each of the elements in the session contributes to building up the 'Cross-Word' with its complete solution. The Cross-Words i.e. what the Cross says, are God's complete solution for sin. Thus the visual aid displays the various elements or clues to our understanding of the Cross and at the same time illustrates the completeness of God's solution for sin in the Cross.

It is important, therefore, that in selecting material for this session, you do not lose the sense of completeness. It may mean that those who have a shorter time available will need to spend more than one session on this subject.

## GRACE

### CROSS-WORDS

Prepare cross-shaped cards with a mixture of relevant Bible verses and short prayers written on them. Prayers should express thanks to God for different aspects of what Jesus did for us on the Cross e.g. showing his love, taking our sin, setting us free, bringing forgiveness, giving us life etc. If your group are all comfortable with reading and/ or praying aloud, give each member a card. Alternatively, to avoid embarrassing those for whom this would be difficult or if you have a large group, use volunteers.

## STARTERS

### REVIEW

Module two looked at Sin and its effects, the first session in this module dealt with God and his love. This session brings the two together, so we need to relate back to what has gone before.

### CLUELESS

On an OHP acetate or flip chart, prepare a large crossword puzzle like the one shown on the 'Takeaways' sheet, without any clues. Ask the group to identify what is wrong. Answer: **No clues - we have a problem with no hope of a solution.**

That's where we were after we had discovered, in the last session, that God is holy and we are sinful. We had a problem and no hope of a solution. But last time we began to get some clues towards the solution, when we learnt that God is not only holy but he also loves us and acts on our behalf.

Now add the clues, but without their 'Cross-Words' clue numbers. We have made progress. We have some hint at the solution, but no clear answer. We still have some work to do.

## MAIN COURSE

### PICTURE IT

Use the clues given in 'Takeaways', which are pictures from the Old Testament that point to Christ and the Cross. You will need to copy and enlarge the individual pictures and their related Bible references or have a copy of the 'Takeaways' sheet for each group member. In small groups, work through the clues together using the following pattern:

Look at the picture and key verse from the Bible passage. Use them both to solve the clue. Then study the passage sufficiently to be able to explain the answer to the clues. The following notes are for your guidance and to prompt groups as necessary.

- **Passover Lamb** – the lamb died; the blood was placed over the doorway; those in the house were saved from death.
  Key idea: **SUBSTITUTE** - the lamb took the place of the firstborn.
- **Atonement Money** – each Israelite, rich or poor, had to pay the same price to ransom his life.
  Key idea: **RANSOM** - a price to buy back a life.
- **Sin Offering** – a sacrifice was made because of sin; the blood of the animal was then sprinkled to symbolise cleansing from sin.
  Key idea: **CLEANSING & FORGIVENESS**.

- **Scapegoat** – the sins of the people were transferred onto the scapegoat, which was then driven away into the desert.
  Key idea: **SIN-BEARING** - taking away the sins of others.
- **Kinsman-Redeemer** –the redeemer paid the price to gain the right of ownership from another.
  Key idea: **PURCHASING** - transfer of ownership.
- **Righteous Servant** – the servant suffers unjustly the punishment which rightly belongs to others.
  Key idea: **SATISFACTION** - the just taking the punishment of the unjust to satisfy the law.
- **Under God's Curse** – the one who hangs on a tree is under God's curse.
  Key idea: **CONDEMNATION** - being subject to the righteous anger of God.

Come back together and pool the results, writing the answers alongside the clues for the moment.

Notice that you will still not be able to fill the words into the cross, because you will have the answers but you won't know how they fit together. This is rather like the people in the Old Testament. They had all these pictures of Christ but they didn't know how to fit them together to make sense of them.

---

PUDDING

## MATCH UP 1

This is a game in which pairs are matched. Each person is given a label on their back on which is written the name of one half of a well-known pair. These may be Biblical characters e.g Adam and Eve, historical e.g. Anthony and Cleopatra, fictional e.g. Jekyll and Hyde, or any other obvious pairings. By asking questions of other people, each group member tries to find their own identity. To make this harder, questions may only be answered with a 'yes' or 'no'. Finally having identified who they are, they must find their 'other half'.

Award a prize to the first matched pair e.g a pair of ear-rings, one each!

## MATCH UP 2

Before the meeting, each of the picture clues already used should be enlarged and pasted onto the left hand side of a card jigsaw piece (use example in 'Takeaways'), ready for this activity. Alongside each picture write the reference of the matching verse(s) from the New Testament and the clue number(s), given on the 'Takeaways' sheet. Separate the picture and reference by cutting the card to form two jigsaw pieces. Mix up the pieces and get the group to match the corresponding halves. For larger groups, you may need to produce more than one set of pictures and references and let smaller teams race to complete their set of matching pairs. To match the halves, your group members will need to use their Bibles.

Having completed the matching, assign to individuals or pairs, one picture and its corresponding New Testament reference. Get them to look up the reference and work out:

- In what way the Old Testament picture illustrates what the Cross is about?

And/Or

- How the Cross fulfils what was fore-shadowed by the Old Testament picture?

If necessary, get them to look back to the Old Testament passages on which the pictures are based and prompt them with the Key Ideas given under 'Picture It'.

CHEESE & BISCUITS

**THE COMPLETE SOLUTION**

Under each of the New Testament references on the 'Takeaways' sheet you will find a clue number e.g 1, which should have been written onto the cards used for 'Match Up 2'. These numbers correspond to those on the 'Cross-Words' puzzle, so you are now in a position to identify which picture clue fits where on the puzzle.

With the help of the group, transfer the answers to the clues onto the puzzle to complete the solution. If each person has their own sheet, they can now complete their own Cross-Word.

Point out that the various pictures in the Old Testament all give clues about the meaning of the Cross. When taken together, they give us the whole picture.

It is worth noting, at this point, that we have looked, in fact, at only a few of hundreds of pictures the Old Testament contains which look forward to the Cross. However, the ones selected represent the key truths.

The Cross itself is the complete solution to the problem of sin.

Re-emphasise the different aspects of the Cross already covered, but stress the need to hold them all together if we are to have a complete picture.

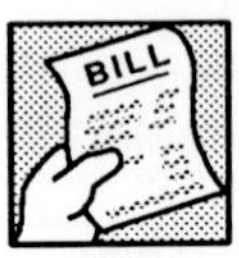


THE BILL

**IN CHRIST**

Conclude the session by pointing out the need for a response.

**2 Cor.5:14-21** is a helpful passage here, for both those who are not yet Christians and those who are. The key words are 'in Christ' or 'in him' (**vv17, 19 & 21**).

In **v17**, point out the 'if'. Being 'in Christ' is not automatic. Although God has provided the complete solution, we need to apply it to ourselves by faith. This is further developed in **vv18-20**. God **has** reconciled us to himself 'in Christ' (**vv17-18**) i.e. He has done his part, but Paul still says (**v20**): 'be reconciled' - this is our part. Forgiveness, new life, reconciliation are all available 'in Christ', because of the Cross, but we need to receive them for ourselves.

But there is another side to the Cross, which is sometimes neglected. This is brought out in **vv14-15**. So far the emphasis has been on Christ as **substitute**, dying in our place, taking our punishment etc. Here the emphasis is on Christ as **representative**. When he died, we died as well. His crucifixion was also our crucifixion. It is only when we recognise that we need to die 'in Christ' that we can truly live 'in Christ'. Refer to **Galatians 2:20** as another relevant verse on this point.

For those 'in Christ', the challenge is **'that those who live should no longer live for themselves but for him who died for them...'(Gal.2:20)**. Part of this is to share **'..the message of reconciliation' (2 Cor.5:19)**.

Close with prayer. You may feel it appropriate to include a prayer of commitment to give a chance for people to respond. However, it may be better to give an opportunity for people to speak to you or other leaders one-to-one before taking this step.

# Takeaways

## CROSS-WORDS PUZZLE

**COMPLETE SOLUTION**

| PICTURE | O.T. PASSAGE & KEY VERSE | CLUE | N.T. VERSE & CLUE No. |
|---|---|---|---|
| Doorway & dead lamb | Ex.12:21-28 Key: v21 | Passover Lamb | John 1:29 Clue: 2 |
| Pile of coins | Ex.30:11-16 Key: v16 | Atonement Money | 1 Pet. 1:18-20 Clue: 5 |
| Altar & bull | Lev.4:13-21 Key: v14 | Sin Offering | Heb. 9:13-14 Clue: 1 |
| Goat | Lev.16:6-10 & 20-22 Key: v10 | Scapegoat | 1 Pet. 2:24 Clue: 3 |
| Body hanging on a tree | Deut.21:22-23 Key: v23 | Under God's Curse | Gal. 3:13 Clue: 8, 9 & 10 |
| Sandal | Ruth 4:1-8 Key: v1 | Kinsman-Redeemer | Rev. 5:9 Clue: 4 |
| Slave | Isa.53:4-11 Key: v11 | Righteous Servant | 1 Pet. 3:18 Clue: 6 & 7 |

| PICTURE | O.T. PASSAGE & KEY VERSE | CLUE | N.T. VERSE & CLUE No. |
|---|---|---|---|
|  | Ex.12:21-28<br>Key: v21 | P_ _ _ _ _ _ _<br>L_ _ _ | John 1:29<br>Clue: 2 |
| 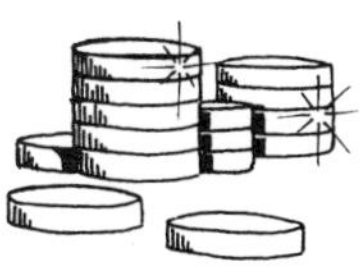 | Ex.30:11-16<br>Key: v16 | A_ _ _ _ _ _ _ _<br>M_ _ _ _ | 1 Pet. 1:18-20<br>Clue: 5 |
|  | Lev.4:13-21<br>Key: v14 | S_ _<br>O_ _ _ _ _ _ _ | Heb. 9:13-14<br>Clue: 1 |
|  | Lev.16:6-10 & 20-22<br>Key: v10 | S_ _ _ _ _ _ _ _ | 1 Pet. 2:24<br>Clue: 3 |
|  | Deut.21:22-23<br>Key: v23 | U_ _ _ _G_ _'_<br>C_ _ _ _ | Gal. 3:13<br>Clue: 8, 9 & 10 |
|  | Ruth 4:1-8<br>Key: v1 | K_ _ _ _ _ _ –<br>R_ _ _ _ _ _ _ | Rev. 5:9<br>Clue: 4 |
|  | Isa.53:4-11<br>Key: v11 | R_ _ _ _ _ _ _ _<br>S_ _ _ _ _ _ | 1 Pet. 3:18<br>Clue: 6 & 7 |

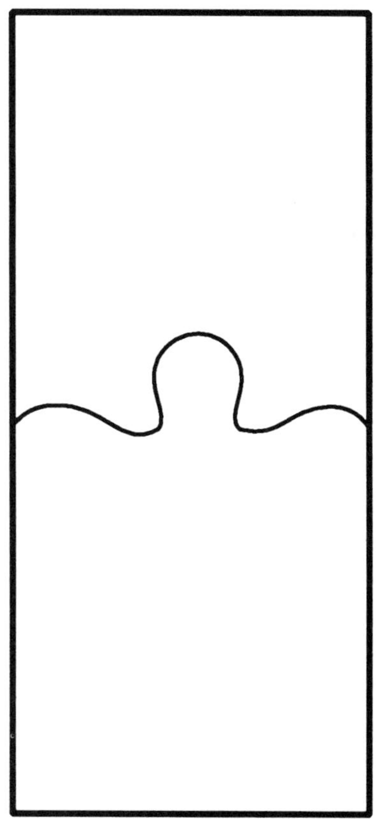

# The Resurrection - Tomb with a View

## TEACHING POINT

**To teach that the Resurrection is central to the Christian faith and demonstrates God's acceptance of Jesus' death as the complete sacrifice for the sins of the world.**

## GROUP ACTION

**For the group to recognise and 'put off' those things which belong to the 'old self' and 'put on' what belongs to new life in Christ.**

MENU

**GRACE**
**A Seed Must Die** 4 minutes (plus two weeks prior)

**STARTERS**
**Tomb With A View** Preparation time only
**Self-Raising** 12 minutes plus cooking time
**If...Then...** 10 minutes

**MAIN COURSE**
**Fact Finding** 30 minutes
**Cross Examination** 15 minutes

**PUDDING**
**Re-Construction** 15-30 minutes

**CHEESE AND BISCUITS**
**Put On...Put Off 1** 10-15 minutes

**THE BILL**
**Put On...Put Off 2** 10 minutes
**Tasty Finish** 5 minutes

## LAYING THE TABLE

The issue of the Resurrection has been the subject of a lot of controversy within the Church in recent years. Some of your group members may feel it is not as important as the Cross and, therefore, it doesn't matter so much whether they believe or not in something that is pretty unbelievable.

One aim of this session is to give group members an appreciation of the importance of believing in the Resurrection of Jesus. We will look, therefore, at the evidence for the Resurrection, to demonstrate that such a belief is supported by the facts. It is important to recognise that belief in the Resurrection is as much a matter of faith as any other aspect of the gospel.

## EQUIPMENT

- ✔ OHP, acetates and pens or flip chart and markers.
- ✔ Bibles
- ✔ Paper & pens/pencils
- ✔ Seeds in a seed tray (prepared a few weeks before) for 'A Seed Must Die'
- ✔ Black paper for 'Tomb With A View'
- ✔ Drawing or picture of Jerusalem for 'Tomb With A View'
- ✔ Map of Jerusalem for 'Fact Finding'
- ✔ Bible Verses on Card for 'Fact Finding'

## MUSIC

All Heaven Declares

He Is Here, He Is Here

Led Like A Lamb To The Slaughter

He Is Lord, He Is Lord

Thine Be The Glory

## COOKING

Although, we might be horrified at the thought of not accepting the Resurrection as a literal, historical event, we may well be guilty of not giving it as much significance as the New Testament writers do. Our tendency to focus so much on the centrality of the Cross, sometimes leads us to neglect the Resurrection.

And yet without the Resurrection, the Cross is incomplete. To the same Corinthian church that Paul wrote, 'I resolved to know nothing among you except Christ and him crucified.', he also wrote, '..if Christ has not been raised, your faith is futile; you are still in your sins.'

When looking to choose a replacement for Judas Iscariot, Peter said they needed someone who '...must become a witness with us of his resurrection' (**Acts 1:22**). And in **Romans 5**, Paul tells us that whilst it is by Jesus' death that we are reconciled, it is through his life that we are saved (**Rom.5:10**). It is clearly vital that we teach both Cross and Resurrection together.

## GRACE

**A SEED MUST DIE**

If you plan to use this activity in this session, you will need to start a few weeks earlier. At the end of an earlier session, explain that you want to introduce something for a future week. Hold a brief burial service for a few seeds, which you plant in a pot or seed tray. Include the reading of **John 12:24**. You or a member of the group will then need to keep the seeds in a warm place and ensure adequate water and light. (To shorten the waiting time, you can use mustard or cress seeds which grow in just a few days).

At the appropriate time, if you plan it properly, the seeds will have germinated and broken through the soil. Bring the pot/seed tray to the session as a symbol of how death has been replaced by new life. Have someone read **John 12:24** again and follow this with prayers of thanksgiving for evidences in the natural world of the cycle of death and new life.

## STARTERS

**TOMB WITH A VIEW**
This is the overall title for the session, but it can also be used as the heading for a visual back-drop. Find a suitable picture of Jerusalem and enlarge it or draw your own sketch, the larger the better. Frame it in black paper to create the effect of looking outwards over the city from the empty tomb. Silhouetted in the entrance to the tomb, you can add the heads of Peter and John looking in. (See on 'Takeaways' sheet.)

**SELF-RAISING**
Divide the group into two or more groups and provide them with bread making ingredients, but only include yeast for one of the groups. Use the ingredients to mix dough and then place them in an oven for about 30 minutes (Gas Mark 6, 400F, 200C), whilst the session continues. If you can, write the words 'He Is Risen' in the top of the dough. Tasting will come later in 'The Bill'.

**IF...THEN...**
This section uses the flowchart on the 'Takeaways' sheet, so you will need enough copies for each person to have one. It is based on a computer programme flowchart, a concept familiar to most teens these days. Working in twos or threes, get the group to work through **1 Corinthians 15:12-19**, filling in the negative implications of not believing in the Resurrection.

When people have completed the flowchart, come together and compare findings. This is probably best done by having a large copy of the diagram on an OHP or flip chart and writing in the answers the group have discovered.

Paul was prepared to stake the whole of the Christian faith on this one issue, but on what evidence?

## MAIN COURSE

**FACT FINDING**
This is where the group play detectives, looking for and evaluating the evidence for the Resurrection and using it to counter the various alternative theories that have been put forward to try to explain what happened to the body of Jesus.

Display round the room cards presenting the various alternative theories to the Resurrection. The following are generally considered to be the most favoured versions:

1) **The disciples stole the body to support Jesus' claim that he would rise from the dead. (Luke 28:11-15)**.
2) **The Roman or Jewish authorities had the body removed and buried elsewhere.**
3) **The tomb was empty because it was the wrong tomb. The women were relative strangers to Jerusalem and, by a**

**combination of their grief and the uncertain light of dawn, they made a mistake and went to the wrong place.**

4) **Jesus did not actually die on the Cross, but swooned from exhaustion and was mistaken for dead. In the cool of the tomb he revived and escaped.**

There is a fifth explanation, namely that the whole story was a deliberate invention of the gospel writers many years after the actual 'events' of Jesus life, which they claim to portray. However, as Prof. J.N.D.Anderson puts it in his booklet, 'The Evidence for the Resurrection', '...there is scarcely a single intelligent critic who would go so far.' That something happened to the body of Jesus to give rise to the claims of the Resurrection is not generally in dispute; the question is, 'What?'.

The group should now be given the task of collecting evidence which they will later use in assessing these various explanations.

Suitable plans and pictures of the different episodes in the whole drama of the Resurrection can enhance the whole atmosphere e.g. a plan of Jerusalem with the sites of the trials, crucifixion, empty tomb etc marked; map showing Jerusalem, Emmaus, Galilee, Damascus with resurrection appearances labelled.

The evidence can be grouped together under a number of headings - **medical, circumstantial, witness testimony, psychological, historical**. It is probably a good idea to split into smaller groups and assign one group to concentrate on each type of evidence.

Copy the following passages **Matthew 26:67-28:20; Mark 14:53-16:14; Luke 22:63-24:43; John 18:19-21:14** (or suitable extracts) and **1 Corinthians 15** onto card for easy access. These contain almost all the information that is needed to carry out the investigation. To make them even more 'user friendly', split the narratives up into sections dealing with the different stages in the story e.g. The Trials, The Crucifixion, The Burial, The Resurrection, Resurrection Appearances. To help the research feel more like a police investigation, the cards could be given headings relating to the time of the events and the scene at which they took place e.g. Thursday morning - High Priest's Residence; Friday morning - scene of death; Friday evening - site of burial etc.

Passages could be marked with fluorescent highlight pens to identify evidence fitting into different categories by a colour coding system e.g. medical - blue; circumstantial - green etc.

Where possible, for simplicity, you could prepare several sets of cards with just one type of evidence highlighted on each.

## MEDICAL

### THE FACTS

- Jesus' last known meal - supper Thursday
- Last known sleep - Wednesday night
- His physical treatment - blindfolded and punched repeatedly, flogged, crown of thorns, spat at and hit on head with a staff, crucified from the third hour (9.00am) to late afternoon, offered but refused pain-killing drugs, spear thrust in his side.
- Death confirmed by Centurion.

### THE QUESTIONS

Assuming Jesus was not dead:

- Would being sealed in a tomb for three days with no food or water have helped or hindered his condition?
- Would a man in such a condition a) be able to move a stone which presented a problem to three healthy women; b) be able to escape from armed Temple guards; c) convince anyone that he had risen from the dead?

## CIRCUMSTANTIAL

### THE FACTS

- The graveclothes - Body wrapped in strips of linen cloth, along with 75 pounds of myrrh and aloes. Linen strips and burial cloth from Jesus' head found in the tomb.
- The tomb - New tomb, therefore no possibility of remains of other burials. Cut into rock and sealed with large stone, therefore no escape routes. Sealed and guarded by Temple soldiers.

### THE QUESTIONS

- What was it about the graveclothes that John saw, which convinced him that Jesus had risen?
- How could Jesus have managed to escape from the tomb?

## WITNESS

### TESTIMONY

The following people all have evidence to give which has a bearing on the case:

**• Pilate • Centurion • Temple Guard • Chief Priests • The women • Peter • Cleopas • Thomas • Eleven • Mary Magdalen • John • Paul • Joseph Of Arimathea**

(For evidence, see 'takeaways' sheet)

### THE QUESTIONS

- How likely is it that the centurion and those burying Jesus were mistaken about him being dead?
- How likely is it that the women were mistaken about the location of the tomb?
- Why did no-one produce the body?
- Who wanted to suppress rumours of a resurrection the most?
- How likely is it that all the reported appearances of Jesus were hallucinations?

## PSYCHOLOGICAL

### THE FACTS

The disciples were changed from a group who fled in panic at the arrest of Jesus and hid behind locked doors for several weeks, to a group who proclaimed from rooftops that Jesus had risen and openly denounced a crowd of thousands for being responsible for his death. Several of them were subsequently martyred for their refusal to stop preaching this message. Paul, in particular, was changed from a persecutor of Christians to Christianity's most ardent follower and most eloquent proponent.

### THE QUESTIONS

- How can the change in the disciples be explained if they knew the resurrection to be a lie?
- Would they have been prepared to die for something of which they were not convinced?
- What transformed Paul, if not the risen Christ?

## HISTORICAL

### THE FACTS

External documents testify to Christians' belief in the resurrection from the earliest days of Christianity. Throughout history and throughout the world people have continued to commit themselves to belief in the Resurrection and their lives have been changed as a result. Many have been prepared to die for their faith.

### THE QUESTIONS

- If the evidence does not support belief in the Resurrection, why has the Christian faith not disappeared?
- If the resurrection is not fact, how do you explain the changes that continue to occur in the lives of Christians?

## CROSS EXAMINATION

Assign the following roles to co-leaders or group members:

Centurion, Mary Magdalene, Joseph of Arimathea, Temple Guard, Peter, John, Thomas, Paul.

Other optional characters, if you have a large group, are:

Simon of Cyrene, Pilate, Nicodemus, Cleopas, Mary the mother of James.

Provide a briefing sheet for each one about their role in the events and the evidence they can give, with the relevant Bible references. Encourage participants to read thoroughly the Bible passages and to make sure that their 'evidence' does not go beyond what the Bible account says.

Allow group members to cross-examine 'witnesses', in turn, about their part in the events. Try to apply the normal rules of evidence i.e. only first-hand experience is valid not hearsay.

---

## PUDDING

### RE-CONSTRUCTION

Your group members might be familiar with re-constructions from T.V. programmes like 'Crimewatch' and documentaries. Use co-leaders or group members to re-construct some of the events. People can either be briefed beforehand and simply role play each scene, or scenes can be acted out as the detail is read from the relevant Bible passage. If using the latter method, have four readers and assign each one a different gospel. In this way, evidence can be pieced together from the different sources to build up the whole picture.

Use suitable props e.g. pieces of linen for graveclothes, large piece of cardboard for the stone etc. to aid the imagination.

After a scene has been enacted, members should be allowed to question the participants to clarify any evidence.

---

## CHEESE & BISCUITS

### PUT ON... PUT OFF...1

Divide the group into teams and provide two piles of clothes for each group - one of old scruffy clothes, the other of decent ones. The first member of each team dresses in the old clothes. When they are ready, blow a whistle to start the race. No.2 must take the old clothes from No.1 and put them on whilst No.1 dresses in the new clothes. When they have finished, No.3 joins them. No.2 now removes the old clothes and passes them to No.3, whilst No.1 removes the new clothes and passes them to No.2. Continue in this way until the last member of the team is wearing the new clothes.

---

## THE BILL

### PUT ON...PUT OFF...2

Dress a group member in old clothes individually labelled with the various sins listed in **Colossians 3:5-9**. Read **Colossians 3:1-14**. As the sins are mentioned, they should be removed and replaced with the new clothes, which are labelled with the virtues listed in **vv12-14**.

Point out the need for the personal 'death' and 'resurrection' illustrated by these verses.

### TASTY FINISH

If you made the bread in 'Starters', then now is the time to see the results. Hopefully, only the dough with the yeast will have risen. Explain that this was only possible because the yeast was present in the dough. This is a picture of life with Christ in us, he is the yeast for us.

Close with a prayer inviting Christ to work in the lives of you and your group members.

# Takeaways

## IF...THEN...

(Flowchart with key words omitted.)

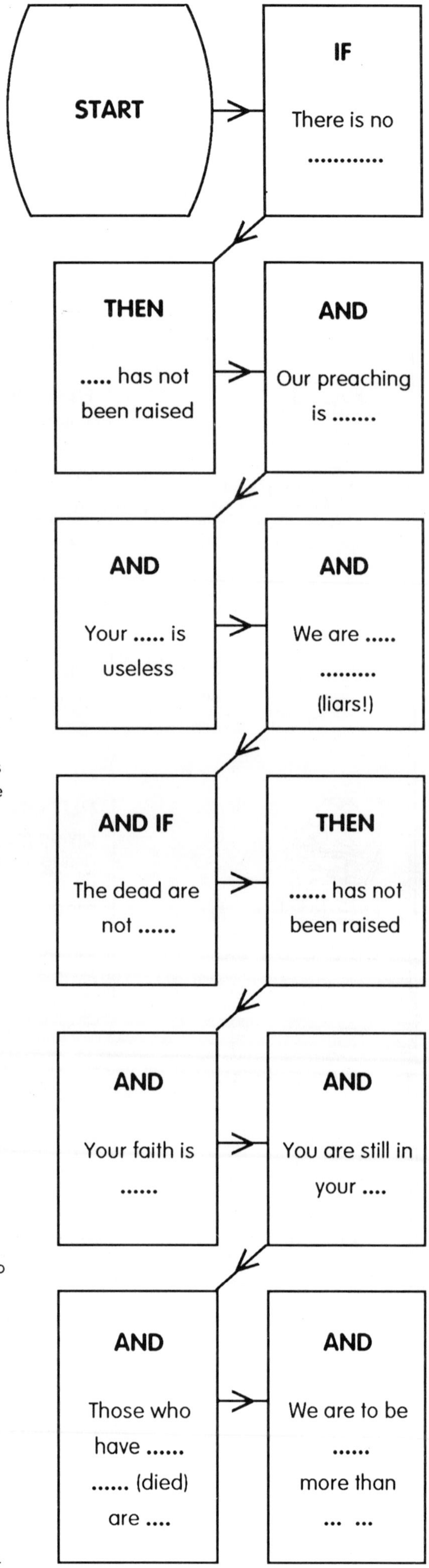

### Witnesses

**Pilate** Ordered the flogging and crucifixion; asked for confirmation that Jesus was dead before releasing the body for burial; authorised the sealing of the tomb.

**Centurion** Supervised crucifixion; pierced his side with a spear; confirmed to Pilate that Jesus was dead.

**Temple Guards** Sealed and guarded the tomb after Jesus' burial; reported events to the chief priests; were ordered to circulate the rumour that the disciples had stolen the body.

**Chief Priests** Supervised the beating of Jesus during his trial; witnessed crucifixion; requested sealing of the tomb; devised the rumour that the disciples had stolen the body then bribed the guards to circulate it.

**Joseph of Arimathea** Asked Pilate for the body of Jesus; along with Nicodemus, prepared the body for burial; provided his own tomb; placed body in the tomb and put stone over the entrance.

**The women** Present at the Crucifixion, they also witnessed the burial personally (Mt. 7:16; Mk. 15:47; Lk. 23:55); returned to the tomb on Sunday; received the message from the angel that Jesus had risen.

**Mary Magdalene** First witness to see the risen Christ.

**Peter** First to enter the empty tomb.

**John** Present at trials and crucifixion; first to reach empty tomb and second to enter; observed graveclothes and became convinced of resurrection.

**Cleopas** With a companion, met the risen Christ on the road to Emmaus; talked for several hours without recognising him; finally recognised Jesus when he broke bread.

**Thomas** Not present when risen Jesus first appeared to the other ten disciples; doubted the reality of their experience; invited to examine the wounds of Jesus in response to his stated condition for believing.

**Eleven** As a group, they met the risen Christ on at least four occasions.

**Paul** Persecutor of Christians who met risen Jesus on the road to Damascus; wrote earliest surviving record of witnesses to the resurrection, listing appearances of risen Christ to Peter, the Twelve, 500 'brothers', and James.

# The Second Coming - Ready Or Not

## TEACHING POINT

**The certainty and climactic nature of the Second Coming of Jesus, and the uncertainty about the timing of it.**

## GROUP ACTION

**To encourage group members to live more godly lives now, in the light of Jesus certain return in the future.**

MENU

**GRACE**
- **Prepare The Way** 5 minutes

**STARTERS**
- **Balloons** 5 minutes
- **Self Portrait** 10 minutes

**MAIN COURSE**
- **Highlights** 15 minutes
- **Guess The Future** 5 minutes

**PUDDING**
- **Statements** 10 minutes
- **Input** 5 minutes

**CHEESE & BISCUITS**
- **Alarm Clock** 3 minutes
- **Memory Verse** 5 minutes

**THE BILL**
- **Cups** 8 minutes
- **Letter** 8 minutes
- **Review** 5 minutes (next week)

## LAYING THE TABLE

Christian youth work is based on the personal relationships built up between the leaders and the young people in the group. But these relationships should also contain some spice. Work on building the sort of relationships with your young people where it is natural and easy to talk about spiritual things, and where it is not a strange or unnatural thing to do. As a result of this session, pray for natural opportunities to talk to one of your young people about what difference the Second Coming is making to their life.

## EQUIPMENT

- ✔ Balloons and felt tipped pens for 'Balloons'
- ✔ Paper cups for 'The Bill'
- ✔ Paper and pens for 'Self Portrait'
- ✔ Photocopies of **Matthew 24:26-31**, and **1 Thessalonians 4:13-5:4**, preferably on card, for 'Highlights'
- ✔ Highlighter pens for 'Highlights'

## MUSIC

Soon and very soon

Lo He Comes

At the Name of Jesus

I cannot tell

Lift up your heads

Prepare the way of the Lord

When the Lord in glory comes

Some of these are hymns, and we suggest them because the words are brilliant. Some youth leaders don't like hymns believing that young people won't sing them. Try some of these, you might be surprised...

## COOKING

The Second Coming is a very important doctrine, as it points us to the future, which is the focus of our faith. Paul summarises this:

**Philippians 3:20** 'But our citizenship is in heaven. And we eagerly await a saviour from there, the Lord Jesus Christ.'

The 3 main Biblical words used to describe the Second Coming are:

1. **Parousia -** This is the commonest term for the Second Coming in the Greek New Testament, and means 'Coming', 'Arrival', or 'Presence'. It was used in the first century for the visit of the Emperor or other important person.
2. **Apocalypse -** This means 'revelation', and refers to the fact that the Second Coming will reveal who Jesus is, and what the world is. These facts are now hidden, but will be revealed for all to see on Jesus' return.
3. **Epiphanea -** This means 'Appearing' or 'Manifestation', as in the drawing of curtains so that you can see what lies the other side of them. It applies to people being able to see what lies beyond death and the end of the world, and so see who Jesus really was and is.

'Main Course' looks at the nature of Jesus' return, and is based on material from **Matthew 24** and **1 Thessalonians 4 & 5**. 'Pudding' looks at the time of the Second Coming, not so that we can spend our time trying to work out when it will be, but rather so that we will always be watchful, ready and waiting. In this section, you may wish to sound a note of caution about speculating about the time of the Second Coming, because:

- 'The last days' can be taken to refer to the time between Jesus' first and second comings, and not just to the time immediately before his second coming (see **Acts 2:17**).
- Jesus discouraged people trying to work out the time of the end.
- Jesus stressed that his return would be unexpected.
- Even Jesus (then) didn't know the time of his return (**Matthew 24:36**)

## GRACE

### PREPARE THE WAY

Use the words of the song 'Prepare The Way Of The Lord' as a prayer. Either do this all together as a group or arrange for individuals to say a verse each out loud.

## STARTERS

### BALLOONS

Give each of your members a balloon and a felt tipped pen. Ask them to write on their balloon all the things that they are going to do in the next week. Ask them to be as detailed as they can, so as to fill up as much space as they can on the balloon. Either now, or during 'Main Course', go around with a pin and pop the balloons. Lead into the session by saying how the Second Coming of Jesus bursts all our plans for the future here on earth.

### SELF PORTRAIT

Give each group member a piece of paper and some drawing equipment. Ask them each to draw an annotated picture of themselves in 20 years time. This could include their husband/wife, number of children, where they hope to be living, what kind of job they hope to be doing, etc. Ask them to share their results with the other members of the group.

Make the point that this exercise assumes that life goes on and that the world will still be here in 20 years time. Show them how the fact of the Second Coming may well alter their plans for the future.

## MAIN COURSE

Start by making the points which arise naturally from the exercises you have done from 'Starters'. Then explain that the Christian Doctrine of the Second Coming of Jesus Christ states that Jesus Christ will return in glory to end the world as we know it, to judge mankind, and to introduce the new Heaven and the new Earth.

Aim to teach your group about the nature of the Second Coming - what it will be like. Most of this teaching will come from **Matthew 24:26-31**, and **1 Thessalonians 4:13 - 5:4**.

### HIGHLIGHTS

We suggest that you photocopy enough copies of these 2 passages to be able to give one to each member of your group. When you copy it, ensure that there is sufficient room for your group to make their own notes.

Explain to your group that you are looking at what the Second Coming will be like. Divide them into groups of 2 or 3, and ask them to look at the passage, and to ring, highlight, underline or otherwise mark those parts of the passage which talk about the following features of the Second Coming:

- Mysterious (eg **Matthew 24:27**)
- Glorious (eg **Matthew 24:30**)
- Decisive (eg **Matthew 24:30, 1 Thessalonians 4:16**)
- Sudden (eg **1 Thessalonians 5:2**)
- Unexpected (eg **1 Thessalonians 5:2**)
- Involving everyone (eg **Matthew 24:31, 1 Thessalonians 5:3**)
- The dead will rise (eg **Matthew 24:31, 1 Thessalonians 4:14-17**)

Ask your members to annotate their passage with the words 'Mysterious' etc, in large letters, so that they get an idea of what it will be like.

It would be a good idea, during this, if you could show on the OHP a copy of what you have given your members, so that you can go through what they have done, and make appropriate comments. (See 'Cooking', for possible content on what you might say).

**GUESS THE FUTURE**

At this stage in the session have a break but before you do, ask your young people to jot down one or two things that they think will happen in the next 15 minutes. These things may include what people will have to drink, what they will say, who will talk to who, or other things they think will happen. Ask them to screw up their pieces of papers and then collect them in.

At the end of the break, inspect the predictions and see how accurate they were. Explain that it is impossible to accurately predict the future. Then lead in to 'Pudding' about when the Second Coming will happen.

## PUDDING

Aim to teach your group about the timing of the Second Coming - when it will happen. This will be based of **Mark 13** and a few other selected passages.

**STATEMENTS**

Give your group copies of the 'Takeaways' Sheet, and ask them to put a tick, cross or question mark against each statement depending on whether they agree, disagree, or don't know. Go through and explain the correct answers giving reasons for what you say.

**Mark 13: 1-37**

Ask your group to look up this passage. Explain that it is a passage which has a mix of material about the fall of Jerusalem (which happened in 70 AD), and material about the end of the world. It's quite easy to separate the two, so as the passage is being read, have someone stand out at the front with 2 large cards, saying 'Fall of Jerusalem' and 'End of the world'. They hold one of these up at the appropriate points as the passage is being read. You could alternatively, use the OHP to do this, but whichever method you use, explain what you are going to do before you do it!

**INPUT**

In a short input from you, explain that there are certain 'signs of the times' which have to take place before Jesus returns. The general areas are:

- Religious apostasy (**Mark 13:5ff**)
- Persecution and the worldwide witness of the church

(**Mark 13:9-11,13,19**)

- Wars and conflict (**Mark 13:7**)
- Disturbances to the natural order (**Mark 13:8,24ff**)

Explain that these are general and not specific signs, and that we are not supposed to try and work out the exact time of Jesus' return by referring to them, that is not why we have been told about them. Rather, they have been given to keep us on our toes, as the last days are the days between Jesus' first and second comings, and these signs are what life will be like in these intervening times. Refer your members to the card handout in 'Main Course' and to those references to the fact that we do not know when Jesus will return (eg **1 Thessalonians 5:1-3**). We must therefore be ready at all times.

---

## CHEESE & BISCUITS

### ALARM CLOCK

The consistent biblical teaching is that we do not know when the Second Coming will happen. To illustrate this, before the start of this session, set an alarm clock to go off towards the end of the meeting, and conceal it in a box or bag. At the start of the session, ask members to vote on when they think the alarm clock will go off. At this point, (or at other regular points during the meeting), remind your group that the alarm has not gone off yet, and that no-one knows when it will go off. Draw the parallels between this and the unknown timing of the Second Coming.

### MEMORY VERSE

**Mark 13:26**

> 'At that time men will see the Son of Man coming in clouds with great power and glory.'

**Philippians 3:20**

> 'But our citizenship is in heaven. And we eagerly await a saviour from there, the Lord Jesus Christ.'

---

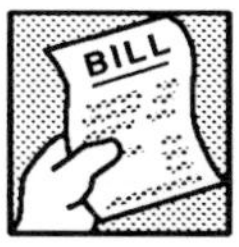


## THE BILL

### CUPS

Give each of your young people a paper cup and a pen that will write on it. (Or else give them a curved shape to cut out which can then be stuck to form a cup shape). Ask your group members individually to write on their cup what they are going to do as a result of this session. Clearly this will be seen by other people, so make sure your members realise this before they start writing.

### LETTER

The proof of the pudding is in the eating, and the proof of the learning is in the doing. Explain that whenever the Second Coming is mentioned in the Bible, it is always to encourage Christians to live more godly lives now so that they will be ready for Jesus when he returns. Therefore the application of this passage is very important. Encourage your members to apply it specifically now, and to do something about it.

Ask your members to write a private letter to Jesus, telling him what they think of this idea of the Second Coming, and what they are going to do to prepare to meet him.

### REVIEW

Next week, go back over what you have covered, and remind your group of the changes that they were going to make to their life as a result of this week's study.

## STATEMENTS

For use in 'Pudding'

Look at the following statements and confirm whether you agree with them or not by placing the relevant symbol in the box.

Yes, I agree (✓); no, I disagree (✗); I don't know (?)

☐ The time of the Second Coming has already been fixed

☐ No-one knows when the Second Coming will be

☐ We should not try to work out when the Second Coming will be

☐ The Second Coming will take everyone by surprise

☐ Jesus talked about the signs of the times to help us see when the Second Coming would take place

☐ It is unlikely that Jesus will return tonight

☐ Some will miss the Second Coming

☐ We must always be ready for the Second Coming

# Judgement - The Verdict

## TEACHING POINT

**All people will come before the judgement seat of the just God, and be judged according to their response to the revealed will of God.Christians will have their work for God assessed and there will be some form of reward for those Christians who have been good stewards of what God has given them.**

## GROUP ACTION

**To understand that God's Judgement is not nasty or vindictive but is based on guidelines he has already laid down and has made known to us.**

MENU

**GRACE**
- **Reflections** 5-10 minutes

**STARTERS**
- **Quotations** 10 minutes
- **Questions** 10-15 minutes
- **Ball Discussion** 5 minutes

**MAIN COURSE**
- **Move It** 20 minutes
- **Bible Study** 15 minutes
- **Agony Aunt** 10-15 minutes

**PUDDING**
- **Fill In** 5 minutes
- **Input** 10 minutes

**CHEESE & BISCUITS**
- **Pictionary** 15-60 minutes
- **Memory Verse** 5 minutes

**THE BILL**
- **Letter To God** 10 minutes

## LAYING THE TABLE

Many modern teaching resources suggest the use of games and activities to help young people learn, and this resource is no different. But it may be appropriate in a session where the content is quite sober, to consider using communication techniques which are more low key. This may be a good session to consider using more straightforward teaching techniques and to have a higher proportion of up-front input. There's nothing wrong with this, particularly perhaps in a session which deals with such a serious issue.

Always have your group members right at the front of your mind when preparing and leading a meeting. Always have in mind those who don't like contributing to a discussion, those who don't like to (or can't) read and write, and those who might struggle with other activities you are suggesting. You don't have to know your members inside out to bear these things in mind. Just remember that you may have people in your group who are not as confident or gifted as you are, and plan alternatives which don't single them out as being less gifted or more introvert, than the rest of the group.

## EQUIPMENT

- ✔ Verses on cards, questions and bowls for 'Move It'
- ✔ Paper and pens for 'Letter To God'
- ✔ Cassette recorder or camcorder for 'Questions'
- ✔ Ball for 'Ball Discussion'

## MUSIC

Jesus shall take the highest honour

Jesus we celebrate your victory

O Lord, the clouds are gathering

## COOKING

When you say 'judgement' the first thought that most people have is a negative one. People often get the wrong idea about judgement, and they confuse it with 'judgmental' - ie they think it means 'condemning'. This means that when the whole subject of judgement is raised, people will often automatically think of God as being a condemning God, and therefore, the whole subject gets a bad press. So right at the start of this session, you will need to explain to your group that the judgement of God is a simple decision, based on guidelines he has already laid down and has made known to us. It is not condemning, but rather it has positive and negative elements.

The 'Main Course' will be teaching the judgement of all who have lived, past and present. The 'Pudding' will be looking specifically at the judgement of Christians.

## GRACE

**REFLECTIONS**

During a time of silence encourage your group to consider, individually, their standing before God - am I a Christian?; what level of commitment do I have to God?; how is God likely to judge my life so far? What more can I do?

Lead them into a time of individual prayer focussing positively on their future response to God.

## STARTERS

### QUOTATIONS
Give out copies of the 'Takeaways' sheet, and ask your group to look at the quotations on it. Give each one a mark out of 10. Don't tell them on what basis the marks are given, so hopefully they will give marks based on what they think of the rightness of what each quotation is saying.

Go through the quotations from the front, and ask what people gave. See if there is any agreement between group members. Focus on the whole area of judgement, rather than on the rightness or otherwise of each particular situation. Avoid red herrings. You may like to use this to begin to talk with your group about the judgement of God, or to go on from this to introduce this meeting's subject of judgement.

### QUESTIONS
Ask your group to think of one question about judgement which they would like answered. Go around with a portable recorder (camcorder if you have access to one), and record their questions. Play back the recording so that people can hear the questions that everyone is asking.

At the end of the session, play back the tape again, and see if the questions have been answered. If not, tie up the loose ends before the session ends, or fix up to meet again (possibly with an 'expert'), to nail these final questions.

### BALL DISCUSSION
Introduce the subject of the judgement of God by getting your group into a circle (or several separate circles if you have a very large group), and throw a ball around the group. When someone catches the ball, they have to contribute something to the discussion. Prime the exercise by asking a question such as 'How can it be right for God to judge all people?' You may also like to have various other questions displayed somewhere in your meeting room, so that those who don't have anything to add to the discussion can pick one of the questions, and so be 'let off the hook'.

---

## MAIN COURSE

Begin by telling your members the teaching points for this session. Stress that the doctrine of the judgement of God is not as terrifying or as un-Christian as some people imagine, but that it is a biblical and just way of dealing with all people, Christian and non-Christian alike.

### MOVE IT
If you have a group of 12 or more, try this active way of looking at the Bible. Write out the verses provided below onto pieces of paper or card, and stick these up at different points around your meeting room. Under each verse, place 2 bowls, one with question sheets on that particular verse in it, and one for group members answers. The members pair up and visit each verse. They collect one question sheet, write down some answers in the space you provide on the question sheet, and place their completed question sheet in the answer bowl. Make sure your members don't just pick up an already completed answer sheet and copy someone else's answer!

**Hebrews 9:27**

- When does the judgement of God happen?
- Who will be involved in the judgement of God?

**John 5:22-23**

- Who was and is the judge?
- Why has God the Father done this?

**Malachi 4:1-2**
- Who is speaking about these events?
- Are these events likely, unlikely, or certain to happen? Why?
- Describe what will happen to the evildoers and those who revere God's name.

**John 5:24-27**
- What do we have to do to avoid condemnation at the judgement?
- What is so important at the end of **v24**?
- What is **v25** talking about?
- Why has the Son got authority to judge?

**Acts 17:31**
- What do we learn from this about the 'day when he will judge the world'?
- What has the resurrection got to do with this?

**2 Timothy 4:1**
- What is the extent of the judgement?
- Who will do it?
- What is the link between the second coming and the judgement?

**Genesis 18:25**
- Why does this verse enable us to face judgement with confidence?

## BIBLE STUDY

If you have a smaller group, you may want to consider having a leader-led Bible study, using the questions which we have suggested in 'Move It' above.

Many young people have a problem over those who have not heard the Gospel. You may want to mention this at this stage, but don't turn this into a session on 'apologetics' (rational justification of Christianity)! Make the following points:

- God will take people's ignorance into account at the judgement (**2 Peter 2:21**).
- God has revealed himself to all through creation (**Romans 1:19-32**), and through the moral law, which we all have an awareness of through our conscience (**Romans 2:14-16**).
- In the end we have to acknowledge that we don't know all the answers, and we trust God that he will do right (**Genesis 18:25**).

## AGONY AUNT

Divide your group up into one or more groups of three, and ask them to discuss if there is anything that bothers them about this doctrine of the judgement of God.

Ask your group to write this down in the form of a letter to an 'Agony Aunt'. If your group don't like writing, ask them to think about what they might say in such a letter, and then record their letter on a cassette recorder, or better still a camcorder. Then pass on the letters, or apportion out the recordings, to other groups, and ask them to write or record their reply to the letter writer for publication. Record and then play back, or read out the letters and their replies.

## PUDDING

This section looks at the judgement which all Christians will face. In 'Main Course' we were able to see that Christians no longer have to face the judgement between eternal life and eternal death, (**John 5:24** - we have already passed over from death to life), but there is still an assessment of the work we have done for God.

### FILL IN

Look at **1 Corinthians 3:10-15**. Either write this out and photocopy it, or write it on a flipchart or OHP, but as you write it, leave gaps where the words 'Foundation', 'Builder', 'Work', 'Reward', and 'Loss' occur. You may like to fill the gaps with little pictures, or leave them blank, and then read the passage. When the blanks come in the reading, ask your members to shout out the relevant words, and to do some relevant hand signs to help them to concentrate and remember what the passage is about.

### INPUT

Read out **2 Corinthians 5:10**.

In a short talk from one of the leaders, make the following points:

- This cannot imperil our eternal salvation (**Romans 8:1**)
- Christians will be judged according to how we have used the gifts, talents, opportunities and responsibilities given to us in this life.
- It will be a fatherly judgement, full of love, compassion and understanding.
- There will be some sort of reward in heaven, but we are not told what this reward will be.

---

## CHEESE & BISCUITS

### PICTIONARY

If you want a raucous break, play Pictionary. Divide your group into groups of 4-6, and arm each group with paper and a pencil. Write out a list of things which the young people can draw, many of which can have something to do with the last things. Suggestions:

- the last day
- good deeds
- justice
- the throne of God
- Jesus

You can organise this in a variety of ways. For example, have it as a competition between the groups, and as they guess a particular picture, the person who gets it runs out to you and gets another subject to draw. The first group to guess all the subjects on your list wins. Or have it less competitive, and simply have some fun trying to guess what the different pictures are.

### MEMORY VERSE

**Genesis 18:25**

'...Will not the Judge of all the earth do right?'

---

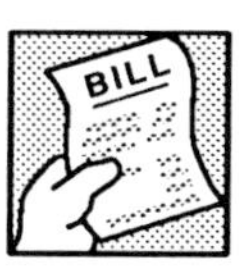


## THE BILL

### LETTER TO GOD

Give your group paper and pens, and ask them to write a letter to God, telling him what they now think of the judgement of God. If you know your group well, you may want to ask for some of them to read out their contributions, so that the rest of the group can benefit.

Pray quietly about what has just been thought and written.

# Takeaways

## QUOTATIONS

MARK OUT OF TEN

☐ 'Life imprisonment for murder should mean life imprisonment, and not getting out after 10 years.'

☐ 'If you don't do any work, you don't deserve to pass your exams.'

☐ 'Why should I get done for copying someone else's homework when everyone else is doing it and they get away with it?'

☐ 'Why should I wait until I'm 18 to go out for a drink, when everyone else goes when they are 17?'

☐ 'It's not fair. She landed the Saturday job because the manager knows her mum.'

☐ 'He works really hard. If anyone deserves to get a job after school, he does. So why can't he get one?'

☐ 'I've never done anyone any harm. I'll be alright when I get to the pearly gates.'

☐ 'But she's such a nice person, I can't believe that God would condemn her.'

☐ 'Convicted terrorists deserve to die.'

☐ 'God's much too nice to condemn anyone.'

☐ 'And be sure, your sins will find you out.'

# Heaven And Hell - The Sentence

## TEACHING POINT

**That all people, who have ever lived, will either spend eternity with God or separated from God. The Bible calls these places, Heaven and Hell.**

## GROUP ACTION

**Aim to show the group what Heaven and Hell are and help them to consider seriously where they are heading. Give them the opportunity to respond to this session.**

MENU

**GRACE**
- **Expectations** 3 minutes
- **Sing It** 4 minutes

**STARTERS**
- **Dress Sense** Announce prior to meeting
- **Sides** 3 minutes
- **Interviews** 5 minutes (plus preparation)

**MAIN COURSE**
- **Explain** 6 minutes
- **Mix Up** 10 minutes
- **Courtroom** Whole Session

**PUDDING**
- **Relay** 10-15 minutes
- **Quotations** 6 minutes

**CHEESE & BISCUITS**
- **Obituary** 5 minutes
- **Egg-Field** 12 minutes
- **Memory Verse** 6 minutes

**THE BILL**
- **Summary** 8 minutes
- **Creed** 15 minutes
- **Faces** 6 minutes

## LAYING THE TABLE

This session may provide you with a natural opportunity to ask your young people where they are heading. Explain the Gospel to them, and show them the two possible destinations involved. There is no need for excessive human pressure, as the Holy Spirit will be speaking as we explain the Bible clearly, but do make it as clear as you can, and give your young people the opportunity to respond should they want to.

This may be a starting point for a personal conversation with one or two of your group members. It should always be our aim to talk to them from time to time at a spiritual level, and a session like this gives an ideal starting point, with a question like 'What did you think of the session last week?'

## EQUIPMENT

- ✔ 2 OHP's/screens or alternatives (eg flipchart or large sheets of paper)
- ✔ Rope for 'Sides'
- ✔ Camcorder or cassette recorder for 'Interviews'
- ✔ Slips of paper for 'Obituary'
- ✔ Eggs and blindfolds for 'Egg-Field'

## MUSIC

All hail the Lamb

Holy, holy, holy is the Lord

Worthy art thou

Thou art worthy

All heaven declares

All these songs are from the early chapters of the book of Revelation. Point this out to your young people, and give them the references. You could turn one of these into the memory verse for this session.

## COOKING

When teaching apparently unpleasant Bible truths, it's even more important than usual to show your young people that these are not your ideas, but you are simply teaching what the Bible says. Stress this, as unpalatable truths are less easily rejected if their source is clear.

This session will concentrate on Hell in 'Main Course', and Heaven in 'Pudding'. Nothing can be more serious than the material which is going to be covered in this session, so take care in your preparation, that you are using material which is not going to make the subject trivial or frivolous.

There have been recent theological debates about the exact nature of hell: whether it will be everlasting torment or annihilation. It is not the place of this resource to probe theological debate. Stress that hell is separation from God for eternity, and that is something to be avoided at all costs.

'Those who remain unrepentant when confronted by God's claim on them, who reject his will when it is made known to them, and who continue through their lives in the blasphemy and rebellion which sin implies, will face God's just wrath.' (Bruce Milne, Know The Truth (IVP 1982), p 274)

Be sure to stress the positive side of this session rather than major on the doctrine of hell. Make sure you spend a lot of time in this session teaching your group about heaven. Hell may hold some form of morbid fascination. But heaven is where Christians are heading, so let's learn about it.

## GRACE

**EXPECTATIONS**
Ask a couple of your group members to pray at the start of the meeting for everyone to be expecting God to speak to them about the response they should make to this session.

**SING IT**
While in an attitude of prayer sing 'All Hail The Lamb' through twice as a group.

## STARTERS

**DRESS SENSE**
The week before this session, suggest to your young people that as this is such a serious subject, that they may wish to turn up in more formal attire than usual. Serious occasions require serious dress. Wear a dinner jacket or equivalent yourself, and at the start of the session, explain to your young people why you are dressed in this way.

**SIDES**
Divide your group into 2, and place a rope across the room, so that it is divided into 2 equal halves, with one half of your group in one half, and the other half of your group in the other half of the room. The aim of the game is to grab people on the other side of the line, and pull them on to your side. The winning team is the one that has the most people after 3 minutes. Team members are not allowed to cower in the corner, and must move around so that they are 'grabbable' by their opponents.

**INTERVIEWS**
Interview young people on what they think heaven and hell will be like. Use a camcorder if at all possible. You could do this outside school one morning or afternoon, **but ask the Headteacher's permission first, and explain clearly what it will be used for**. Ask well ahead of time, so that the Head has sufficient time to tell other staff members.

Play back these interviews at the start of the meeting, and use them to introduce the subject of heaven and hell.

## MAIN COURSE

**EXPLAIN**
Start by explaining that just as in 'Sides' above, where everyone was either on one side or the other, so at the end of the world, the judgement of God will mean that all people, past and present, will end up in one of two destinations, heaven or hell. Explain that the term hell can be quite an emotive subject, but that we want to use it because the Bible uses it to describe the eternal destiny of those who are separated from God.

It would be useful to have two OHP's and screens (or flip charts) for this session. Use them throughout the session by displaying information about hell on one, and using the other to display information about heaven. This would be an effective way to emphasise the contrast between the two.

**MIX UP**
Give your young people a copy of the 'Takeaways' sheet and ask them to unscramble the sentences so that they make coherent sense, match the sentence with the selection of verses (don't allow them to open their Bibles for the first 5 minutes of this exercise - that might constitute cheating.), and note down what each verse teaches them about hell.

Recap the main lessons learned, and stress the seriousness of the situation for those who do not know Jesus. Write a summary of the answers on the first OHP, and keep this turned on for the 'Pudding'.

**COURTROOM**

You could run the whole session as a legal case, where your group are on trial, accused of sin against the holy and perfect God. The verdict is either innocent or guilty, and the sentence is either life with God in heaven if innocent, or life without God in hell if guilty.

Think through the possibility of setting up your meeting room as a courtroom, and use the session to sum up what you have covered on JUDGEMENT in session 9, and to focus on the sentence of the court. Stress that there are only two possible outcomes.

---

## PUDDING

Explain to your group that it's very difficult to describe what heaven will be like. That's because it's far outside any experience we have ever had. The Bible therefore tends to draw word pictures to describe it, and in interpreting these, we must be sure not to take them too literally, nor too sceptically.

**RELAY**

Put the question 'What will heaven be like?' onto the second OHP. Divide your group into 2 or more teams of between 3 and 6. The aim of this game is that the members go to one of the leaders, collect a slip of paper with a Bible verse on it, go back to their group, look up the verse and answer the question on the OHP, and then (and only then) another member from the group collects another verse, etc. Stress that although this is a relay, it is not a race. Give them time to look at the verses, and to see what they say. If you meet in a home, get the members to collect the verses from another room. These are the verses. Write them onto cards or photocopy them onto sheets for your group members.

**Matthew 24:35** **1 John 3:2** **Luke 23:43**
**Revelation 19:7** **1 Corinthians 15:42-44** **Revelation 21:4**
**1 Corinthians 15:51-55** **Revelation 22:3-5**

Alternatively you could give each group just 2 verses to look at, and give them a piece of OHP acetate and pen. Ask them to write their findings on the acetate and then put it on the OHP. You'll have to read all these as you recap and make the main points about what heaven is like. Or, once all the groups have finished, collate the information onto the second OHP, and draw the contrasts between heaven and hell.

**QUOTATIONS**

Borrow a book of Christian quotations from your minister, and look up a selection on heaven. Display these around your meeting room, and read these out to your group at this point in the meeting.

> eg. 'The essence of life in heaven is to see and know God. It will be an endless exploration of unutterable beauty, love, kindness, power, joy and grace which is God himself.' (unknown)

Use some of the biblical quotations about heaven too!

Make sure at the end of this teaching section that your young people realise that we cannot decide which way people are heading. That is, in the end, God's decision. We have a responsibility to make sure that we are right with God, and we can know in our hearts whether we are heading for heaven, but we can't make that judgement about other people. That's God's job.

## CHEESE & BISCUITS

### OBITUARY

Explain to your group what an obituary is, and then ask them either to write their own, or to write one for another member of the group. These should be quite short (50-60 words). Or lead your group in the writing of their own personal epitaph as follows:

- On a piece of paper, write your name
- Underneath that write your date of birth
- Underneath that, write today's date
- Underneath that, write a one or two word description of yourself
- Then write 'RIP', draw a gravestone shape around it, and tell your group that they have just written their own epitaph.

### EGG-FIELD

Divide your group into pairs, or if you have a large group, ask for volunteers, and go outside and find a piece of flat ground.

Mark a start and finish, and place between 6 and 12 eggs on the ground to form an obstacle course. Blindfold one person in each pair, and the sighted one has to guide the blindfolded one through this egg-field without treading on any of the eggs. (The leading may be done physically or verbally)

Play this for a bit of fun. Refer to it later on when you want to illustrate the need to trust Jesus Christ, putting your faith in him, as the way of avoiding hell, and booking your place in heaven.

### MEMORY VERSE

**1 Thessalonians 1:9-10**

'They tell how you turned to God from idols, to serve the living and true God, and to wait for his Son from heaven, whom he raised from the dead - Jesus, who rescues us from the coming wrath.'

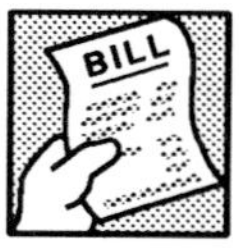


## THE BILL

### SUMMARY

Ask your members to write down a summary of what they have learnt in this session.

### CREED

Ask your members to work in groups of 3 or 4, and to write their own creed which summarises what they have learnt, either in this session, in this block of three sessions, or in this whole course about Christian doctrines. You may need to explain what a creed is, and for instance give them some directions like:

- Start with 'We believe...'
- Keep sentences very short - keep it to the bare essentials
- Each section should be a short summary of what we believe about a particular aspect of Christianity.

You may need to plant a leader in each group, to keep down the heresy, and to help your group with what is quite a difficult, but a very rewarding task.

Ask each group to say their creed together, and if there is a particularly good one, get your whole group to say it together.

### FACES

Ask your members to draw a face which sums up how they now feel about the doctrines of heaven and hell (a small selection has been provided on the 'Takeaways' sheet. Ask them to put a small caption under each face to explain why they are feeling this way.

# Takeaways

## MIX UP

**Unscramble the mixed up sentence, match it up with the right verse, then note down what it teaches you.**

**1** Hand sin better to you maimed two hell fire out it if where never hands causes life go to it for enter to off your you is with cut goes the than into.

**2** Darkness where that servant and throw gnashing will teeth into weeping of outside be worthless the there and.

**3** No ever smoke torment or night beast the day worship image or name and rises of rest there is the who those and his mark who for ever their for anyone for the receives of his and.

**4** Contempt everlasting dust multitudes the awake to sleep to shame everlasting and life earth the of who will others in some.

**5** There be teeth of furnace the weeping them throw will will where gnashing and they into fiery.

**Verses**

Daniel 12:2 Mark 9:43 Matthew 13:42 Revelation 14:11 Matthew 25:30

# TEST 1

## Part 1 - Example Answer: Essay - Mark: 3

There are too many people today in the U.S.A and Europe who are needing to lose weight. They must do something about it. I'm sure people agree to this.

Firstly, many people are eating fast food. This makes them get obese. People should to eat healthy foods then they wouldn't get obese and have problems with their health. There's so many calories in fast food and it's too iresponible of schools to serve burgers and things like that in the canteen.

Another reason why people get obese is the drinking. Alcohol is fatening and so are soft drinks, even. People are not realising that when they are drinking alcohol, this makes them get obese.

I belive that schools should tell students about obesity. When children are learning what makes them get obese from a young age then they are less likely to be obese when they are older.

So we should educate children and stop them eating fast food because when they grow up, they are going to become obese.

### Examiner comments:

| Subscale | Mark | Commentary |
|---|---|---|
| Content | 3 | The introduction clearly introduces the topic of obesity and its prevalence in the U.S.A. and Europe and the need to tackle the problem. All main topic issues are then covered from the effect of fast food (para 2) and alcohol (para 3) on obesity, as well as introducing the writer's own opinion on the subject 'I belive that schools should tell students about obesity' (para 4). Whilst a solution is offered to weight problems connected to fast food consumption 'People should to eat healthy foods then they wouldn't get obese,' (para 2) no solution to the effect on alcohol consumption and obesity is offered, the writer merely stating the link between the two 'Another reason why people get obese is the drinking.' (para 3). In addition, the conclusion summarises the effect of fast food on obesity, proposing a solution, but fails to refer to the role of alcohol in obesity. The writer also does not take a clear personal stance on the issue in the conclusion, instead stating a general proposal 'So we should educate children.' |
| Communicative Achievement | 3 | In places the register is too informal as the writer directly addresses the reader, 'I'm sure people agree to this,' (para 1) and uses inappropriately informal lexis 'burgers and things like that...' (para 2). Too frequent use of the active tense instead of the more formal passive e.g. 'They must do something about it,' (para 1), 'it's too iresponible of schools to serve burgers and things like that in the canteen...' (para 2), makes the essay too informal on occasion. The introduction of new ideas is clearly signposted with markers e.g. 'Firstly...Another reason...I belive that...' and the ideas are then developed clearly and coherently, in topic-related paragraphs. There is a clear introduction, although the view expressed in the conclusion is more general, than personal. |
| Organisation | 4 | The topic is clearly stated in the introduction and the causes of obesity - fast food consumption and alcohol - are discussed in topic - related paragraphs, which each deal with one idea, followed by the writer's opinion 'I belive that schools should tell students about obesity,' (para 3) and a clear conclusion. There needs to be more linking words though, to give cohesion to the essay which can seem quite disjointed as a result in places, e.g. 'Firstly, many people...This makes them get obese. People should to eat healthy foods...There's so many calories' (para 2). |
| Language | 3 | There are several misuses of the present continuous in this essay, e.g with stative verbs 'who are needing to...' 'are not realising,' and other instances where the present simple should have been used, instead e.g. after conditional forms 'When children are learning what makes them get obese from a young age then...' and when describing a habit/routine 'many people are eating fast food...' Other grammatical mistakes are present e.g. '..there's so many calories in...' should to eat healthy foods,' but they do not impede comprehension. There are some instances of errors in vocabulary e.g. 'I'm sure people agree to this...' 'so are soft drinks, even.' as well as in spelling 'iresponible', 'fatening', but they are relatively minor. There is an absence of linking words e.g 'because,' 'as,' which could join sentences making the essay seem less disjointed. |

# TEST 1

## Part 1 - Example Answer: Essay - Mark: 2

I don't know whether you've noticed it like me, but there's so many obese people . Being obese harms the health and as a result we need to do something to stop it. Fast food and drinking are large reasons why people get obese.

Everywhere there are fast food places. It's too easy to get and eat food that causes you problems to your health and makes you to get fat. I know that when I eat burgers I put on weight and I think not just me but everyone does. So this should be stopped .

Another thing that is making people to get obese is the alchohol. There's so many calories in drink. You know, people are not thinking of this when they drink, then they are suprised when they get obese. They must stop to drink so much alchohol if they want to be O.K.

Finally I reckon that if schools teach children how to eat rigtht then they won't be having obesity problems when they are older.

So I think that drinking and fast food and education too are important to stop people becoming obese.

### Examiner comments:

| Subscale | Mark | Commentary |
|---|---|---|
| Content | 2 | The problem of obesity and the need to tackle it is referred to in the introduction. The two problem areas linked to obesity-namely fast food and drinking are reviewed respectively in paragraphs 2 and 3, with the writer as required, offering their own viewpoint on the issue of obesity, in paragraph 4. These ideas are briefly summarised in a clearly-defined conclusion. However, in the introduction, the prevalence of the problem is referred to, but not its distribution i.e. in the U.S.A. and Europe. The connection between fast food and obesity is made in paragraph 2, but no clear solution as to how to tackle this is offered, the writer merely stating 'so this should be stopped.' The conclusion is also too brief and merges several issues together, referring to negative (fast food, drinking ) and positive (education) influences together as being 'important' but not clarifying how or re-stating a solution to these issues. |
| Communicative Achievement | 2 | The register in many instances is too informal, with the writer inappropriately giving personal examples 'I know that when I eat burgers I put on weight and I think not just me but everyone does,' (para 2), and addressing the reader 'I don't know whether you've noticed it like me...' (introduction) ... 'You know...' (para 3). In addition, phrases used are sometimes too informal 'Another thing,' ... 'I reckon...' Reference points of personal and demonstrative pronouns are not always clear, e.g. 'Being obese harms the health...we need to do something to stop it...' (para 1) ... 'So this needs to be stopped.' (para 2). |
| Organisation | 3 | There is a clearly defined introduction. The main body of the essay is organised into distinct topic-related issues, although the solution to the problems raised in each paragraph is not always clear. The conclusion is clearly outlined, although the content is somewhat muddled, referring to both positive and negative influences on obesity as being 'important' but not clarifying how. |
| Language | 2 | Language is limited to everyday vocabulary but often sentence structures are incorrect. 'It's too easy to get and eat food that causes you problems to your health.' (para 2) 'Another thing that is making people to get obese' (para 3). There are also many grammatical errors, throughout, with plural forms 'there's so many obese people...' (para 1) ... 'there's so many calories in...' (para 3) and frequent misuse as well as misconstruction of the infinitive 'makes you to get fat.' (para 2) 'They must stop to drink...' (para 3). Tenses are misused, often the present continuous being wrongly substituted for the present simple, 'Another thing that is making people to get obese,' ... 'people are not thinking of this.' (para 3). There are also vocabulary errors 'large reasons' ... 'fast food places' as well as misspellings 'alchohol' ... 'suprised' ... ' rigtht'. |

# TEST 1

## Part 2 - Task 2 - Model Answer: Review

This is an example of a very good answer. It uses an appropriate informal style for a review that is probably aimed at young people and uses a good range of vocabulary and grammatical structures appropriate to the audience and the publication. There is clear organisation into an introduction, main paragraph and conclusion. It begins with a title and finishes with a recommendation.

**Metropolis - A Great New Band**

Last weekend I saw a live performance by the band "Metropolis". I had not planned to see a concert, and indeed, I had never heard of the band. Why I went is a long story; a friend of a friend knew someone who knew one of the band members and said we should check it out. It has been a long time since I have been so pleasantly surprised!

The band was fantastic. They were very unique, and played a style of music that cannot be categorised. There was a lead singer with a beautiful mysterious voice, who sang mostly using abstract sounds instead of words. And then there was a man with a synthesizer and drum machine, and another with a computer who was busy sampling the other two musicians, changing the sounds a bit, and then adding what he came up with to create a really funky sound. It was all improvised and very creative! It was great value for money, too, since the concert was free!

If you ever get the chance to see "Metropolis" perform, even if you have to pay, by all means do it! You will not regret it.

## Part 2 - Task 2 - Example Answer: Review - Mark: 3

This is an adequate attempt at a review. It uses an appropriate, fairly informal style and it is well-organised into an introduction, main-body paragraph and conclusion in which a recommendation is made. Linking expressions are generally used well (however, so, unless). However, frequent grammatical errors distract the reader and prevent this review from receiving a higher mark (i.e. 'was a disappointment performance' 'look like having fun' ambiguity about bored/boring). The past tense is not used consistently, particularly in the case of irregular verbs.

**Stacy Kay**

The band I saw was Stacy Kay. I have many of their albums and I enjoy very much. However, this band was a very disappointment performance.

The band was boring. The singer, named Stacy Kay like the band looked like she was sleeping. She did not look like having fun and it make us all feel like not having fun. The guitarist was good but he never danced he just stand and played. The drummer was awful, although he had funny hair. I like however the dress that Stacy wear. It was long and she looked like a movie star from long time ago. It is too sad that she was boring. But I liked the drummer's hair best of all. Too sad that he couldn't play drum.

So, I don't know what to say I cannot recommend it. The albums are greats and the style is nice but this live band was so bored. Maybe the day was bad for them I don't know. So, unless you want to go and see funny hair and nice dress, I say just buy the album and miss the performance. That is the best choice.

# TEST 1

## Part 2 - Task 3 - Model Answer: Report

This is an example of a very good answer. It is organised into an introduction, three main body paragraphs and a conclusion which have clear headings. The introduction and conclusion - first and last paragraph - of a report sometimes have headings but not always. The main-body paragraphs should always have headings. Each part of the question is answered. The style is appropriate for a report addressed to a principal and a variety of vocabulary and grammatical forms are included. There is good use of language for making formal recommendations.

I am writing this report to inform you about what subjects students at my school would be most interested in learning in a new elective class.

**What I did**
During lunch break I asked my classmates to fill out a questionnaire about what new class they would like. In total, I asked one hundred and forty students to fill out the questionnaire.

**What I found out**
The most common suggestions were a football or a volleyball class. This is surprising, because we already have a football team as an after-school activity. However there are no volleyball facilities at our school, so this is an interesting suggestion. The second most popular choice was media studies; of particular interest were films and the internet.

**Recommendations**
Another new football coach seems unnecessary. Instead, I would recommend hiring someone to teach a class on media studies, because there is a lot of interest in this subject too. I would also suggest creating a volleyball team as an after-school activity, because it would cost very little.

In conclusion, I think it is clear that students would benefit most if you hired someone to teach media studies, and perhaps also expanded the after-school sports program.

## Part 2 - Task 3 - Example Answer: Report - Mark: 3

This is an acceptable report. It is the correct length and satisfies the requirements of the question. The text is organised into paragraphs with headings that reflect their content. The content is generally understandable; however, there are weaknesses in grammar and vocabulary that impede expression of more complicated ideas. An attempt is made to use linking expressions (i.e. finally, therefore, on the other hand) however they are not always used appropriately and formal expressions of recommendation are lacking. Better use of formal language would have improved the report.

This report is to say what subjects the students will want to learn and will be useful for them.

**Subjects**
I think that all the students they like the sports best of all. Of my friends, the boys like the football and the girls like the volleyball. Everyone would like the hiring a physical education teacher to develop these sports. Also all like computers, for games mostly, but we like them generally and I am sure that students would be very enthusiastic with a class teaching them of computers.

**Benefits**
Therefore, sports are very good because they offer the benefits of exercising the body. It is something very important. On the other hand, the computers can benefit the whole of the future live. They will help with the jobs and so make the student lives better.

Finally I think the teacher of computers the school should hire because the student like and it will be too useful in the all of their lives. The sports are very good and popular for the students but useful only for exerciseing the body and not for the future jobs.

## Part 2 - Task 4 - Model Answer: Letter

The letter has a nice mixture of formal to more informal expressions, that would be expected in a letter to a friend, describing a formal exhibition. There is a wide range of vocabulary used accurately and grammatical forms are varied and correctly used. All the content is relevant to the task and no information from the task has been omitted. The content is also well-organised, each paragraph dealing with a separate issue.

Dear Gabriel,

How are you? It's been ages since we were last in contact! Anyway I just felt I had to write and tell you about a fabulous art exhibition I went to last weekend at the Dorchester Hotel.

What I loved most, was the variety of art on show - from sculptures to paintings and installations, all by up-and-coming artists who were being showcased in this exhibition-some of them for the first time. All of the artists were obviously highly-talented.

Although there were so many amazing different exhibits on show, I have to say, I was most impressed by the sculptures-especially the ones made from recycled or 'found' objects. They were most original!

As for the paintings, well they were probably a bit too modern for my taste. They were nevertheless well-executed and quite interesting. I much preferred the mixed media section, though, which incorporated collage into painted images.

If I hadn't been on such a limited budget I would definitely have bought something. Well that was just a brief run down of what I saw and I hope it will encourage you to visit an exhibition next time one is in town.

All the best,

Anna

## Part 2 - Task 4 - Example Answer: Letter - Mark: 3

The style of the letter is informal as to be expected in a letter to a friend, but on occasion, slang is used which is too informal for a written letter. All the content is appropriate to the task and all the relevant material is mentioned, however the content is not always well-organised; the reference back to the sculptural exhibits in paragraph 3, which is discussing the painting exhibits, results in a confusion of content. Vocabulary contains some more sophisticated lexis but in some instances there is over-repetition of words and incorrect linking words are used. There are also occasional misspellings and incorrect use of lexis, although the general meaning is still clear. Grammatical forms are varied, but with errors.

Dear Patrick,

Hi how are you doing? Hope you've been keeping well? You know you really missed out last weekend when you have decided not to go to the art exhibition at the Dorchester Hotel!

You know, you would have loved the art displays-especially the sculptures. I thought they were really great! They were made of all sorts of strange stuff-made from recyclable rubbish, not alone the usual sorts of materials like wood and stone. This kind of thing was completely new to me!

Then there were the paintings. There was a lot of abstract type art - which isn't to my like but I guess the artists had talent. I reckon the sculpture was better though. Actualy I saw one or two sculptures that I liked to buy-but they were too much money! There was also lots of other stuff for sell.

Moreover I also enjoyed the 'mixed media' section that was inclusive of installations. These installations used light and sounding to make an amazing atmospheer. It was too exciting to expereince! I wish you were there! Oh well maybe another time!

Hope to see you again soon!

Best wishes,

Jamie

# TEST 2

## Part 2 - Task 2 - Model Answer: Article

This is an example of a very good answer. It has an eye-catching title and is the correct length. It is effectively organised into an introduction, main-body and conclusion. The first part of the introduction catches the reader's attention with a generally-agreed-upon statement. It makes use of a semi-formal style appropriate for an article for a news magazine about a serious subject.

**Everyone's Responsibility**

These days the environment is a very serious issue. It seems to be in the news every day. All the politicians are arguing about what to do about it, but governments do not seem able to agree on any measures. It may seem quite hopeless, but there are a lot of ways each of us can make a difference.

Our personal choices can help to protect the environment. Recycling household rubbish makes a big difference because it saves space in landfills, and also helps to keep resources from being used up. Also, how we get around makes an impact; by choosing to walk or cycle when we can, or by using public transport, we can cut back on air pollution. Finally, the simple act of switching off lights and the television when we are not using them, also helps to save electricity and reduce waste.

As you can see, there are many things we can all do to help the environment. It is the responsibility of each and every one of us.

## Part 2 - Task 2 - Example Answer: Article - Mark: 2

This is an example of an article that does not pass. It is not of adequate length and it borrows heavily from the prompt, and uses language repetitively. A lack of preciseness in vocabulary and grammar frequently prevents understanding. It is inadequately organised, with introductory and concluding paragraphs absent, while the existing paragraphs do not contain single clear ideas.

**How to Improve the Environment**

This is for ideas from our readers about how to improve the environment. The first idea is not to throw rubbish. People throw rubbish on the ground and the sea and the environment is very bad. People must not throw the rubbish they must to put the rubbish in the place. The cars how also to improve the environment. Take the bus improve the environment. The cars are everywhere pollute the environment very bad.

I like to ride the bicycle very much and it improve the environment. to recycle improve the environment, the papers the glass the tins. To not buy stuff when you do not need this is better. This is very helping the environment.

# JUSTIFICATIONS OF THE ANSWERS

## for Paper 1 - Reading & Use of English & Paper 3 - Listening

# TEST 1

### Reading & Use of English Part 5

**31.** The correct answer is **C**. Strides are quick, long steps. It is not B because "leaps" means jumps in the air over a long distance, which would be unusual in the context. It is not A as "brooms" are brushes used to sweep the floor. Yells are loud shouts, either in anger, pain or excitement; he is not shouting but rather walking.

**32.** The correct answer is **A**. Line 8, column 1: "Nobody much here yet, said Mr. Watson". The room into which he is shown is described as long and bare, so for this reason wouldn't be B. The text describes areas of the school as "vast", "long" and "large"; the opposite of cramped or small. For this reason, it can't be C. As students are only just starting to return to the empty school, it can neither be noisy nor be full of activity as D suggests.

**33.** The correct answer is **A**. Lines 22-23, column 1: "The headmaster glared amicably at the two children, filling them with fear by the roar of his voice". It isn't B as the text says he looked "amicably", which means in a friendly way. For the same reason it can't be C either. The headmaster is said to have roared - to have made a very loud sound. It doesn't mention whether he is big and powerful (ruling out D), but we can assume he has a loud and strong voice.

**34.** The correct answer is **B**. His tormentor is Venning who teased Philip with jokes, pressured him to see his foot and then kicked him in the leg. The text says that he was nursing his foot when a third boy arrived and Venning, his tormentor, left. For this reason the answer can't be either A, C or D.

**35.** The correct answer is **C**. Lines 23-25, column 2: "...he noticed that the pair were talking about him, and he felt they were looking at his feet. He grew hot and uncomfortable". He grew hot and bothered because he felt awkward and self-conscious that people were talking about his foot. For this reason the answers can't be A, B or D.

**36.** The correct answer is **B**. Lines 37-40, column 2: "The boy looked down quickly and reddened. Philip saw that he felt he had asked an unseemly question. He was too shy to apologise and looked at Philip awkwardly". This boy was embarrassed while Venning had been curious. It isn't A as the subject of the foot keeps coming up in conversation. The boys show little sympathy, so C is incorrect, but neither do they react as if it is something terrible and disgusting, so choice D is also incorrect.

### Reading & Use of English Part 6

**37.** The correct answer is **B**. The text speaks about a static line, used when the writer skydived. The gap must be filled by B as it describes what a static line is. Other options can be eliminated as they do not explain what a static line actually is.

**38.** The correct answer is **G**. The subject of this paragraph is the writer's experience of his or her first jump. This choice has something to do with the first jump - the others may be eliminated. The "still" which appears after the gap suggests that this sentence will contradict what comes before, so, choice G is most appropriate. The first experience is a sharp memory, still, a bit of it is missing because of pure terror!

**39.** The correct answer is **D**. This paragraph describes a sequence of jumps involving increasing time in free fall, which is exactly the meaning put across by choice D.

**40.** The correct answer is **C**. The paragraph is talking about more advanced training, such as learning to go faster, and then describes a painful error that everyone makes "at least once". Choice C describes the physical sensation of that mistake. It also fits because, several lines before, ear discomfort is mentioned, which is echoed again in choice C. Choice F may be eliminated because the gap occurs at the end of the description of the mistake, not in the middle as would be required for choice F. Choice G may be eliminated because at this point in the text the writer has quite a lot of experience.

**41.** The correct answer is **F**. Another mistake is being described; however, the gap here occurs in the middle of the explanation of what happened; the writer deployed the canopy, and a problem occurred; that is, the bag wrapped around his/her leg. Although it could have been very dangerous i.e. "not good at all", in the end it was ok. The key here is the flow of the narration of the fearful experience. Choice C would disrupt the chronology, while choice F helps it to flow.

**42.** The correct answer is **E**. The correct choice must provide an altitude since the gap is followed by "from this altitude". Also, sunset is mentioned in choice E and echoed later in the paragraph.

### Reading & Use of English Part 7

**43.** The correct answer is **C**. "...I had to attend regular meetings with an advisor, which I hated at first..."

**44.** The correct answer is **B**. "But as soon as we set out I realised I was quite out of my depth..."

**45.** The correct answer is **A**. "Luckily my husband has no problem with spiders, and is tolerant of my phobia!"

**46.** The correct answer is **B**. "...to have the opportunity to join a trek for charity."

**47.** The correct answer is **A**. "Luckily my husband has no problem with spiders, and is tolerant of my phobia!"

**48.** The correct answer is **C**. "I was just so terrified that I would fail."

**49.** The correct answer is **D**. "The feeling was exhilarating..."

**50.** The correct answer is **D**. "My fear of heights was affecting my life..." and "...so I put myself into difficult situations on purpose."

**51.** The correct answer is **C**. "...I could get a free computer, or something."

**52.** The correct answer is **D**. "I got a trusted friend to go with me..."

### Listening Part 1

**1.** The correct answer is **A**. We are told that the title is "Getting the Most out of Your Guitar". If you get the most out of something, you use it (in this case play it) in the most effective way possible. Therefore choice B is not a good answer; no mention is made of music. Choice C may be eliminated because the salesperson asks "Is it a recent publication?" A publication is a book or magazine which has been published. Also "available in paperback now" is another clue that it must be a book.

**2.** The correct answer is **C**. "...this makes what the minister said wrong..." and "...difficulties for the government..." both indicate that the topic of discussion is political. Choice A is not correct because it is "...currently happening..." or happening now. Choice B is not a good answer because while the dispute is related to shipbuilding, he is talking about the dispute itself.

**3.** The correct answer is **C**. "Not since Geoff got round to fitting the new windows..." Choice A is not a good answer because weather is discussed only in relation to the windows. Choice B is not a good answer because she wore a coat before she got new windows, but she does not mention buying one.

**4.** The correct answer is **B**. The speaker mentions "...Anne's staggering breakthrough..." A 'breakthrough' is an important development or achievement and something 'staggering' is surprising and amazing. Choice A is incorrect because Anne started her career there and hasn't left. Choice C is not correct because although the meeting is being held at "...short notice...", which means without much advance planning; no mention is made of lateness.

**5.** The correct answer is **C**: "... they become a habit". Choice A is not correct: " ... we actually enjoy them" therefore not boring to everyone. Choice B is wrong: "... the plot is often repetitive and predictable."

**6.** The correct answer is **A**. The mother says "He's one of her favourite actors." and "It's just come out, hasn't it?", so we can assume he asks to go to see a film at the cinema. No mention is made of the other answer choices.

**7.** The correct answer is **B**. "a blast" is a big explosion, especially caused by a bomb. Choice A is not correct because he found "remains of a...vehicle scattered over a wide area"; a crash would not do this. Choice C is not correct because there is no mention of any fire.
**8.** The correct answer is **B**. "The line's a foot under water" means that the track that the train runs on has flooded. Choice A is incorrect because there had been snow but it melted and choice C is incorrect because no trains are running, so accidents won't happen.

## Listening Part 2

**9.** "...the Thorndale clinic, situated on the outskirts of **Bristol**..."
**10.** "...the Thorndale clinic has the highest success rate in treating abusers of **alcohol** and tobacco."
**11.** "...the Thorndale clinic has the highest success rate in treating abusers of alcohol and **tobacco**."
**12.** "Addicts attending a **ten-day course** of treatment..."
**13.** "For example, a one-hour session for smokers involves smoking rapidly without stopping well beyond the point where they **want no more**."
**14.** "In fact, they are not allowed to stop smoking until they have been **physically sick**."
**15.** "...many people find the course too painful to complete, and those who do **give up early** are not considered cured..."
**16.** "On the other hand, smokers who keep going to the end of the course are **most unlikely** to want a cigarette again."
**17.** "...'patients' are encouraged to drink excessively in the setting of a bar. During this stage they are carefully monitored by **trained personnel**."
**18.** "Nearly all subjects feel **great embarrassment** when faced with forgotten scenes..."

## Listening Part 3

**19.** The correct answer is **H**. "...because I needed a medical certificate." and "...an official piece of paper from any qualified doctor..."
**20.** The correct answer is **E**. "...they'd give me something to put me to sleep and when I came round everything would be over and all I would see would be a few stitches." The speaker was operated on.
**21.** The correct answer is **D**. "When, at last, I managed to find the right room I almost didn't recognise her." He expected to recognise her because he knew her well, so, of the options, it is most likely that she is a relative.
**22.** The correct answer is **F**. "...the call on my answerphone said there was this leaking roof in one of the wards." and "...I told them to get someone else to do it." The speaker was called to fix the roof.
**23.** The correct answer is **C**. "The address on the package says room 4J." and "...I take it up there and then there's nobody there to sign the documents to say they've received it."

## Listening Part 4

**24.** The correct answer is **A**. She says "Well, I have seen better films. I mean, it wasn't as good as..." so choice B is not correct. However, she concedes that "The dinosaurs were good." so choice C may be eliminated. Her feelings are neutral.
**25.** The correct answer is **C**. We may find the correct answer by the process of elimination. Choice A is not correct because the course he did was "computer graphics" which is how the dinosaurs - the subject of the current conversation - were created. Choice B is not correct because he is adding information to what Mrs Turner said, not contradicting her.
**26.** The correct answer is **C**. He says "...they looked much better on the big screen than they did on my mate's pirate video - but at least I could smoke at my mate's house." He mentions an advantage of going to the cinema and also an advantage of staying at home.
**27.** The correct answer is **B**. She says "No, I wasn't! What are you talking about?" and "I wasn't covering my eyes, I was laughing." Choice C is not correct because she says "Well, at least it wasn't too long..." which means she is happy that it was short.
**28.** The correct answer is **A**. We know from the previous question that Wendy claims that she was not frightened. Mrs Turner, on the other hand, says "Well, I couldn't look sometimes. I mean it was only a P.G. film but some of the scenes were...well...pretty..." In other words, she was frightened at times. Choice B is incorrect because this was a subject Wendy and Adrian were arguing about. Choice C is incorrect because Mrs Turner states that the film was P.G. as if this is a fact and no one contradicts her.
**29.** The correct answer is **B**. Mrs Turner says "Why don't we go for a quick one at the King's Head?" 'In context, we can infer that the King's Head is a pub and we can also guess that 'a quick one' refers to a drink of some sort.
**30.** The correct answer is **C**. Adrian says "...I'm afraid you're not insured to drive my car and if the police stopped us we'd both be in trouble." Choice B is not correct because she says "I'll have a fruit juice and I can drive us home." She offers not to drink. No mention is made of choice A.

# TEST 2

## Reading & Use of English Part 5

**31.** The correct answer is **A**. Paragraph 3: "He pushed his bowl aside, took up his hunk of bread in one delicate hand and his cheese in the other, and leaned across the table." This would suggest they are in a place where food is provided and they are chatting over lunch. However, the discussion is about work, which rules out options B and C and leaves us with the workplace cafeteria. The "noise" mentioned on line two rules out option B.
**32.** The correct answer is **C**. Paragraph 3: "He had brightened up immediately at the mention of Newspeak", in other words, he was very happy Winston had asked about his work. Also, Paragraph 5 "He continued speaking with a sort of pedant's passion." A pedant is someone who is too academic and concerned with rules and details. It isn't A as the text says he eats hungrily, but doesn't mention if he likes the food. B is incorrect as it is Syme who is doing the most talking. D is also incorrect since Syme leaned across the table in order to speak without shouting.
**33.** The correct answer is **B**. Paragraph 6: "Of course the great wastage is in the verbs and adjectives." In other words, there are a lot of verbs and adjectives to be got rid of, so these will be targeted the most - but not just the adjectives, which rules out A. And while Syme says "there are hundreds of nouns that can be got rid of as well', we can infer that this number is not as significant as the "great wastage" of verbs and adjectives he alluded to, ruling out C. Syme also mentions that antonyms should be done away with, which excludes D as a possible answer.
**34.** The correct answer is **D**. Paragraph 8: Syme comments on Winston's attitude: "I've read some of those pieces that you write...they're translations. In your heart you'd prefer to stick to Oldspeak, with all its vagueness and its useless shades of meaning." Winston is using Newspeak, but it is clear to Syme that he does not like it. Winston expresses neither excitement or disagreement in the conversation, eliminating answers A, B and C.
**35.** The correct answer is **B**. Paragraph 10: Syme says to Winston: "Don't you see that the whole aim of Newspeak is to narrow the range of thought?" The language is simple and has a limited number of words in order to stop people from thinking at all.
**36.** The correct answer is **C**. Last paragraph: "Every year fewer and fewer words, and the range of consciousness always a little smaller." He envisions that language will be so limited people won't be able to think at all. This is the opposite of choice A. Choice B is incorrect because the crimes in question are "thought crimes" which are not physical so cannot be violent. D is incorrect because people will not even "understand such a conversation as we are having now".

## Reading & Use of English Part 6

**37.** The gap is best filled with choice **F**. The sentence that follows mentions the particular features of the mountain - "its symmetrical cone" this would then fit in with F that says it is a familiar landform to Aucklanders. The landform is visible in "plain view" from downtown Auckland, as it also says in the previous sentence.
**38.** The correct answer is **A**. The sentence before says that the volcano wasn't always the way it is seen today and A says that it did

not exist when the first inhabitants, the Maori, came to the surrounding lands. A is then the most logical answer.

**39.** The correct answer is choice **E**. This sentence goes on to provide further information of what possible effects occurred from the volcano, which fits in here with the text describing how the smell of sulphur dioxide would have filled the air from the steam.

**40.** The gap is best filled with choice **D**. The text describes how people were trying to flee from the erupting volcano, D says that they were paddling for safety. For this reason D is the most logical answer.

**41.** The correct answer is **G**. G is the topic sentence; claiming that people returned after the eruption, and the text follows on from this to give evidence of their return in the form of footprints preserved in the volcano's dust. Choice C may be eliminated because "The impressions" have not yet been explained, so would make little sense here at the beginning of the paragraph - the reader would wonder "What impressions?".

**42.** The gap is best filled by choice **C**. The paragraph is speaking about the footprints that remained, and C refers to "The impressions" of the footprints preserved in the ash.

## Reading & Use of English Part 7

**43.** The correct answer is **A**. "Perhaps the answer is to make the best of the present and stop hankering after the past."

**44.** The correct answer is **E**. "I would never have ended the relationship with the love of my life."

**45.** The correct answer is **A**. "I'd persuade my dad to stop smoking, so that he wouldn't die so young."

**46.** The correct answer is **D**. "...see Asia but steer clear of package tours."

**47.** The correct answer is **A**. "...have two wonderful grown-up children and two precious grandchildren."

**48.** The correct answer is **B**. "I would not exchange today for any previous era. I have studied a lot of history..."

**49.** The correct answer is **B**. "...eighteenth and nineteenth centuries - exciting, but too many petticoats to wear, never mind about corsets."

**50.** The correct answer is **D**. "Imagine coming home after a long voyage, and telling the people in the pub all about your travels!"

**51.** The correct answer is **E**. "...register 250 of the best internet domains possible, so by now I'd be a..."

**52.** The correct answer is **C**. "...you would be denounced as a devil; tortured, quartered and drawn, and then burnt at the stake!"

## Listening Part 1

**1.** The correct answer is **B**. "If you urgently need to see a doctor, dial...for doctors Smith and Parker". Choice A is not correct because you are advised to "go to 217 George Street." Choice C in incorrect because you should dial "622909".

**2.** The correct answer is **B**. "Looking though the chain-link fence..." indicates that they are outside the factory grounds looking in. Choice A is therefore incorrect. Choice C is incorrect because the nearby town is where the bodies have been taken for identification, not where the broadcast is happening from.

**3.** The correct answer is **C**. "...you'll have to go today or tomorrow because Friday's a public holiday..." So, we have today, tomorrow, then Friday, therefore today must be Wednesday. Also, we know that yesterday was Tuesday because the son says: "I couldn't go yesterday; it was closed." and "No, it's shut all day Tuesday."

**4.** The correct answer is **A**. His car is parked "...on the high street, you know, beside the Green Lion pub." Choice B is incorrect because the man says "No, not the one on Baker Street..." and choice C is incorrect because it is parked in the High Street.

**5.** The correct answer is **B**. "...we're currently carrying out a survey to determine...an average family's washing needs." Choice A is incorrect because he observes that she has already bought the washing powder and choice C is incorrect because he tells her "...it will not be necessary for one of our representatives to visit your home."

**6.** The correct answer is **C**. She says "I was working at the desk that day..." and "two officers brought a suspect into the station..." We know in this case that 'station' refers to the police station, not a railway station, because a suspect had been brought in by officers. A suspect is someone believed to have committed a crime.

**7.** The correct answer is **C**. We are told that the man gave "...a very impressive performance..." and he also says "...things that we do on stage..." Because he performs on a stage, he must be a theatre actor rather than a film star so choice B may be eliminated. Choice A may be eliminated because singers do not usually work with directors.

**8.** The correct answer is **A**. "The building has been hailed as a masterpiece, although I personally have reservations because it lacks the colour and flamboyance..." and therefore choice C is clearly incorrect. Choice B is incorrect because she says the gardens are "...particularly noted for the unusual layout..." which does not necessarily mean that they are beautiful.

## Listening Part 2

**9.** "TV, radio and **newspapers** are the three main forms of media "

**10.** " Politicians use it in their political **campaigns** in order to gain support"

**11.** "Entertainers and celebrities use it to promote themselves and keep themselves in the **public eye**."

**12.** "**4%** had no opinion either way".

**13.** "which they were most influenced by...over two thirds asked said **TV**".

**14.** "carefully chosen or edited **images** can deceive us".

**15.** "turns fact into **fiction**".

**16.** "awarded **one million pounds** when...said he was a homosexual".

**17.** "get away with making a public **apology**".

**18.** "newspapers...tend to fall into two groups; the **tabloids** and the so called quality newspapers".

## Listening Part 3

**19.** The correct answer is **G**. "Brian mentioned you in his speech...he still likes your cooking best." and "Of course, Dad was there..." indicate the speaker is addressing her mother.

**20.** The correct answer is **B**. The speaker says "when we get married a few little things are going to change..." so it must be her boyfriend she is speaking to.

**21.** The correct answer is **F**. The speaker asks the other person how he/she met Brian and provides the same info about herself - they didn't know each other.

**22.** The correct answer is **C**. "Did you take all these pictures yourself? You are clever." This would be inappropriate to say to an adult! Also, Julie is the other person's Auntie, he/she also has a granny and grandad, which suggests he/she is still a child.

**23.** The correct answer is **E**. "If you hadn't given me the Friday off...", so we can assume it is her boss.

## Listening Part 4

**24.** The correct answer is **A**. She says: "I'm fed up with staying in nearly every night. Since John and I broke up..." Choice B is not correct because she had split up with her boyfriend (see above). Choice C: there is no mention that she had hurt herself.

**25.** The correct answer is **B**. He is trying to change the subject: "Anyway, enough of my personal life. What about you..." There is no mention in the text about the other two choices.

**26.** The correct answer is **A**. "Well, well. That's why you *(referring to Mark)* are never home these days when I try to phone you"

**27.** The correct answer is **C**. Dave says: "We're trying to decide where to go on holiday." Choice A is not correct because Dave says: "I'm not saying we won't get married." Choice B is not correct: "We're trying to decide where (they have decided they will go) to go on holiday."

**28.** The correct answer is **C:** Mark: "...and I had to leave early because the smoke was making my asthma bad. I could hardly breathe and felt terrible the next day." The other two options are not mentioned.

**29.** The correct answer is **B**. She says: "The best cure for a broken heart is a new romance" so she is optimistic about the future and not sad or nervous.

**30.** The correct answer is **B**. "I'll see if I can arrange for him to be at the Christmas party..." The other options are clearly wrong.

# TEST 3

## Reading & Use of English Part 5

**31.** The correct answer is **B**. Paragraphs 1 and 2: "I hope I will not grow any more - as it is I can't get out at the door...Alas, it was too late to wish that! She went on growing and growing..." - Alice couldn't leave the house because she had grown so large she was not able to get out. For this reason answers A, C and D can't be correct.
**32.** The correct answer is **A**. Paragraph 2: "she tried the effect of lying down with one elbow against the door, and the other arm curled round her head. Still she went on growing, and, as a last resource, she put one arm out of the window, and one foot up the chimney". She tried her best to feel comfortable in the house, but it was impossible.
**33.** The correct answer is **B**. Paragraph 4: " 'It was much pleasanter at home,' thought poor Alice". Alice goes on to say how her life will be now that she is stuck in the house and what will happen to her. She carried on arguing each side of the conversation until the Rabbit turned up. For this reason the answer can't be A. There is no talk in the text about an old woman and Pat is the Rabbit's helper, so it can't be C or D.
**34.** The correct answer is **B**. Paragraph 8: "Mary Ann! Mary Ann!' said the voice...Alice knew it was the Rabbit coming to look for her." The Rabbit calls for Mary Ann and the text says that Alice trembled knowing that the Rabbit was in fact calling her. We can gather from this part of the text that A, C and D can't be correct.
**35.** The correct answer is **C**. Paragraph 11: " 'I'm here! Digging for apples, your honour!' 'Digging for apples, indeed!' said the Rabbit angrily." When you dig for something, you make a hole in the ground in order to uncover what is there. As we know apples grow on trees and aren't found in the ground; Pat's comment is therefore meant to be foolish. Pat doesn't make his actions secret, so A must be incorrect. Pat isn't hiding because he announces where he is when the Rabbit calls, so B is incorrect. And D is incorrect as Pat doesn't say he is growing food, but seems to be searching for it.
**36.** The correct answer is **C**. The last paragraph: "An arm, you goose! Who ever saw one that size? Why, it fills the whole window!" Normally an arm isn't the size of Alice's, so the Rabbit can't believe what he sees and he wants a second opinion.

## Reading & Use of English Part 6

**37.** The correct choice is **B**. The text before the gap introduces the concept of a lucid dream, and begins to describe an experience, ending with the discovery of two fish. The gap begins a new paragraph, and following the gap we are told the writer's second reaction to the discovery of the fish. We would expect the gap to give the writer's first reaction. The only other possible reaction is choice A, which may be eliminated because the second reaction is to wonder, so the sense of understanding conveyed in A does not fit. B is appropriate; first she was shocked, then she started to wonder.
**38.** The correct choice is **A**. The writer is still trying to make sense of the extra fish. First, she is shocked, then she starts to wonder, then she realises she is dreaming and it all makes sense. As said in the Q.37 justification notes, A is also a reaction, but now it fits appropriately.
**39.** The correct choice is **E**. Since the sentence before mentions the writer's husband the correct answer must also include the same subject of husband and family. The writer spoke to her dream-family, and choice E shows the response of her husband.
**40.** The correct answer is **G**. The subject of the sentence before the gap is lucid dreaming, as is the subject of the sentence after the gap, so the correct answer must also refer to or involve this subject. The sentence before gives "an example of lucid dreaming" and choice G explains what this concept actually is.
**41.** The gap is best filled by choice **F**. Before the gap, we are told of two techniques to use to learn to induce lucid dreaming. Choice F refers to "these habits" meaning the two techniques. Also "tipped off" is used in sentence F and is also echoed in the following sentence through the phrase "...which alerted me". Choice D is wrong because it refers to noticing something odd while awake in a conscious state as opposed to while sleeping in a dream state.
**42.** The correct answer is **C**. The sentence before suggests that once you have mastered the ability to lucid dream, there are no limits on what your imagination can create. Choice C takes this idea further by suggesting some things which could be possible "from flying, to inventing, to art".

## Reading & Use of English Part 7

**43.** The correct answer is **A**. "...manta rays." and "For a few minutes we were companions..."
**44.** The correct answer is **A**. "...but were content to let me swim on a parallel course..."
**45.** The correct answer is **D**. "I liked New York even more than I expected..."
**46.** The correct answer is **C**. "...that although hippos may seem harmless, if threatened, they could easily kill a man!"
**47.** The correct answer is **B**. "...writing an article while monsoon rains pounded on the windows all around me."
**48.** The correct answer is **D**. "...I was on my own and this seems like a better way to get to know a city: less being sociable..."
**49.** The correct answer is **B**. "...5,000 temples on every side..."
**50.** The correct answer is **B**. "...I gave a friend a nine-hour account of every moment. The motorbike ride through Sukhothai; the first long lazy evening in an expat's teak house in Sunkumvhit; the flight into the otherworldly charm of Rangoon and the Strand Hotel, and the pulse of warm activity around the Sule Pagoda at nightfall."
**51.** The correct answer is **D**. "...to live. It's fighting for the top spot with San Francisco, with the next position occupied by Paris."
**52.** The correct answer is **C**. "Our guides..."

## Listening Part 1

**1**. The correct answer is **C**. "When he last saw his mummy, he says, she was choosing some pears."
**2**. The correct answer is **B**. "...it's your price-beater guarantee ... I went into Lunthams and saw them there for only nine ninety-nine." Choice C is not correct because "...it works perfectly. That's not the problem at all."
**3**. The correct answer is **B**. "And the flight number...BA 893. And take-off time?" This suggests she's going by plane and not by train or coach.
**4**. The correct answer is **C**. The policeman says "...we would like to speak with him on a rather urgent matter." and is refering to "...a Mr Winston of number 43 just across the street there." Mr Winston is the man's neighbour.
**5**. The correct answer is **B**. "...we want to hear from any single parents out there who are listening and, in fact, we have one on the line right now. Hello, Mary..." Someone who is single is not married. Choice C is incorrect because there's no mention of the frequency with which Mary listens to the programme.
**6**. The correct answer is **A**. "...we recommend you carry 10 gallons of bottled water." Choice B is not correct because he only mentions that you can't drink salt water and Choice C is incorrect because he is advising on how *not* to run out of water by recommending to carry ten gallons of bottled water.
**7**. The correct answer is **B**. One of the women says "Oh, look, here's your bus coming now." and the other woman says "And I hope you don't have to wait too long for yours." which shows that they are taking different buses. Choice A is not correct because the woman giving directions says "...you get out there in front of the war memorial. You can't miss it." If the other woman was familiar with it, she would not have needed this reassurance. Choice C is incorrect because they can't be going to the same place since they are taking different buses.
**8**. The correct answer is **A**. We may come to this conclusion by a process of elimination. B may be eliminated because he says "But why would they want to know mother's maiden name?" so he can't be speaking to his mother. C may be eliminated because he says "Sophie's grown up now. She's left home. It's not really any of my business..." so we can presume that Sophie is his daughter. Also, he mentions Sophie, so can't be talking directly to her. That leaves us with option A, his wife.

## Listening Part 2

**9.** "...several kinds of insect, including bees, have been observed performing a **special dance** to tell each other where they can find nectar and pollen..."
**10.** "Many people think that certain birds like parrots can speak...Such animals are only capable of **copying** the sounds of human speech but have no understanding..."
**11.** "...primates are capable of communicating a small number of **basic ideas** using a range of simple sounds..."
**12.** "...none of the groups of monkeys observed so far have developed any form of **grammar**..."
**13.** "They can manage the vowel sounds...and so on, but lack the necessary voice equipment to reproduce our **consonants**."
**14.** "But what makes these noises more amazing is that dolphins do show an **awareness** of when to use such phrases..."
**15.** "These are fast clicking and squeaking noises that whales make underwater and the sounds themselves actually contain **more information** than human speech."
**16.** "Of particular interest is a species called the bottle-nosed whale whose songs have many of the **characteristics** of human..."
**17.** "...we are the only species that has developed proper grammatical languages...because of the **large communities** that we live in."
**18.** "If, for any reason, a young child does not get enough **contact** with other people...he or she may never develop speech."

## Listening Part 3

**19.** The correct answer is **A**. "I have to babysit...many jobs around the house...difficult to get any spare time".
**20.** The correct answer is **D**. "he needs; feeding, changing, bathing etc."
**21.** The correct answer is **C**. "they were always fighting...noisiest house"...living in same house "now...he comes to visit sometimes" therefore living apart.
**22.** The correct answer is **F**. "three generations under one roof".
**23.** The correct answer is **E**. "enough of us to make a basketball team so we play as a family" therefore large family. "Two children would be enough for me though" therefore many children; brothers and sisters.

## Listening Part 4

**24.** The correct answer is **B**. He says "It's enough to make anyone depressed. I haven't got a good word to say about it myself." Choice A is incorrect because he never says that it is entertaining - just silly. Choice C is incorrect because he says "...that's a good thing, otherwise all the kids would be spending all their pocket money on it." Young people can't play so it can't be bad for them.
**25.** The correct answer is **A**. "Over twenty million people entered last week, which is a lot if you consider that it's only open to people over eighteen."
**26.** The correct answer is **A**. She says "...this week was special. I just thought I was going to be lucky..." Choice B is incorrect because Camelot is the lottery company, and the money has gone there, not Tina.
**27.** The correct answer is **C**. Tina says "They don't keep the money, they give it all to charity and the arts." Choice A is incorrect because this is what the man says. Choice B is incorrect because it is the opposite of what Tina claims in the quote above.
**28.** The correct answer is **B**. He tells her he played "...just once. The lads and I at work did have a go when it started."
**29.** The correct answer is **A**. His dad says that "God helps those who help themselves." and he brings this up to support the idea that "I don't think it's right. Somebody getting all that money...for doing nothing." so choice B is not a good answer. Choice C is incorrect because Barry says the chances of winning are low but he has changed his topic by the time he brings up the quote from his dad.
**30.** The correct answer is **C**. She says "Well, I was thinking of giving it a miss next week, anyway. Maybe that's what I'll do."

# TEST 4

## Reading & Use of English Part 5

**31.** The correct answer is **D**. Column 1, lines 11-12 and lines 22-23: "I want...to let in a little more light here... A broad ray of light fell into the room...". When Monsieur Defarge first came into the workshop there was obviously not enough light as he asks the shoemaker if he can let some more in. The answer is not A as the text gives the impression that the place is silent and empty. The answers are not B or C, as these issues are not mentioned in the text.
**32.** The correct answer is **C**. Column 1, lines 26-28: "He had...exceedingly bright eyes." and "they were naturally large, and looked unnaturally so." His eyes are given a more lengthy description than his other features, indicating they were his most distinctive characteristic.
**33.** The correct answer is **D**. Column 2, lines 26-27: "He glanced at the shoe with some little passing touch of pride." The sentence suggests he showed some emotion when describing the kind of shoe he was making. His actions weren't overly enthusiastic but revealed his sense of satisfaction with the work. For this reason the answer isn't A or B. Monsieur Defarge had to encourage the shoemaker to describe the shoe to Mr. Lorry, so the answer is also not C as he didn't show eagerness to promote the shoe.
**34.** The correct answer is **B**. Column 2, line 21: "I forget what it was you asked me. What did you say?" The shoemaker was not able to focus on Monsieur Defarge's questions and his mind was clearly elsewhere. It is not A, which suggests he deliberately avoided giving an answer. Also it's not C, as he did eventually answer Monsieur Defarge's questions. And it is also not D as the shoemaker didn't give any indication of extra anxiety in response to the questions.
**35.** The correct answer is **B**. Column 2, lines 25-26:
"I never saw the style. I have had a pattern in my hand." The text suggests that the shoemaker had never seen any women wearing the style, but had the pattern written down, which he then copied. The text also says the design was in the present style, meaning modern and not traditional. For these reasons the answer can only be B and not A, C or D.
**36.** The correct answer is **D**. Column 2, lines 34-36: "Did you ask me for my name?...Assuredly I did...One Hundred and Five, North Tower." As the story illustrates, the shoemaker was not very good at communicating. He was absorbed by his work and did not pay much attention to his company. He didn't seem used to being asked questions and even when he was asked his name he replied with his address. For this reason D is the most suitable answer; A, B and C are incorrect.

## Reading & Use of English Part 6

**37.** The correct answer is **F**. The sentence before refers to borrowing and repaying money. Sentence F then introduces a problem, and after the gap, we are told reasons why problems might arise and why people who borrow money might not be able to repay it.
**38.** The correct answer is **A**. The topic of the paragraph is *debt and what happens when people become too heavily indebted.* The sentence before uses the phrase 'draw a line', and choice A follows on from this term and explains what it means. Similarly, the sentence that follows the gap briefly explains the meaning of bankruptcy.
**39.** The choice that best fits the gap is **B**. The topic of the paragraph is how poor people are affected by debt. It therefore makes sense to fill the gap with B which goes on to explain how poor people can be affected.
**40.** The correct choice for the gap is **D**. The previous sentence mentions the role of the IMF in the case of 1982 with Mexico and its debt. It says that it stepped in to help. Choice D continues this theme by describing exactly how the IMF helped. It also introduces "other struggling countries" which is necessary so that the phrase "these countries" in the following sentence has something to refer back to.
**41.** The correct answer is **G**. The gap is in the position of the topic sentence of the paragraph, and the following sentences support the concept of declining standards of living. Importantly, choice G uses the word 'however' to transition from the idea of help in the previous paragraph. The programme, which may have begun positively, actually produced worse effects as choice G indicates.

**42.** The correct answer is **E**. The previous sentence speaks about HIPC; the IMF's new programme to help poor countries, that unfortunately doesn't seem to work. Choice E concludes that more needs to be done about the growing debt crisis. It is also a fitting closing sentence for the piece.

## Reading & Use of English Part 7

**43.** The correct answer is **B**. "...a former staff member of the IMF, Pauly is in a unique position to give a fresh perspective."
**44.** The correct answer is **A**. "...industrialized nations moved to create the IMF in the midst of World War II in the belief that an organisation that balances international monetary policy would help prevent future wars."
**45.** The correct answer is **D**. "It deserves a wide audience."
**46.** The correct answer is **B**. "...the demise of fixed exchange rates in the 1970s."
**47.** The correct answer is **A**. "Louis Pauly obviously wanted to startle people..."
**48.** The correct answer is **A**. By process of elimination - no personal opinion offered here.
**49.** The correct answer is **D**. "...very interesting and readable book..."
**50.** The correct answer is **C**. "...how the global markets of today have been shaped by central banks, the IMF, the G-7, and the policymakers of the world."
**51.** The correct answer is **C**. "...described the evolution of the international markets over the past fifty years." and "...over the past seventy-five years."
**52.** The correct answer is **D**. "...significant to anyone interested in..." and "...and the future of democracy in advanced industrial states."

## Listening Part 1

**1**. The correct answer is **B**. The person who answered the phone says "...I had intended to stick with the original price but let's say 75 pounds." and so must be selling the item. Choice A is incorrect because the caller is enquiring about the item and so must be interested in buying it, however we are not told if the caller makes any decision so choice C is not a good answer.
**2**. The correct answer is **C**. "...we should still be arriving in Malaga five minutes ahead of schedule."
**3**. The correct answer is **C**. The doctor says "...if you do decide to go out at all - I mean, out of the house - in the open air, especially in the daytime, just...er...take good care...."
**4**. The correct answer is **A**. "...these bags weigh 32 kilograms. That's more than twice the normal baggage allowance for this flight."
**5**. The correct answer is **A**. "But, I'm afraid there will be no improvement in north-eastern England and Scotland for a day or so." Choice B is incorrect because it is the east Midlands that should get much brighter. Choice C is not correct because most of the country is rainy as is the north east.
**6**. The correct answer is **B**. We have to assume they sell office supplies, since they used to sell office cleaning supplies. Choice C is incorrect because they aren't office cleaners, but used to sell cleaning supplies. Choice A is not a good answer because they sell items from a catalogue. No mention is made of organising parties.
**7**. The correct answer is **C**. We are told that Jack is "...getting the sack..." which means he is being fired. We are also told that "...Colin's being too hard on him." Finally, the man says "Couldn't you have a word? I mean, he listens to you." which means he wants the woman to have a word with Colin about Jack.
**8**. The correct answer is **A**. "Oh, good. Then you can get a copy of today's 'Andover Gazette'." Choice B is not correct because the speaker says: "...if they haven't got one, get us a copy of 'Today'..." (which also renders choice C wrong).

## Listening Part 2

**9.** "...people celebrate Guy Fawkes Night. The celebration centres around the burning of a **life-sized model** of a man, with a black hat and beard, called 'Guy'."
**10.** "The model has been specially made for this **purpose**."
**11.** "...but not so much fun for cats and dogs, which are usually **terrified** by sounds of exploding fireworks and skyrockets."
**12.** "In 1605, the king, James I, and his government, were Protestants and they made life rather difficult for the country's **Catholics**..."
**13.** "...a group of prominent Catholics met secretly and decided that the king and his government **must die**."
**14.** "...the conspirators bought a house beside the parliament building, which already had **a tunnel** going into the Houses of Parliament from its cellar."
**15.** "...Catesby and his companions moved huge barrels of highly **explosive gunpowder** along the tunnel and placed them...under the government building."
**16.** "Guy Fawkes had the important job of watching the street outside the conspirators' house and warning the others of any **approaching danger**."
**17.** "...but Guy Fawkes has remained the most famous, probably on account of his being **caught first.**"
**18.** "...Catholics and Protestants have learned to live together in peace and so the celebration itself is mostly **harmless fun**."

## Listening Part 3

**19.** The correct answer is **D**. The recipe only involves putting ingredients together. There is no cooking.
**20.** The correct answer is **A**. "...gelatin is made from the hooves of cows, so, unfortunately, some people won't be too keen on this." Vegetarians would not eat gelatin.
**21.** The correct answer is **B**. "...you will only really be able to make this recipe from May to early July; after that, raspberries can be used instead up to late August."
**22.** The correct answer is **E**. "...indeed it has such a simple method that they could even make it themselves."
**23.** The correct answer is **F**. "Now, these are about one pound fifty for a fifty gram packet, so you'll not want to waste any."

## Listening Part 4

**24.** The correct answer is **C**. "I'm talking to you on my mobile and the train keeps going into tunnels and we get cut off." Choice B is not correct because another passenger speaks to her, but he does so after her phone call has ended.
**25.** The correct answer is **A**. He asks, "Isn't this the train to Salisbury?" Choice B is not correct because the train they are on goes to Brighton. Choice C is not correct because the train divided at Redhill.
**26.** The correct answer is **A**. He says "...but that's impossible..." and "I can't believe this is happening."
**27.** The correct answer is **B**. "...if this is the Brighton train, I haven"t got the right ticket." Choice C is incorrect because the man's bank card is the thing that is plastic.
**28.** The correct answer is **A**. "...we should be arriving in Balcombe in just a minute." Choice B is incorrect because the last (previous) stop was Three Bridges. Choice C is incorrect because the final stop is Brighton.
**29.** The correct answer is **C**. She says "...I'll be taking the connecting service to Lewes..."
**30.** The correct answer is **B**. She says "...I could phone through to central enquiries and make sure." and he responds "If it wouldn't be too much trouble."

# TEST 5

## Reading & Use of English Part 5

**31.** The correct answer is **C**. "When an early, heavy snowstorm last autumn...eventually chased me from the backcountry back to the station and its comforts [the station being referred to is Abisko]"
**32.** The correct answer is **B**. "The Aurora may be old hat to those who live this far north, but for the rest of us it is an unforgettable experience." The "but" signals a contradiction will be made, so, both "old hat" and the correct answer must contradict "an unforgettable experience", as choice B does.
**33.** The correct answer is **B**. "For travellers from afar it's a spectacle that has us shivering on the deck...The lights here are so mesmerizing we quickly forget the discomfort of the cold." - "the lights" is another name for the aurora.
**34.** The correct answer is **A**. "this quirk of weather" refers to the always-clear skies around lake Abisko, and a quirk is an unusual happening or aspect of someone's character, so in this case, an "unusual feature" of the weather is the best choice.
**35.** The correct answer is **C**. "it's Abisko's remote location, and its unique infrastructure that make it such a prime vantage point...It is dark; Abisko is far from any city lights that might dim the show. The station operates a ski lift to the top of Nuolja Peak...a cafe at the top of the mountain has been turned into a viewing platform for the Northern Lights, called the Aurora Sky Station. Also, the station posts "forecasts each night", therefore A, B and D are incorrect. The highway makes the station exceptional for its comfort, service and ease of access, but none of these factors will help to ensure a good viewing or make one more likely.
**36.** The correct answer is **A**. Early on in the text the author calls Abisko "the crown jewel of the Swedish mountain lodges" and "I'm back for a second time" so clearly the impression is positive, and praise for the place continues throughout the text. B is incorrect because it is "Much more elaborate than many wilderness huts". C and D are not mentioned.

## Reading & Use of English Part 6

**37.** The correct answer is **D**. The gap must be filled by something that could be achieved with a scientific research permit. Because it is ok to kill whales for research, this would allow Japan to hunt them legally.
**38.** The correct answer is **B**. We are told, in the sentence before the gap, that trade within Japan and Korea is allowed. Using "However" to indicate a contrast in meaning, choice B follows this information with the fact that they may not trade internationally.
**39.** The correct answer is **E**. Because of "on the other hand" located immediately after the gap, we would expect some information that gives an idea that is in contrast with the idea in this sentence - that opponents say "lethal sampling" is not necessary. Choice E informs us of reasons some people think that "lethal sampling" is required.
**40.** The correct answer is **G**. "samples of sushi" from the previous sentence tie in with "the sushi" in choice G. And "illegally traded" in choice G ties in with "criminal proceedings" in the sentence following the gap. Choice A might also appear to fit, as the two choices are very similar, but the emphasis in A is where, geographically, the meat came from, while the emphasis in choice G is whether or not the sushi was legal.
**41.** The correct answer is **A**. This paragraph is about the source of the meat. Also, the mentioning of the DNA results link Sentence A with the sentence before gap 41. Choice G may seem to work, but it is not the best choice; see Q.40 above for discussion.
**42.** The correct answer is **C**. Before the gap we are told that information is not available, and choice C says that scientists urgently need the same information.

## Reading & Use of English Part 7

**43.** The correct answer is **A**. "...not because I knew anything about it, just because it's considered one of the seven wonders of the world, you know."
**44.** The correct answer is **B**. "My favourite building, this year at least..."
**45.** The correct answer is **D**. "...that used to be used by fishermen"
**46.** The correct answer is **B**. "Gehry was the first person to use a computer modelling system called CATIA..."
**47.** The correct answer is **D**. No mention is made in text D of a designer; the building is very old so it is most likely unknown.
**48.** The correct answer is **B**. "...the Sky Church – a high-tech cinema with a 70 ft high ceiling and the world's largest LED screen."
**49.** The correct answer is **C**. "...a real character and his buildings are all so creative and progressive..."
**50.** The correct answer is **C**. "...forested roofs..." and "...the high-rise meadow house..."
**51.** The correct answer is **D**. "...was kept closed to the public."
**52.** The correct answer is **A**. "I would love to get married there one day..."

## Listening Part 1

**1**. The correct answer is **A**. "...a good set of tyres with at least five millimetres of tread can and will save your life." Choice B is not correct because "Whether it be another vehicle, a child crossing, or an unexpected bend in the road..."; children crossing are just one of many things to watch out for. Choice C is incorrect because there could be problems "...even if you never touch a drop of alcohol...".
**2**. The correct answer is **B**. "Look, I've been supporting this team longer than you have." They both support the same team, therefore choice A is incorrect. Choice C is incorrect because the pronoun 'we' is used with Man. United, which indicates their support.
**3**. The correct answer is **B**. "...you won't find it anywhere at this...bargain basement price..." Choice A is incorrect because "...you've all seen it before on TV anyway..." and choice C is incorrect because it is "...exactly the same quality as all the others..."
**4**. The correct answer is **A**. "...ever since we were at school together..." Choice B is incorrect because the speaker and the groom are the same age; see above. Choice C is incorrect because George is the groom, not the speaker.
**5**. The correct answer is **A**. "...I've got a mind to write to Tomlinson's right now and tell them just what I think of them." Tomlinson's is the name of a tour provider. Choice B is incorrect because "...the scenery was nice and some of the local people were friendly" so the country had some positives. Choice C is incorrect because "it wasn't a total disaster".
**6**. The correct answer is **C**. "...you have overcharged us by $14." Choice A is incorrect because "...everything was supplied as ordered..." and choice B is incorrect because "...No, it was for this morning, so that's fine...".
**7**. The correct answer is **B**. The clue is that one list of fillings is requested on brown bread, then other fillings are requested "both" on white bread. "both" indicates 2 (two white sandwiches and one brown; therefore, 3 in all).
**8**. The correct answer is **B**. "...a letter arrived from a former neighbour in Naples where Dino had turned up..." Choice A is incorrect because his owners were in Germany, which he left. Choice C is incorrect because he was described as "streetwise" because he managed to find his way all the way home to Italy from Germany.

## Listening Part 2

**9.** "An incredible 62% of **British adults** say that the stars are of some interest to them..."
**10.** "...only 3.5% would use them to choose a husband or wife and only 2.9% of people would refer to them in making **business decisions**."
**11.** "Psychologists now widely agree that both early life experiences and time of birth are a great influence on the development of a person's **character**."
**12.** "...this does not make the whole of a person's character, but rather the **foundation or base** on which later changes are made."
**13.** "...made a statistical comparison between people's **choice of career** and their zodiac sign."
**14.** "An astonishing 20% of **artists and entertainers** were born in the period between the 12th of July and the 20th of August."
**15.** "This, in fact, is the most positive connection we have found so

far. But there have been others although they have been **less obvious**."

**16.** "We looked at keen sports players...and found a sizable number were born in the **winter** months..."

**17.** "...so far, we haven't found any professions containing large percentages of one particular star sign, which is a little **disappointing**..."

**18.** "...because our modern technological world has removed us further and further from the **effects of nature**."

## Listening Part 3

**19.** The correct answer is **H**. "...all cuddled up together. Makes me wonder how some people can hate them so much..." People often hate mice and spiders, however spiders don't cuddle.

**20.** The correct answer is **C**. "He squawked every so often..." a squawk is a loud noise made by a bird. Also, parrots are the only pet listed here sometimes known to talk.

**21.** The correct answer is **B**. "...yapping and barking..." are sounds made by a dog.

**22.** The correct answer is **F**. "He's not a bit like you'd imagine...if you are brave enough to hold him, he's actually quite soft and furry and really quite warm." One might not expect a fish or spider to be warm, but the fish may be eliminated because it would not be furry.

**23.** The correct answer is **D**. "I can spend hours in front of the tank..."; only fish are kept in tanks and come in lots of colours.

## Listening Part 4

**24.** The correct answer is **A**. "Not so loud, darling - people are looking." He is speaking so loudly that the other people can hear him and are looking to see what the fuss is about.

**25.** The correct answer is **A**. "...I don't think he'd be too happy." Choice B has the opposite meaning and so is incorrect. It would matter - he wouldn't like it - so choice C is incorrect.

**26.** The correct answer is **C**. Joel says "...I used to be a vegetarian..." Choice A is incorrect because Joel is a waiter now.

**27.** The correct answer is **C**. "...you could try writing the numbers a bit more clearly. Er, can you deal with this, dear? I've left my reading glasses in the car." Although he blames the numbers, the fact that he needs his glasses and his wife can see them indicates that the problem is with his vision and not with the numbers so choice A is not a good answer.

**28.** The correct answer is **B**. "...and one banana split." then "...and don't forget the extra cream."

**29.** The correct answer is **A**. "...all our meals are assembled in advance and nothing extra can be added - or removed."

**30.** The correct answer is **C**. He says "My word, that's very efficient. Even the officer's canteen in Stanbroke isn't that fast." Although his attitude for most of the exchange could be described as one of annoyance or perhaps even anger, at the end his attitude changes completely.

# TEST 6

## Reading & Use of English Part 5

**31.** The correct answer is **C**. To pave a road means to cover it with flat blocks of stone or concrete, so that it is easy to travel on, so, to "pave the way" for something means to prepare things so that something may happen more easily.

**32.** The correct answer is **C**. "new technology allowed viewers to move from the role of passive media consumers to active participants."

**33.** The correct answer is **A**. "We're trained to make a split between private and public surveillance". Choices C and D, both apply to public surveillance only, and B is incorrect because while people are not worried about private surveillance, they don't like the idea of public surveillance at all.

**34.** The correct answer is **C**. "The cast members on these shows are constantly talking about how great the experience is and how much they have grown personally because of it. It connotes honesty...It becomes a form of therapy or almost a kind of extreme sport ...". Advertising is not mentioned.

**35.** The correct answer is **A**. "students are trained to separate the world of academics from the world of popular culture. They tend not to think of that part of life using theories they have learned in class." Choice B is not correct because this is what students accuse others of doing. Choice C is incorrect because while "Andrejevic says he encourages his students to look beyond the characters and the surface glamour of reality television" this does not mean that they do. D is incorrect because this was true in the past, but today "young people form lines snaking for blocks" in their efforts to get on reality shows.

**36.** The correct answer is **D**. He says "it's time to start worrying about it as a form of social control" and that he "encourages his students to look beyond the characters and the surface glamour of reality television and consider the broader issues of surveillance, privacy, democracy and technology", he also says that "it's a good place to examine and inspect our culture".

## Reading & Use of English Part 6

**37.** The correct answer is **F**. The "but" after the gap indicates that we must expect two contrasting statements. Choice F tells us that she was completely unknown, while after the gap we learn that she rapidly became very famous. Although choice G may seem promising, it does not set up the contrast required by the "but".

**38.** The correct answer is **G**. The topic sentence basically says her rapid rise to fame is something new; choice G builds on this statement, and the sentences after the gap explain the reasons why her rise to fame was so fast.

**39.** The correct answer is **A**. The sentence after the gap contains an un-introduced "them" who had expectations about what Boyle's performance would be like. Choice A provides us with an appropriate subject for the "them" to reference - "the audience and panel". This choice might not be immediately obviously because it does not mention the subject of the paragraph - appearance and fame - directly, but in context, it does have to share this subject.

**40.** The correct answer is **C**. Now, in this paragraph we are introduced to the subject of serial killers. The gap is placed so that it must contain the paragraph's topic sentence. Each sentence in the paragraphs supports the idea that serial killers become famous. Only choice C can fulfil the role of topic sentence for this subject. B and D also share the subject of serial killers, but both compare them with something else, which is not done in this paragraph.

**41.** The correct answer is **D**. This paragraph gives examples of how no one else can match serial killers' fame; choice D sums the paragraph up, and ties in nicely to the subject of Boyle's exceptional fame in the next paragraph with the phrase "at least until now".

**42.** The correct answer is **B**. Much of this paragraph compares Boyle's fame with that of serial killers, as does choice B, which also provides an appropriate ending for the text.

## Reading & Use of English Part 7

**43.** The correct answer is **B**. Nothing at all positive is said.

**44.** The correct answer is **A**. "Don't blink or you'll miss it!"

**45.** The correct answer is **B**. "In this heavily processed and polished Disney product..."

**46.** The correct answer is **D**. "...from 1941..."

**47.** The correct answer is **C**. "...got me to shed a tear and sit on the edge of my seat, but the film isn't flawless, not by a long shot."

**48.** The correct answer is **C**. "...the special effects are impeccable."

**49.** The correct answer is **B**. "...it is beyond the scope, or intention, of the movie to sharpen this into an ironic or satirical point."

**50.** The correct answer is **C**. "...a message we want to be spreading, and more so, promoting? What about taking responsibility for yourself?"

**51.** The correct answer is **D**. "...stunning and sophisticated as any movie ever made, yet it moves at a pace that can keep the MTV generation riveted to the screen."

**52.** The correct answer is **A**. "...everyone has his or her secret reasons for what they do. But the wisdom of Miller's Crossing is that it understands that the human heart sometimes keeps those reasons a mystery..."

## Listening Part 1

**1.** The correct answer is **C**. "You said something very important about the core laws and I was just wondering...Could you possibly go back over this?" Choice A is incorrect because although the student misunderstood a word, it is not what the student was asking. Choice B is not correct because "I missed some of what you said; it was very fast." This means the student didn't have time to write it down, not that the student didn't understand.
**2.** The correct answer is **B**. "...we in the L.D.P. believe" - the personal pronoun 'we' is the clue; it shows affiliation. Also you must extrapolate from the abbreviation because we are not told the exact name of the party. The correct answer choice is the only one that shares the same initials. Choices A and C are incorrect because these parties are mentioned but criticised; they are opponents.
**3.** The correct answer is **A**. "They have over twice the number of rooms we have..." Choices B and C are incorrect because the other hotels "...offer very much the same facilities and standards".
**4.** The correct answer is **C**. "How many times have I told you not to touch things that don't belong to you?"; her tone is angry. Choice A is incorrect because the child's safety is not a concern here, as far as we know and choice B is incorrect because there is no explanation given, just orders.
**5.** The correct answer is **C**. "...they were wonderful...fixed it right there in front of me, and I didn't have to pay a penny." Choices A an B are incorrect because she "was worried" and she "was furious" but the problem was solved.
**6.** The correct answer is **A**. "I want to go to Radleigh Road number two-six-nine..."
**7.** The correct answer is **B**. "...but with the card it's only six fifty" and "I did also have to pay ten pounds to buy the card".
**8.** The correct answer is **C**. He says "...the song that everyone loved when they first heard it, but I think we're all ready for a new number 1, aren't we?" He is speaking for everyone, but also for himself.

## Listening Part 2

**9.** "no **brakes** on board".
**10.** "the minds that come up with" (ie think of) "all this... the shores of Utah's **Great Salt Lake**."
**11.** "can make you **sick** but they won't... we won't do that we refuse".
**12.** "the cars are easy ... the real art comes in designing the **track**" therefore most difficult.
**13.** "uses **gravity**".
**14.** "maximum speed ... record is **85 mph**".
**15.** "you're able to comprehend...there's a lot more kind of **fear**".
**16.** "**40 plus (+) mile** an hour screamer"
**17.** "the next generation ... maybe a coaster with a **virtual reality** helmet".
**18.** "coaster will go faster when the air is **warm but dry**".

## Listening Part 3

**19.** The correct answer is **D**. "I don't seem to remember a single person actually saying thank you and really meaning it."
**20.** The correct answer is **F**. "I was all set to have another unexci-ting Christmas" and "...they'd noticed that I was going to be alone that day and would I like to join them. And of course, I had a wonderful time."
**21.** The correct answer is **A**. "It isn't over yet. I mean we've had the actual festivities on the 25th, but there's so much more to Christmas than that."
**22.** The correct answer is **B**. "It wasn't as good as it's been in the past. For a start the telly was pretty disappointing" and "there's been nothing to watch all Christmas."
**23.** The correct answer is **C**. "But what's most distressing is..."

## Listening Part 4

**24.** The correct answer is **C**: "Jim Adams: Hi, this is "Say it like it is", the programme in which your comments about what's been on Radio One for the last week are read." Choice B is wrong: the programme is not direct it by the audience. Choice A is also wrong: "based on weather this time" therefore NOT always.
**25.** The correct answer is **B**. Mrs Kent says: "I'm more concerned about the present day situation...should...focus on short-term weather forecasts". She is is worried about the weather. Choice A is wrong. Mrs Kent says: "Some experts may tell us what the weather may be like in the next century but I'm more concerned..." therefore she is not an expert herself. Choice C is also wrong: Ice Age information was from the previous speaker - John Holmes.
**26.** The correct answer is **B.** "all those conversations about the weather would disappear" said as a negative point. Choice A is wrong: Tom does not mention food at all (Jim Adams says "food...seems to be a favourite to introduce the next readers". Choice C is also wrong: Tom Sheridan: "...would disappear" therefore are still talking about the weather.
**27.** The correct answer is **A.** "the producer of our cookery show here today, Mr Paul Spenser". Choice B is wrong: he's the producer of the show - not a listener. Choice C is also wrong: says it has to be easy for the beginners - it will get more difficult.
**28.** The correct answer is **A.** Jane says: "...we depend on libraries for our books". Choice B is wrong: "...too expensive to buy...depend on libraries" therefore she thinks borrowing books should be free. Choice C is also wrong: "...20p is too much" so she is against the idea that libraries should charge.
**29.** The correct answer is **C.** An elderly listener: "Why shouldn't others pay...they pay in...Discos...why not at libraries". Choice B is wrong: No mention of not liking pubs. Choice A is also wrong: "Why shouldn't others pay...they pay in...Discos...why not at libraries".
**30.** The correct answer is **A.** Most letters read out were complaints i.e. negative reactions. Choice B is wrong: There are not any real personal problems mentioned. Choice C is also wrong: There is no mention of money worries except paying for library books which is, at present, a rumour i.e. don't have to pay yet.

# TEST 7

## Reading & Use of English Part 5

**31.** The correct answer is **A**. "...worlds inside a bigger world they knew little about. The only world that mattered was the one that you could see in your immediate surroundings." While C may seem likely to be true, it is not actually mentioned, so is not a good answer choice.
**32.** The correct answer is **A**. "Statesmen and women saw that the way forward lay in bringing the world closer together. World War Three was to be avoided at all costs, they said." B is incorrect because this happens much later. C is not correct because they wanted to prevent it, which is a form of interest -they were interested in preventing conflict if you like. D is incorrect because they were becoming more "interdependent" which is the opposite of independent.
**33.** The correct answer is **C**. "Their task is to preserve world peace and prevent conflict, but the dream never quite became a reality as this body has very little 'real' power - it just does a lot of talking." A is incorrect because, although this is the dream, it didn't quite happen. B is incorrect, because "the nearest thing we have ever had to a world government" implies that it might be close but it isn't quite world government. D is incorrect because "the U.N. was to share power, responsibility and decision making for world affairs equally between all the members of the new global village".
**34.** The correct answer is **B**. To "take shape" means something develops or begins to appear in its final form.
**35.** The correct answer is **C**. "Technology was the most powerful tool for uniting people in the last century, and the first to create a truly global community."
**36.** The correct answer is **D**. "We may be closer; we may live in a global village; maybe we're getting there, but there's still a lot more to do." This is neither very positive nor very negative. It is balanced and realistic.

## Reading & Use of English Part 6

**37.** The correct answer is **A**. The sentence before the gap ends with "it's all or nothing up there" and A echoes this with "...it seems to be nothing instead of all".

**38.** The correct answer is **D**. We would expect the gap to be filled by an explanation of the reason for the enthusiasm referred to and the paragraph is about "those patient folk" so it would make sense that they "waited a long time" and something they wanted (they wanted snow) finally happened.

**39.** The correct answer is **C**. The gap is followed by "Back then...", so the missing sentence must be about the past which eliminates all but choices C and E. Choice E is not a good choice because it talks about childhood memories, which do not fit so well with crowded shops and overflowing cafes. The "glory days" of skiing would be a time when skiing was very popular, which fits better with the description after the gap.

**40.** The correct answer is **E**. We would expect the gap to give a reason why the author would be saddened by a lack of snow, and because the sentences following the gap speak of a time in the past, the gap must as well. E satisfies these requirements, and also fits nicely with the subject of the author's children not having an opportunity to enjoy snow which is mentioned later in the paragraph.

**41.** The correct answer is **B**. Before the gap, the author tells us that his children might not have the "same innocent sense of delight that I once did" and after the gap says that "it isn't fair". The unfair thing that caused the previously mentioned loss, is explained in choice B.

**42.** The correct answer is **F**. "One of them" refers to "those hopeless romantics". The author is not ready to give up hope for winter sports in Scotland.

## Reading & Use of English Part 7

**43.** The correct answer is **B**. "What I admire about my people is their diversity."

**44.** The correct answer is **B**. "I'm also quite proud of the monarchy. So many countries have abandoned the monarchical system, and I think that's sad."

**45.** The correct answer is **D**. "People from all over the world come to visit our wildlife reserves..."

**46.** The correct answer is **C**. "Of course, as we have become wealthier, our lifestyles have changed, too."

**47.** The correct answer is **D**. "...but it's sad to think this is all the rest of the world knows about us."

**48.** The correct answer is **C**. "...how far we have come in such a short space of time."

**49.** The correct answer is **A**. "...being in such close proximity to both Africa and the Middle East has given us a unique perspective."

**50.** The correct answer is **B**. "I am afraid that the more involved we become in the European Union, the less distinct we are as a nation."

**51.** The correct answer is **A**. "It's just a shame the present isn't quite as glorious as the past."

**52.** The correct answer is **A**. "And history is everywhere you go here, too; it's alive."

## Listening Part 1

**1.** The correct answer is **C**. "...it will cut a substantial slice off your family's electricity and water bills...economical with both water and energy making running costs a third less..." Choice A is incorrect because it is "...a more expensive model..." and choice B is incorrect because "...it has the same features as all our other models and does the job just as well."

**2.** The correct answer is **C**. "Penelope Parchment has a particularly difficult case to solve..." Detectives solve cases. Choice A is incorrect because "Alvin Major's guests tonight include..." Alvin has the talk show, not Penelope. Choice B is incorrect because no mention is made of a comedy show.

**3.** The correct answer is **A**. "...it makes more than fifty cups..." Cups go with coffee. Choice B is incorrect because bowls would go with soup and choice C is incorrect because glasses would go with juice.

**4.** The correct answer is **B**. "Cookery courses for the new year are in Chinese, South American and Indian cuisine..." Choice A is incorrect because the Indian cookery class will "...last an extra 2 weeks beyond the usual 5 week duration". Choice C is incorrect because "...Indian cookery course on Mondays, Wednesdays and Saturdays..."

**5.** The correct answer is **A**. "I think it made a lot of things unnecessarily difficult" He did not find it completely useless: "Mind you, it does have some useful diagrams that helped me pick up the fingering", so choice B is incorrect. Choice C is not a good answer because he suggests "...if I were you, I'd spend my money on having some actual lessons".

**6.** The correct answer is **A**. When he says he can't come she responds "Still, you deserve a break..." and "Will you be going abroad?" Choice B is not correct because: "You've been quite run down recently - and we don't want you getting ill." While 'run down' is not exactly well, it is not serious enough to be considered 'unwell'. Choice C is incorrect because he has been working a lot but that's not the reason he can't come to the dinner; see above.

**7.** The correct answer is **C**. "...you go all the way up St Mark's Hill, over the top and right down..." Choice B is incorrect because "...if you get to the river, you know that you've gone too far".

**8.** The correct answer is **B**. The teacher says "...haven't you been missing your classes quite a lot recently?" Choices A and C are incorrect because when the student says "...I promise I'll try to pay more attention and bring the right books next time..." he responds: "...that's not the problem...".

## Listening Part 2

**9.** "...that of fractures - or to put it more simply - **broken bones**."

**10.** "...performing the two vital functions of **support** for the body and protection for the internal parts of the body..."

**11.** "Bones are...made up of a **hardened** outer layer of cells around a soft material in the centre..."

**12.** "The bone marrow, incidentally, performs the equally vital function of producing **new blood** cells."

**13.** "Bones do not break easily." and "the bones...can actually **bend** to a surprising degree..."

**14.** "...locate any fractures before attempting to **move** the victim."

**15.** "further movement of the damaged area will result in **'multiple** fractures' - in other words - many small breaks..."

**16.** "If the victim is conscious...he or she will be able to tell you the **position** of any fractures"

**17.** "But, in the case of an unconscious victim, a different procedure should be followed. After checking...as described in **previous programmes**, the next step..."

**18.** "in the case of an unconscious victim...methodically feel each major bone in the body noting any **change in shape** that would indicate the presence of a break."

## Listening Part 3

**19.** The correct answer is **F**. "The fabric was too wet and I just couldn't get things to come out without creases..."

**20.** The correct answer is **B**. Clues include "...rather than send everything to the laundry..." and "hanging everything out afterwards."

**21.** The correct answer is **A**. "In the end, we did end up having to call a professional plumber out..."; plumbers fix leaking taps.

**22.** The correct answer is **C**. "You rub and rub until you think you've finished and then ten minutes later, when you go outside, you see a bit you've missed."

**23.** The correct answer is **E**. "...wallpapering is so much easier than it looks..."; wallpapering is included within decorating.

## Listening Part 4

**24.** The correct answer is **B**. He says "Quick, pretend we haven't seen him." and therefore choice A is not a good answer. Choice C is incorrect because he says "...hang on...hey! That's Carl." He recognises him fairly quickly.

**25.** The correct answer is **A**. When Andrea mentions it he says "Oh, God." which indicates he dislikes even the thought of it and when Carl says "it didn't seem to sell too well" Bob replies "I'm not surprised".

**26.** The correct answer is **C**. Carl asks "Are you interested in country

music?" and Andrea responds "Is that what all this is? All country music?" and Carl does not contradict her so we can assume her assumption is true.
**27.** The correct answer is **A**. "...then one day, I got talking to my claims officer...er...about my collection...and he suggested that I did this..." Choice B is incorrect because although he was talking about his collection, no mention is made of him selling it or wanting to sell it.
**28.** The correct answer is **A**. "After 'Acres' closed down..." and "pays even less than 'Acres' did." Acres is referred to in the past tense, therefore it no longer exists.
**29.** The correct answer is **B**. "Oh, I spent my redundancy money on a holiday." and "Well, yeah, yeah, it didn't quite cover the car."
In other words, he spent some of the money on the car, but most of it was already gone.
**30.** The correct answer is **A**. Bob says "Oh, er...I don't know about that. I'm not sure all that standing around in the cold would be good for my poor circulation." He does not really like the idea.

# TEST 8

## Reading & Use of English Part 5

**31.** The correct answer is **B**. A "paradox" involves two facts that contradict each other. Choice B is the only choice that has two such facts.
**32.** The correct answer is **D**. British students have "conditions most educational researchers would say are far more likely to help them succeed."
**33.** The correct answer is **D**. "classroom management seems to be a whole lot easier in places like Korea,...belligerent and disrespectful students appear to be the norm these days. Teachers in Britain seem powerless to control what happens anymore."
**34.** The correct answer is **A**. "The traditional family unit still remains relatively intact in Korea. Few children come from broken homes," while in Britain "one in every two marriages fails and divorce rates are sky high".
**35.** The correct answer is **C**. "Asian students tend to put their education before literally everything else. They do very few extracurricular activities and devote far more time to their studies than their British peers".
**36.** The correct answer is **C**. The author says "is it perhaps about time we stopped comparing and started trying to combine the best bits of both"; this implies that both could be improved.

## Reading & Use of English Part 6

**37.** The correct answer is **E**. The sentence before the gap mentions "upcoming holidays", choice E describes the writer on the way to Sidney, and, after the gap, the author describes the excitement of finally being there. So, choice E fits nicely in the sequence of the narration.
**38.** The correct answer is **G**. Choice G ties the paragraph which it completes to the first sentence of the next paragraph, which repeats the same idea while adding more detail. "No sooner" in the following sentence means immediately, which is certainly not long to wait.
**39.** The correct answer is **D**. The sentence before the gap mentions the Lyrebird's "spectacular plumage" which means amazing feathers. Choice D continues on the same topic - the bird's "bright, colourful feathers". The author says the feathers by themselves would have made the journey worthwhile, and the sentence after the gap indicates that, in spite of this, things were going to get even better.
**40.** The correct answer is **A**. A reason is given for why they remained undetected. The male Lyrebird was completely absorbed in his performance and so didn't notice them.
**41.** The correct answer is **B**. Here, Mark tells the author that the bird has fooled him with its song, which, as we learn after the gap, leads him to realise that what he was hearing was the bird and he was not actually being shot at.
**42.** The correct answer is **F**. It makes sense that witnessing something extremely rare would be a very important moment in the author's career which is what the following sentence confirms.

## Reading & Use of English Part 7

**43.** The correct answer is **A**. "...do make sure you put on an extra layer if you are going out."
**44.** The correct answer is **C**. "...please ensure that you apply protection to your skin if you are going to go outside during the day for any significant length of time."
**45.** The correct answer is **A**. "...clear skies will see night-time temperatures plummet below freezing..."
**46.** The correct answer is **B**. "...a flood warning is in place..."
**47.** The correct answer is **A**. "...markedly colder than recent weeks."
**48.** The correct answer is **D**. "...remember that with the warmer temperatures comes an increased risk of tropical storms..."
**49.** The correct answer is **D**. "This could fall as snow over the mountains..."
**50.** The correct answer is **B**. "The signs are not good for the winter sports industry..."
**51.** The correct answer is **B**. "...most of central Canada will be dry, though the coastal regions can still expect to experience some light showers..."
**52.** The correct answer is **C**. "...record highs..."

## Listening Part 1

**1**. The correct answer is **C**. "...I can't give you a point for that..." Points are given on quiz shows. Choice A is incorrect because no mention is made of phoning in. Choice B is incorrect because knowledge is being demonstrated, not talent.
**2**. The correct answer is **B**. "It really isn't the same any more...you do have to wait longer for everything and there isn't the same selection as before - especially the desserts..." and therefore A is incorrect. Choice C is incorrect because "it's still good value".
**3**. The correct answer is **A**. "life on the outside" and "the day I got out" indicate he was in jail, so he must be a criminal and he calls himself "a celebrity" so he is famous for some reason. Choice B is incorrect because no mention is made of a detective, only a "...detective writer", which means the same thing as crime writer; and Sam Beesly is the "...detective writer".
**4**. The correct answer is **A**. "So, how did you know that I was his daughter?" indicates they have never met, otherwise it would not be surprising if he knew who she was. Choices B and C are incorrect because actually the man was the woman's father's "arithmetic and geometry" teacher.
**5**. The correct answer is **C**. "If you open your books to page 62, you will see two contrasting maps of the region." Geography includes the study of maps, demography and land usage.
**6**. The correct answer is **C**. "This service is now running about 7 minutes late and will now depart at 7:22..." Choice B is incorrect because the train "...will now depart at 7:22 from platform 3 as advertised"; 'as advertised' means there is no change of platform.
**7**. The correct answer is **B**. "Yes, I know it was advertised on television but the distributor...Well, I'm sorry, too"; The caller clearly wants the disc right now. Choice A is incorrect because although the speaker is trying to be polite, the response of "Well, you'll just have to do that, won't you?" indicates that the caller probably said something that was not very polite.
**8**. The correct answer is **B**. "Well, if you don't go round there and talk to them, ...I will." Choice A is incorrect because it is the students next door making noise, not the husband. Choice C is incorrect because she wants him to "...go straight to the source of the trouble" [in other words, confront the problem directly].

## Listening Part 2

**9.** "...a shower of meteors or **shooting stars**."
**10.** "To imagine what is happening, it helps us to imagine a car driving fast along the road. In a way, our planet Earth is like that **car**."
**11.** "In many ways, the meteors are similar to the swarm of **insects**..."
**12.** "In fact, meteors are mostly tiny pieces of **iron** that look like little stones."
**13.** "...the Earth...does follow the same circular route around the sun once every year. This enormous circular path is called the Earth's '**orbit**'."

**14.** "...when the earth approaches one of these stones, it is pulled **downwards** towards our planet by a strong force called gravity."
**15.** "This is about a hundred times faster than **a jet plane**."
**16.** "Now, because it is going through the air so fast, the shooting star starts to become **hotter and hotter**..."
**17.** "...the outside of this piece of iron gets very hot indeed and as a result, it gets soft and **melts** and then starts to burn."
**18.** "...fortunately for us, most meteors are so small that they have completely burned up, long before they could ever **reach the ground**..."

## Listening Part 3

**19.** The correct answer is **G**. "...and Sally braked..." so Sally was the driver of the car, not the speaker.
**20.** The correct answer is **B**. "...going from carriage to carriage..." Carriages are unique to trains.
**21.** The correct answer is **E**. "...in the end, I had no choice but to set off on a four-mile march..." To 'march' means to walk somewhere quickly, in a determined way, so the speaker went on foot.
**22.** The correct answer is **F**. "...the chain had come off..." Bicycles have chains.
**23.** The correct answer is **A**. "We'd taxied to the end of the runway..."; a runway is where a plane takes off and lands.

## Listening Part 4

**24.** The correct answer is **B**. After Charles introduces himself, the bartender says: "What can I get you then, Mrs Miller?" Choices A and C are incorrect because: "The farm - I know very well...but you, I don't." He knows they are not locals and he is surprised to hear they live at Draycott farm.
**25.** The correct answer is **C**. Charles says "Of course, I did actually meet the poor man once - worked there on summer picking strawberries."
**26.** The correct answer is **A**. "About the suicide you mean? Yes. What a terrible tragedy"; the owner killed himself.
**27.** The correct answer is **A**. "...and he would have wanted the farm to go to someone from Willowdale...which you are not." While choice B is true, this is not the reason that Bill thinks they shouldn't have the farm. Choice C is incorrect because Bill says that he is being frank, which means that he is stating things in an open and honest way.
**28.** The correct answer is **B**. Charles says "...that Draycott farm won't be a farm any more and..." and Bill replies "...That is what people have been saying". Choice C is incorrect because although Bill says "and he would have wanted the farm to go to someone from Willowdale...which you are not." This only means he does not think the farm was taken over by the right people, NOT that Charles and Daphne didn't actually take it over. Clearly, they did. They have a "fancy estate agent", after all.
**29.** The correct answer is **A**. "So we wanted to get away from the city and make a healthier life." Choice B is not correct because Charles' work is flexible; he can work wherever he is so it's not a reason they needed to move to the country. Choice C is incorrect because they have "...every intention of using the shops and the local services." In other words, since they live there, they will support the local community but this does not mean they moved there for the purpose of doing so.
**30.** The correct answer is **C**. After he hears about the high salary, Bill says "Well, that is rather generous" which, is the first positive thing he has said. Choice A is incorrect because he expresses suspicion from the start and choice B is incorrect because, although he changes his attitude, he does not indicate that he is sorry for his previous negativity.

# TEST 9

## Reading & Use of English Part 5

**31.** The correct answer is **C**. "...questions about family history and lifestyle to determine a person's RealAge".
**32.** The correct answer is **D**. If people are buying the books, and taking the test, and it has even been on Oprah's show, then people must be interested. A is not correct, because in this paragraph no value judgement is made. B is incorrect because while we know about current profits, no mention is made of past or future profits. C is not correct because the future is not mentioned at all; we don't know how things will develop nor is it speculated about.
**33.** The correct answer is **D**. "Each lifestyle factor interacts with other factors in a complex way. RealAge does try to address this, adjusting some of the factors for age..."
**34.** The correct answer is **A**. "RealAge, unfortunately, is not transparent about how it uses information..." and "This is not specified to those who become members..." "Transparent" means clear, open, and easily understood, and "specified" means explained.
**35.** The correct answer is **B**. "Users' health histories, which they provide while taking the test, are used by the website to generate personalized content, including health tips, but also including highly targeted advertisements." "Personalized" and "highly targeted" are key words here that mean something is individualized to cater to the needs or tastes of a particular person. This eliminates A because the tips contain 'personalized content' and are therefore not random. D is wrong because the website does not provide 'information' about products but rather advertises them.
**36.** The correct answer is **C**. Overall, the review would not be regarded as very positive (ruling out D). That said, the writer has some positive comments to make in the final paragraph (ruling out A) and, although he expresses his doubts or scepticism about the test in said paragraph, his criticism isn't very strong and he doesn't emphasise these doubts. Therefore, while he may be slightly sceptical or doubting, he is not very much so (ruling out B). If anything, he is 'somewhat positive', ceding that 'the test can be...fun' and that people who use it 'will probably be healthier and better off for it'. This is not a comment filled with lots of doubt; indeed, it is fairly committal, bordering on a mild endorsement, and is followed not by warnings but a caveat to simply take the usual and obvious precautions as with any service of this kind.

## Reading & Use of English Part 6

**37.** The correct answer is **C**. The topic sentence of this paragraph states that the pattern is not only present in this time and place. Later in the paragraph, place is discussed, so this gap must concern time. Something that is permanent does not change with time, making C an appropriate choice.
**38.** The correct answer is **B**. The gap is surrounded by the topic of *fewer children and lower birth rates*, so it follows that the correct choice would share this topic. Choice D might also be considered, but while it sort of fits, the topic of the paragraph is that lower birth rates are one factor that causes an ageing population, so the goal is to point out that lower birth rates do indeed exist. There is no mention anywhere in the paragraph of the government's level of influence on birth rate, so D does not support the paragraph's aims.
**39.** The correct answer is **A**. The second gap in this paragraph deals with the second factor - people living longer. Life expectancy at a past time is mentioned before the gap, and after the gap "similar increases" in life expectancy are mentioned, so we would expect the gap to provide us with proof of an increase in life expectancy. Choice A does just this, with "it" refering to life expectancy today and in the future. It makes sense for "it" to refer to life expectancy, because "it" is measured in years.
**40.** The correct answer is **F**. The topic of the paragraph is *changes causing concern.* Before the gap we are given a statistic in the past, in the form of a ratio. We would expect the gap to provide us with a worrying example of how this ratio is changing - from 5 to 1, decreasing to 2.5
to 1 - as choice F does. Other choices that show changes do not ex-

press them in a way that fits this ratio.

**41.** The correct answer is **G**. The paragraph where the next two gaps are located discusses what might be done about the problem, and a number of options are given. The first gap is sandwiched between a sentence about huge tax increases, and enormous spending cuts, so we would expect the correct choice to transition between the two ideas, which choice G does using "An alternative approach...". Choice E has a similar role, but instead transitions between spending cuts and a deficit, which is required for gap 42.

**42.** The correct answer is **E** which uses "instead" to provide a transition between impossible budget cuts, before the gap, and irresponsible dept, after.

## Reading & Use of English Part 7

**43.** The correct answer is **B**. "Since we didn't have one of those side-rails..."

**44.** The correct answer is **A**. "...called my grandmother to verify a date..."

**45.** The correct answer is **D**. "What I saw was horrible."

**46.** The correct answer is **C**. "The earliest thing I can remember is sitting in my crib, in a house we moved out of when I was about nine months old..."

**47.** The correct answer is **A**. "My mum got kind of quiet..."

**48.** The correct answer is **B**. "...mom in her bright sunny room, working at her desk on some bills."

**49.** The correct answer is **D**. "...a lot of people have clear memories of their early childhood. I don't. Instead they are flashes of events over a period of time."

**50.** The correct answer is **C**. "...when I was in my twenties I walked into a public place with my mother and stopped and said, "We used to have this tile in our kitchen.""

**51.** The correct answer is **B**. "...this was great fun to fall out of bed so slowly!"

**52.** The correct answer is **D**. "Despite my dislike for the sun they are all sun-drenched - I don't have many memories of winter in my early years..."

## Listening Part 1

**1**. The correct answer is **A**. "...but if your car remains there, the floats won't be able to get past..." Choice B is incorrect because "Sorry, we appreciate this is your legal parking space..." Choice C is incorrect because if the car remains where it is "...then everybody will be complaining." They have not begun complaining yet.

**2**. The correct answer is **B**. "Now, if you look here into the battery compartment, this should be put in this way round..." Choice A is not correct because when the same battery is used or inserted correctly they "have power". Choice C is incorrect because the speaker says "Oh, don't worry about the film, I wound it back into its container."

**3**. The correct answer is **A**. Cecilia is concerned about her "Swiss Cheese plant". The programme is neither about cheese or Switzerland but a living thing which grows in the garden.

**4**. The correct answer is **A**. "...the flash disturbs other visitors and damages the colouring in our priceless antique paintings." A flash is used to take a photograph inside. Choice B is incorrect because no mention is made of smoking and choice C is incorrect because we are told there is no problem with the man who has brought his dog because "...he is not using a flash".

**5**. The correct answer is **A**. "...we can meet at quarter to four..." Choice B is incorrect because it is "the departmental heads meeting at 4:15" and choice C is incorrect because no mention is made of 4:45.

**6**. The correct answer is **C**. "...Horden's Limited should provide compensation of..."; compensation is money paid out because of a mistake or bad service. Choice A is incorrect because no mention is made of there being too many clients and choice B is incorrect because the company was "not directly responsible".

**7**. The correct answer is **A**. "...her fur did come out such a beautiful, snowy white colour..."; cats have fur, while children and parrots do not.

**8**. The correct answer is **B**. "...the Brain-Booster is capable of raising your intelligence level by as much as 40 I.Q. points..." Choice C is not correct because it works "...without affecting other brain functions such as memory".

## Listening Part 2

**9.** "The strap, as they call it, was a thick piece of leather... especially designed for **hitting** small children with, on the palms of their hands."

**10.** "Nowadays, if you do something wrong at school, you're unlucky if you even get a **telling off**."

**11.** "I'll never forget the first time it happened to me...I came to school in **the wrong shoes**..."

**12.** "I saw this and many other examples of our school's discipline system as **very cruel** and unfair."

**13.** "All the other members were like me. They had **young children**..."

**14.** "...in 1979, **the government** put an end to the strap..."

**15.** "My own son and daughter have turned into **lazy**, irresponsible young adults..."

**16.** "...who really have no idea **how lucky** they are."

**17.** "...I've begun to think - to wish - that they'd never **changed the law**."

**18.** "...we wouldn't have all the **teenage crime** if those teenagers concerned had...been given the strap."

## Listening Part 3

**19.** The correct answer is **D**. "...some of these bells weigh as much as 40 kilograms."

**20.** The correct answer is **E**. "...since international trade in ivory has been made illegal, few of these instruments have been made."

**21.** The correct answer is **F**. "...the drum can be displayed outside a building of importance to drive away the evil spirits..."

**22.** The correct answer is **B**. "...not only its appearance but the tuning as well are similar to that of a classical guitar..."

**23.** The correct answer is **A**. "The curved base and supporting structure of this instrument are made of matured rose-wood while the nails ...are traditionally made of ebony...Four different trees are used to make the blocks themselves...hammers are fashioned by hand from willow"

## Listening Part 4

**24.** The correct answer is **B**. The passenger says "I'm visiting a friend who says he can get me a job." Choice A is incorrect because "Well, actually I'm not exactly on holiday."

**25.** The correct answer is **B**. The flight attendant says "More like five and a half hours and that's if there are no delays..."

**26.** The correct answer is **A**. "it's the same distance but from London to Athens we have a tail wind which makes it quicker...but on the way back that becomes a head wind which slows us down."

**27.** The correct answer is **C**. She says of the longer flights "Well, actually they're better..." and "And sometimes, if you're lucky, you even get a two-night stop-over."

**28.** The correct answer is **A**. She tells the man that she stays over for two nights "About once a week usually".

**29.** The correct answer is **C**. "I'm doing Moscow tomorrow, that's one...and it's a nice place..." She's going and says it's nice so she is looking forward to it. She knows it is nice so she must have been before, therefore, choice B is not correct. Choice A is incorrect because she complains about the weather, not the living conditions.

**30.** The correct answer is **B**. "...but it's a bit chilly around this time of year." 'Chilly' means 'rather cold'.

# TEST 10

## Reading & Use of English Part 5

**31.** The correct answer is **A**. "Music enwrapped her" means that it occupied her completely, and her mind was carried away somewhere by the music and not focused on reality. B is not correct because she agrees, saying "I expect so". C is not correct because she is already in the concert hall, and the concert is in progress. While D is true, it is not the reason she was not able to speak about him.
**32.** The correct answer is **D**. "For the Andante had begun", the "for" here has the meaning of "because" and the "Andante" is a passage in the piece of music being performed.
**33.** The correct answer is **B**. Although she found the music a bit boring, she was not bored by the people. She thought "How interesting that row of people was! What diverse influences had gone to the making!"
**34.** The correct answer is **B**. The goblins "were not aggressive creatures; it was that that made them so terrible to Helen".
**35.** The correct answer is **D**. The goblins observed that "there was no such thing as splendour or heroism in the world" and "Helen could not contradict them, for, once at all events, she had felt the same, and had seen the reliable walls of youth collapse." If you say the walls of something collapse, it means you can no longer believe in that something.
**36.** The correct answer is **A**. "tangible" = something clear enough to be seen, felt or noticed; something concrete and physical. She reaches out as if there was a physical thing that she could touch.

## Reading & Use of English Part 6

**37.** The correct answer is **E**. The topic of this paragraph is "musical utterances" in the "animal kingdom". E is a better choice than B, because it mentions birds and animals, covering more of the animal kingdom than B, which only concerns birds. Although choice C also mentions members of the animal kingdom, it may be eliminated because it is speaking about drumming, which is not an utterance, or a sound produced with the voice.
**38.** The correct answer is **B**. This paragraph talks specifically about birdsong, which makes choice B, which lists species of birds, most appropriate. Also, the sentence following the gap, speaks about "the latter" (which means the second of two) topics and "human music" which is the second of two topics in choice B, fits nicely with the meaning of the next sentence.
**39.** The correct answer is **G**. The topic of the paragraph is instrumental sound which eliminates all but C and G. Choice C may be eliminated because it contains the word "other" which requires a specific animal to have been mentioned previously. Also, in choice G, the words "limited to" agree with the word "rare" in the sentence before the gap.
**40.** It follows that **C** is the correct answer in the second gap in this paragraph about instrumental sound. The "other" species mentioned before are the great apes. Also, the list of drumming species fits with the modification in the following sentence using 'however', followed by statement of the fact that only a couple of species drum with both hands.
**41.** The correct answer is **F**. This gap is in the position where we would expect a topic sentence. The following sentences would lead us to expect the meaning to concern ideas about the function of music. F has this meaning, and also ties in with the previous paragraph by mentioning "since Darwin posed the question". Choice A also shares the subject, but because of the "However", it cannot take the position at the beginning of the paragraph.
**42.** The correct answer is **A**. The initial "However" makes it appropriate for a sentence at the end of a paragraph, emphasizing that although the paragraph mentions several ideas, we still don't know the answer. The subject matter both sums up the paragraph, and the whole article.

## Reading & Use of English Part 7

**43.** The correct answer is **B**. "But can music ever be separated from its political context?"
**44.** The correct answer is **B**. "Song was a communal act of expression that shed light on the injustices of Apartheid, playing a major role in the eventual reform of the South African government."
**45.** The correct answer is **C**. "...it's my job to help others get the best possible start in life. It seems music has a role to play."
**46.** The correct answer is **B**. "I had a glimpse of this first-hand growing up in South Africa..."
**47.** The correct answer is **A**. "...deprived boys and girls could receive strong skills to overcome poverty with the collective learning experience of music."
**48.** The correct answer is **A**. "...by the work of a charity called the National System of Youth and Children's Orchestras of Venezuela, popularly known as "The System"."
**49.** The correct answer is **A**. No mention is made of Ann's occupation.
**50.** The correct answer is **A**. "...a quote in which he highlighted how these feelings affected the poor, much more..."
**51.** The correct answer is **B**. "If you want to know more, let me recommend Amandla! A Revolution in Four-Part Harmony..."
**52.** The correct answer is **C**. "This seems to be true for classical music, but not other styles of music because of classical music's complicated structure."

## Listening Part 1

**1.** The correct answer is **B**. "...if you can just try changing the contrast and brightness controls, they're on the back of that model, and try repositioning the aerial..."
**2.** The correct answer is **C**. "I had a shocking temperature...and a couple of days I felt so dizzy I couldn't even stand up"; it sounds like he had the flu or a similar illness. Choice A may be eliminated because "...feeling hot and cold all the time and shivering..." refers to how he felt when he had a temperature, not the weather.
**3.** The correct answer is **A**. "Can I take this over there to show my friends?" The answer comes from the context; since they are discussing price and choice of meals, it makes sense that "this" would be a menu.
**4.** The correct answer is **C**. "...no work begins before 7am but we can check with the foreman to see if this rule has in fact been broken..." Choice A is not correct because the topic of discussion is noise in the morning;. Choice B is not correct because when the speaker says "I think you'll find that if there's been no damage..." the "if" implies that damage is not the problem.
**5.** The correct answer is **B**. "I just wondered if you could read through it and see if I've made any spelling mistakes." Choice A is incorrect because Amanda says "I've just finished typing this letter". Choice C is incorrect because when the man asks if she wants his opinion she responds "Well, not really. I do know how to write a letter."
**6.** The correct answer is **A**. "...the West Bromwich Albion - Wolverhampton game which has been delayed by flooding of the pitch..." Choice B is incorrect because "The Fulham Brighton and Hove Albion match was postponed due to rain..." and choice C is incorrect because both of the above games are scoreless, so this is not different.
**7.** The correct answer is **B**. "This song is for Simon and anyone else with cerebro-spinal arthritis."
**8.** The correct answer is **A**. "...your tail-lights are not functioning." Choice B may be eliminated because the policeman says "Otherwise, there'll be an accident."; there hasn't been one yet.

## Listening Part 2

**9.** "Good morning, I'd like to welcome you to **Trinity** college."
**10.** "For you, the **history** students, most of your seminars will be held..."
**11.** "...your seminars will be held from **9-12.30**..."
**12.** "... in rooms **201** and **95**."
**13.** "...who will just be here for the **eight week** course that you are following."
**14.** "The highlight of this is always the trip to **the British Museum** on Saturday 5th July."

**15.** "This museum is particularly famous for the Parthenon Marbles and the **Egyptian Mummies**..."
**16.** "The canteen is open daily from 12-**2.30 p.m.** and again from **5**-8 **p.m.** although on Fridays..."
**17.** "These are available every day and all are free with the exception of the **aerobic classes**."
**18.** "...you can find the accommodation officer in Room 16 in **Western House**."

## Listening Part 3

**19.** The correct answer is **A**. "...just after the New Year sales..." and "he picked up a crystal decanter, looked at it and then put it back on the shelf" indicate she is in a shop.
**20.** The correct answer is **D**. "...after quickly phoning his mum, I asked Sam to take care of my group"; she is looking after children.
**21.** The correct answer is **E**. "...in the back" and "I pulled over" indicate a large vehicle such as a bus.
**22.** The correct answer is **C**. "...like other products when it comes to market research...". Executives conduct market research.
**23.** The correct answer is **F**. "In legal terms..." and "...custody of the child. And according to her rights, she should have...".These are all concerns of a lawyer.

## Listening Part 4

**24.** The correct answer is **C**. Patty says "...We met at the Thomas' Christmas party last year..."
**25.** The correct answer is **A**. To call someone a rocket scientist is an idiomatic way of saying they are very smart. Also, the children are very young, so B and C are not possible.
**26.** The correct answer is **C**. Norman says "...just what every seven-year-old needs." which is sarcastic - it means the opposite - and follows this with "It never caused me any trouble not knowing three languages." Choices A and B are incorrect because it is Patty who says "And you know, the younger you start..." and "...languages are so important these days."
**27.** The correct answer is **B**. Patty says "Oh Linda, you ought to find out about these things. He expects to learn from you, not be your teacher." Choice C is not correct because Patty went to night school in order to help her son and brings this up as an example.
**28.** The correct answer is **B**. Linda says "I could never manage that - what with the hours I work." which means she doesn't have time because she works so many hours. Also, Patty says "So you're still doing six nights a week?" and Linda replies "I'm afraid so." Choice C is not correct because Linda says "Still, tomorrow night's my night off."
**29.** The correct answer is **A**. Norman says "Is your husband still sending you the maintenance cheques every month then?" and Patty replies "...he's my ex-husband now, but he does still send the cheques..." Choice B is incorrect because Patty mentions "Stewart's school fees" and choice C is incorrect because no mention is made of Patty working as a teacher.
**30.** The correct answer is **C**. Norman says "Does Stewart ever have time to play?" Choice B is incorrect because he says "No, I mean play with other kids, kick a ball around, get in fights..." and choice A is incorrect because he says "...all he seems to do is one lesson after another. What a way to spend a childhood".

# TEST 1

*I am going to give you the instructions for this test.*
*I shall introduce each part of the test and give you time to look at the questions. At the start of each piece you will hear this sound:*

— *** —

*You will hear each piece twice.*

*Remember, while you are listening, write your answers on the question paper. You will have **five** minutes at the end of the test to copy your answers onto the separate answer sheet.*

*There will now be a pause. Please ask any questions now, because you must not speak during the test.*

PAUSE 5 SECONDS

*Now open your question paper and look at **Part One**.*

PAUSE 5 SECONDS

*You will hear people talking in eight different situations. For Questions **1–8**, choose the best answer (**A**, **B** or **C**).*

***Question 1***
*You are in a shop when you overhear this man answering the telephone.*

PAUSE 2 SECONDS

— *** —

Hello, Hammerstones, can I help you? Yes, we can take an order. Is it a recent publication? ... Okay then, do you know the name of the author? ... Aha, and the title? ... 'Getting the Most out of Your Guitar'. Yes, I am familiar with that title. It is actually available in paperback now ... Okay then ... If you'd like to leave your name and telephone number, ... *FADE*

PAUSE 2 SECONDS

— *** —

TAPE REPEAT
PAUSE 2 SECONDS

***Question 2***
*You are listening to the radio when you hear this man speaking.*

PAUSE 2 SECONDS

— *** —

Well Giles, what is currently happening in the Cumberland dry-dock dispute is nothing new. There has been a long history of industrial problems in British shipbuilding and this makes what the minister said wrong on a number of counts. In fact, this statement could be going to cause serious difficulties for the government. Rodwyn Lewis has managed to get a number of backs up in the union, which is not going to help his government solve the dispute.

PAUSE 2 SECONDS

— *** —

TAPE REPEAT
PAUSE 2 SECONDS

***Question 3***
*You are sitting in a cafe when you hear this woman speaking.*

PAUSE 2 SECONDS

— *** —

Well, I'm not in the slightest bit bothered about the cold weather this year. Not since Geoff got round to fitting the new windows. I mean the old ones were letting in the rain. Last winter it got so cold that I ended up having to wear a coat in our front living room and what with Samantha being only two-and-a-half well, we just had to do something about them. Anyway, Geoff's marvellous when it comes to jobs round the house. I mean he had them up and finished in a week - good thing it wasn't snowing then.

PAUSE 2 SECONDS

— *** —

TAPE REPEAT
PAUSE 2 SECONDS

***Question 4***
*Listen to this woman introducing a college lecture.*

PAUSE 2 SECONDS

— *** —

Good evening, everybody. Er, this won't be very long. Er, I'd just like to say thank you to all of you for managing to turn up at such short notice. I'm sure you won't be disappointed. I'm sure by now all of you must have heard about Anne's staggering breakthrough in the field of micro-neurosurgery. And, I can tell you, as a personal friend of hers, that Anne started her career right here. So it's very fitting that I should be introducing - right now - Anne Suiter.

PAUSE 2 SECONDS

— *** —

TAPE REPEAT
PAUSE 2 SECONDS

***Question 5***
*You will hear someone talking about soap operas.*

PAUSE 2 SECONDS

— *** —

Nowadays our TV's seem to be showing soaps every day for most of the day. Soaps from America, Australia or the continent. The characters tend to be stereotypes and the plot is often repetitive and predictable. So why then do we rush back to our homes after work to see what has happened to the characters that we love to hate? Maybe because we actually enjoy the lack of challenge that they offer, and although we may protest that we aren't really interested, they become a habit and we suffer from withdrawal symptoms if we don't get our daily dose of bad acting. No one believes they are real characters of course - or do they? Many characters actually receive fan mail and if one dies, some fans are unhappy for weeks.

PAUSE 2 SECONDS

— *** —

TAPE REPEAT
PAUSE 2 SECONDS

***Question 6***
*You are staying in the home of a British family. You hear the mother answering the phone.*

PAUSE 2 SECONDS

— *** —

Hello, Sevenoaks 9818 ... oh, oh, yes, hello Steven. No, I'm afraid Audrey's not in right now. Can I give her a message? ... No, she's not doing anything tomorrow night. ... Oh, yes. I'm sure she'd love that. He's one of her favourite actors. It's just come out, hasn't it? ... Look, I'll tell her when she gets in to give you a ring, okay? ... All right! Bye.

PAUSE 2 SECONDS

— *** —

TAPE REPEAT
PAUSE 2 SECONDS

***Question 7***
*Listen to a policeman being interviewed on the evening television news.*

PAUSE 2 SECONDS

— *** —

Well, I didn't so much see the blast as hear it. I was on duty at the time and walking along Tarrant Street when it happened. Of course, I went to investigate and found the remains of a light vehicle scattered over a wide area. There was also some damage to nearby buildings. I immediately radioed the station and requested assistance and then proceeded to cordon off the street. Fortunately, there was no evidence that anybody had been in the vehicle at the time.

PAUSE 2 SECONDS

— *** —

TAPE REPEAT
PAUSE 2 SECONDS

***Question 8***
*You overhear this exchange in a major London railway station.*

PAUSE 2 SECONDS

— *** —

***C*** *= Commuter* ***P*** *= Porter*

**C**: Um, excuse me. Did I just hear that the Preston/Lancaster service has been cancelled again?
**P**: Well, sir, it won't be running today.
**C**: Would that be because of the snow in the Tring Gap? You've had three days to get that line clear.
**P**: Well, actually sir, the snow melted earlier today and that part of the line's a foot under water now and if we did run any trains along there we'd be having an accident and I'm sure that you wouldn't want that ... *FADE*

PAUSE 2 SECONDS

— *** —

TAPE REPEAT
PAUSE 2 SECONDS

*That is the end of Part One.*
*Now turn to* ***Part Two****.*

PAUSE 5 SECONDS

*You will hear part of a radio talk about an institution that helps addicts. For questions* ***9-18****, complete the sentences with a word or short phrase.*

*You now have 45 seconds in which to look at Part 2.*

PAUSE 45 SECONDS

— *** —

***I*** *= Introducer* ***J*** *= Jane*

**I**: Why do perfectly sane, normal people pay up to a thousand pounds a week to make themselves sick? Jane Seaworthy has been finding out.
**J**: Well, actually, the people attending the Thorndale clinic, situated on the outskirts of Bristol, all have a problem and it's a problem that has become increasingly common in the last two decades - that of addiction. There are over fifty 'addiction clinics' operating in the United Kingdom but what makes Thorndale so special is a new kind of treatment that they have been applying with remarkable success. The new system being used here is called 'Aversion Therapy', although the idea itself is not new. And of all the clinics treating addicts of various kinds worldwide, the Thorndale clinic has the highest success rate in treating abusers of alcohol and tobacco. Addicts attending a 10-day course of treatment live, eat and sleep in the same building and, unlike other systems, are encouraged to indulge in their addiction instead of treating subjects with drugs that reduce their dependence, this course sets out to induce in its patients a strong feeling of disgust directed towards the object of their addiction. For example, a one-hour treatment session for smokers involves smoking rapidly without stopping well beyond the point where they want no more.
In fact, they are not allowed to stop smoking until they have been physically sick. As you can imagine, this is not a pleasant process. It has to be repeated three times a day for the entire ten day period in order that the subjects develop a strong enough hatred for their earlier addiction. Unfortunately, many people find the course too painful to complete, and those who do give up early are not considered cured, as they will most likely return to their former habit. On the other hand, smokers who keep going to the end of the course are most unlikely to want a cigarette again. The treatment for alcoholism has to be somewhat different, mainly because alcohol abuse involves loss of memory. This problem is overcome in a simple way. A group of 'patients' are encouraged to drink excessively in the setting of a bar. During this stage they are carefully monitored by trained personnel. Their behaviour is also recorded on video cassette and the following day they are shown their 'drunken performance' from the night before. Nearly all subjects feel great embarrassment when faced with these forgotten scenes of uncontrolled drunkenness. Usually, a ten-day course of treatment is all that is required to shift a patient's emotional attitude to drinking.

PAUSE 10 SECONDS

*You will hear the piece again.*

— *** —

REPEAT INSERT

PAUSE 5 SECONDS

*That is the end of Part Two.*
*Now turn to* ***Part Three****.*

PAUSE 5 SECONDS

*You will hear five different people talking about visits they have made to a hospital. For questions* ***19-23,*** *choose from the list* ***A-H*** *the reasons why each attended the hospital on the occasion described. Use the letters only once. There are three extra letters which you do not need to use.*

*You now have 30 seconds in which to look through Part 3.*

PAUSE 30 SECONDS

— *** —

**Speaker 1**
PAUSE 2 SECONDS

Well, the last time I went to the hospital was because I needed a medical certificate. I'd just been offered the job in Kuwait and they needed an official piece of paper from any qualified doctor saying that I had healthy lungs, heart, liver and good eyesight. And well, I couldn't go to my regular doctor because I had already given his name as a reference. And well, I was a bit nervous because if the doctor didn't declare that I was perfectly healthy, I wouldn't get the job.

**Speaker 2**
PAUSE 2 SECONDS

I'd always thought they'd give me something to put me to sleep and when I came round everything would be over and all I would see would be a few stitches. But these days it's all done with a local anaesthetic so you stay awake through the whole thing and you can see everything they're doing. Of course, they tell you that you don't have to look but you can't really look anywhere else, can you? Of course, you don't feel anything, but it's a bit scary.

**Speaker 3**
PAUSE 2 SECONDS

I didn't know what to expect. I mean, when somebody has such a big operation nothing really prepares you for ... what happens afterwards. It's not a bit like it is on telly. When at last I managed to find the right room I almost didn't recognise her. It really was a bit of a shock but the staff all seemed really pleased with her progress and were even talking about ... er ... going home in just a few days. I don't know about these things and I believed what they said. If I'd known what was going to happen, I'd have stayed there all night just to be with her, right up to the end.

**Speaker 4**
PAUSE 2 SECONDS

Well, the call on my answerphone said there was this leaking roof in one of the wards. 'A drip' they called it. Well, it hadn't been raining much so I suppose it didn't seem too bad to them. But when I got up there, the whole roof was in a shocking state. It's a good thing I looked at it when I did because one heavy rainstorm and all that lot was going to collapse, and with all the patients in their beds underneath. I mean, I know the 'National Health' hasn't got much cash these days but they should have had the whole roof fixed. So, in the end, I told them to get someone else to do it. And I'll tell you another thing - I'm going private from now on.

**Speaker 5**
PAUSE 2 SECONDS

The address on the package says room 4J. Anyway, I've been to the hospital loads of times to visit my gran. So I know the layout pretty well. Anyway, I find room 4H in no time - it says 'check-ups' on the door so it can't be the room I want but then there's no room 4I or 4J and room 4K is the maintenance office and they certainly don't want a box of surgical knives. So, after I've been looking for a good ten minutes, I ask someone and they tell me, as though everyone knows, 'it's on the next floor, of course'. How was I to know? Anyway, I take it up there and then there's nobody there to sign the documents to say they've received it. So, I have to come all the way back to ... *FADE*

PAUSE 10 SECONDS

*You will hear the piece again.*

— *** —

TAPE REPEAT
PAUSE 5 SECONDS

*That is the end of Part Three.*
*Now turn to **Part Four**.*

PAUSE 5 SECONDS

*You will hear three people, Wendy, Mrs Turner and Adrian, discussing a film they have just seen at the cinema. For questions **24-30**, choose the best answer **A**, **B** or **C**.*

*There will now be a pause of 1 minute for you to look through Part 4.*

PAUSE 1 MINUTE

— *** —

***W** = Wendy **M** = Mrs Turner **A** = Adrian*

**W:** What a load of old rubbish. You hated it too, didn't you, Mum?
**M:** Well, I have seen better films. I mean it wasn't as good as 'Aliens' or that 'Werewolf' film, you know the one.
**A:** Oh, come on, some bits were brilliant. What about the scene where the accountant is ...
**W:** Well, you always like these mindless special-effects movies; I mean, where was the acting?
**M:** The dinosaurs were good. The last film I saw with dinosaurs - you could see they were made of rubber but these ones looked real. It's amazing.
**A:** It's all done with computer graphics. I will say they looked much better on the big screen than they did on my mate's pirate video - but at least I could smoke at my mate's house.
**W:** Well, if everyone was smoking in the cinema you wouldn't be able to see the picture, would you? Anyway, that's one movie I won't be bothering to take out on video.
**A:** You just didn't like it because you were frightened.
**W:** No, I wasn't! What are you talking about?
**A:** I saw you covering your eyes!
**W:** I wasn't covering my eyes, I was laughing.
**M:** Well, I couldn't look sometimes. I mean, it was only a P.G. film but some of the scenes were ... well ... pretty ...
**W:** You mean hilarious. Well, at least it wasn't too long. Look, it's only quarter past ten.
**M:** Ooh, yes. Ten minutes till last orders. Why don't we go for a quick one at the King's Head?
**W:** Adrian can't. Don't you remember? He's driving.
**M:** Don't worry. I'll have a fruit juice and I can drive us home.
**A:** That's very kind of you, Mrs Turner, but I'm afraid you're not insured to drive my car and if the police stopped us we'd both be in trouble.

PAUSE 10 SECONDS

*You will hear the piece again.*

— *** —

REPEAT INSERT
PAUSE 5 SECONDS

*That is the end of Part Four.*
*There will now be a pause of five minutes for you to copy your answers onto the separate answer sheet. Be sure to follow the numbering of all the questions. I shall remind you when there is one minute left, so that you are sure to finish in time.*

PAUSE 4 MINUTES

You have one more minute left.

PAUSE 1 MINUTE

That is the end of the test. Please stop now. Your supervisor will now collect all the question papers and answer sheets.

# TEST 2

*I am going to give you the instructions for this test.*

*I shall introduce each part of the test and give you time to look at the questions.*

*At the start of each piece you will hear this sound:*

— *** —

*You will hear each piece twice.*

*Remember, while you are listening, write your answers on the question paper. You will have **five** minutes at the end of the test to copy your answers onto the separate answer sheet.*

*There will now be a pause. Please ask any questions now, because you must not speak during the test.*

PAUSE 5 SECONDS

*Now open your question paper and look at **Part One**.*

PAUSE 5 SECONDS

*You will hear people talking in eight different situations. For Questions **1–8**, choose the best answer (**A**, **B** or **C**).*

***Question 1***
*You need to see a doctor urgently. You telephone a surgery and hear this answer-phone message.*

PAUSE 2 SECONDS

— *** —

You have reached the East Street Surgery answering service. Doctors Marsh, Green and Clifford are not available for consultation at this time. If you urgently need to see a doctor, dial Reading 622909 for doctors Smith and Parker or go to 217 George Street. If you wish to leave a message at this surgery, please speak after the tone.
PAUSE 2 SECONDS

— *** —

TAPE REPEAT
PAUSE 2 SECONDS

***Question 2***
*You hear part of a news broadcast on TV about an accident at a chemical factory.*

PAUSE 2 SECONDS

— *** —

It's been three hours since the first casualties were brought out and we have been informed that there are many more victims still inside the compound. Looking through the chain-link fence, I can see the head of one body lying on the ground only a hundred yards or so from where I'm standing. Even the grass at my feet was badly scorched by the blast. All the bodies so far have been taken to a nearby town for identification. So far, no effort has been made to cap the leaking column but we've been informed that a team of German scientists are on their ... *FADE*

PAUSE 2 SECONDS

— *** —

TAPE REPEAT
PAUSE 2 SECONDS

***Question 3***
*You are staying in Britain with a host family. You hear the father speaking to one of his children.*

PAUSE 2 SECONDS

— *** —

***D** = Dad* ***S** = Son*

**D:** When are you going to get your hair cut? It's not long till school starts again. I thought you were going to do it yesterday.
**S:** Er, well, I'll have to go tomorrow or the next day. I couldn't go yesterday; it was closed.
**D:** I thought it was always shut on Wednesday afternoons.
**S:** No, it's shut all day Tuesday.
**D:** Well, look, you'll have to go today or tomorrow because Friday's a public holiday and everything will be closed then.
**S:** Not everything, Dad. The pubs will be open.

PAUSE 2 SECONDS

— *** —

TAPE REPEAT
PAUSE 2 SECONDS

***Question 4***
*You overhear a man at a call box telephoning an emergency breakdown service to ask for a mechanic to fix his car.*

PAUSE 2 SECONDS

— *** —

Hello ... yes ... er, it's my car ... Er, no, I can't get it to start ... No, I've tried that already ... Yes, it's a 1963 Hillman Avenger ... Er, where? ... It's parked right opposite the chemist ... No, not the one on Baker Street, the one on the high street, you know, beside the Green Lion pub.

PAUSE 2 SECONDS

— *** —

TAPE REPEAT
PAUSE 2 SECONDS

***Question 5***
*Listen to a man outside a supermarket talking to a housewife.*

PAUSE 2 SECONDS

— *** —

Excuse me, madam. I wonder if you could spare me a few minutes. I see you've bought an automatic washing powder for use in a standard front-loading washing machine. You see, I work for the British Energy Conservation Council and we're currently carrying out a survey to determine how much energy is required for an average family's washing needs. I must assure you that if you do agree to participate in our questionnaire right now, it will not be necessary for one of our representatives to visit your home. Now, if I could just have your name and address and possibly your telephone number ... FADE

PAUSE 2 SECONDS

— *** —

TAPE REPEAT
PAUSE 2 SECONDS

***Question 6***
*You are with a group of friends. One of them is telling you about something that happened to her at work.*

PAUSE 2 SECONDS

— *** —

Well, I was working at the desk that day and well, it had been quite a busy morning and it must have been about 11 o'clock when two officers brought a suspect into the station. They'd received a 999 call from a woman living in Maple Road and as soon as I saw him, I just burst out laughing because I suppose it's not often that the head of Much Hadham CID gets pulled in on his day off.

PAUSE 2 SECONDS

— *** —

TAPE REPEAT
PAUSE 2 SECONDS

***Question 7***
*Listen to this man being interviewed on the radio.*

PAUSE 2 SECONDS

— *** —

***L** = Lucy* ***S** = Sebastian*

**L:** And that was a very impressive performance but you've been involved in a bit of controversy recently.
**S:** You mean in 'The Silent Revolutionary'?
**L:** Well, ... yes, one critic described it as the most utterly unpleasant ninety minutes he'd ever endured.
**S:** Well, it always was the intention of Tim Broke, the director, to be shocking but perhaps he did misjudge the audience's reaction to some of the things that we do on stage.
**L:** But I gather you've been playing to nearly empty houses recently.
**S:** Well, hum ... *FADE*

PAUSE 2 SECONDS

— *** —

TAPE REPEAT
PAUSE 2 SECONDS

***Question 8***
You are on a bus tour of a British historical city. You are currently looking at Saint Christopher's Memorial Hospital.

PAUSE 2 SECONDS

— *** —

The building just coming up on our right is the Saint Christopher memorial hospital. Founded in the late 1930s, it is considered to be one of the finest examples of this style of architecture. It is particularly noted for the unusual layout of its ornamental gardens, which are at their best in the late spring. The building has been hailed as a masterpiece, although I personally have reservations because it lacks the colour and flamboyance of many of the ... FADE

PAUSE 2 SECONDS

— *** —

TAPE REPEAT
PAUSE 2 SECONDS

*That is the end of Part One.*
*Now turn to **Part Two**.*

PAUSE 5 SECONDS

*You are going to hear somebody giving their opinion about the media and its influence on society. For questions **9-18**, complete the sentences with a word or short phrase.*

*You now have 45 seconds in which to look at Part 2.*

PAUSE 45 SECONDS

— *** —

There is no escaping the fact that the media has become one of the most powerful influences in our lives. TV, radio and newspapers are the three main forms of media that we have daily contact with. Because of their importance it is inevitable that controversy will often go hand in hand with such a powerful force.

The media is not always used wisely or responsibly and is often a source of gossip, scandal or propaganda. Politicians use it in their political campaigns in order to gain support. Entertainers and celebrities use it to promote themselves and keep themselves in the public eye. This is of course to their advantage but on the other hand they are also open to the disadvantages of publicity. Private lives are brought out into the open and the word private no longer suits the situation. Celebrities find themselves being followed and photographed at all times of day or night and in the most personal situations. A survey has been carried out asking people what they thought of this invasion of privacy and a massive 85% thought that celebrities were asking for it, 11% believed they were still entitled to their privacy and 4% had no opinion either way. The survey also asked which form of media people felt they were most influenced by. Over two thirds of the people asked said TV, rather than radio or newspapers.

This then leads us to the question of how reliable the information that we get from TV is. The belief that if we can see through images what is happening we cannot be tricked or lied to, is a fallacy. Carefully chosen or edited images can deceive us more than words. It is in fact the images that are not shown which often speak the truth. Some channels have even been accused of showing scenes that were not actually from the place being reported about. This kind of false information turns fact into fiction but how is the viewer meant to distinguish between the two? That is the problem. Radio and newspapers, on the other hand rely on words to get their story across and if they intentionally lie they run the risk of being taken to court later. This of course happens regularly, particularly when a celebrity is involved. One rock singer was recently awarded one million pounds when a tabloid paper said he was a homosexual. Sometimes the papers are lucky and get away with making a public apology and withdrawing what they have previously said about somebody. A distinction has to be made between newspapers though as they do tend to fall into two groups; the tabloids and the so called "quality newspapers". The question is though, can we really trust anybody to tell us the facts objectively?

PAUSE 10 SECONDS

*You will hear the piece again.*

— *** —

REPEAT INSERT

PAUSE 5 SECONDS

*That is the end of Part Two.*
*Now turn to **Part Three**.*
PAUSE 5 SECONDS

*You will hear five different women talking about the same wedding. For questions **19-23**, choose from the list **A-H** who the speaker is speaking to. Use the letters only once. There are three extra letters which you do not need to use.*

*You now have 30 seconds in which to look through Part 3.*

PAUSE 30 SECONDS

— *** —

**Speaker 1**
PAUSE 2 SECONDS

Well, it really was a pity you couldn't be there. Brian and Julia looked so wonderful and everything went off perfectly. The vicar gave a beautiful address and the reception was gorgeous. Everyone commented on the bridesmaids' dresses. They wore pale yellow just like you wanted, oh, and I almost forgot, Brian mentioned you in his speech. He said Julia's got everything a wife could offer, but he still likes your cooking best. I think he meant it, too. Of course, Dad was there with ... er ... but I don't suppose you want to hear about that.

**Speaker 2**
PAUSE 2 SECONDS

Brian's not going to have an easy time of it. After all, Julia's not going to coddle him like that mother of his does. And it's a good thing too if you ask me. It's about time he learnt to be useful around the house. Seventy years of feminism doesn't seem to have done much for our family either. Still, when we get married a few little things are going to change. There'll be no more nights out with the lads - not when I'm in charge - and I'll tell you another thing, if I were Julia, I'd be keeping a good eye on one of those bridesmaids, too.

**Speaker 3**
PAUSE 2 SECONDS

So you must have known Brian for quite some time now. Has he always been this handsome? ... No, don't tell me, I can imagine. Well, anyway, I met him a couple of years ago when they moved our unit up to head office and he was already working there as entertainment officer. You know, all the big firms have them these days. He organises surprise parties and hires entertainers and kissagrams and then comes round the office collecting money for them afterwards, but I suppose you know all this already.

**Speaker 4**
PAUSE 2 SECONDS

Did you take all these pictures yourself? You are clever. And look there's one of me. I don't remember you taking that one. Oh, and here's one of everybody outside the church. Your Auntie Julia would probably like a copy of that one and so would your granny; mind you, it's a pity it's got your granddad in with that Marjorie. Oh, could you be a darling and get some copies done? We could send them for Christmas. They always send you something nice.

**Speaker 5**
PAUSE 2 SECONDS

It was really one of the best weddings I've ever been to. The service was short; the bride arrived on time; the groom was sober; the food was excellent; the speakers were funny - not like my wedding at all. They really must have put so much thought into it, and so much preparation. Which must show that they're serious about each other because so many young people aren't these days. The only sad thing is that they live so far away. I mean if you hadn't given me the Friday off, I simply wouldn't have been able to get there on time.

PAUSE 10 SECONDS

*You will hear the piece again.*

— *** —

TAPE REPEAT
PAUSE 5 SECONDS
*That is the end of Part Three.*
*Now turn to **Part Four**.*

PAUSE 5 SECONDS

*You will hear three friends talking about their relationships. For questions **24-30**, decide which of the choices **A**, **B** or **C** is the best answer.*

*There will now be a pause of 1 minute for you to look through Part 4.*

PAUSE 1 MINUTE

— *** —

*A = Anne* *M = Mark* *D = Dave*

**A:** I'm fed up with staying in nearly every night. Since John and I broke up life has been really boring. How about you two, how's your love life these days? Mark you're grinning, you must be happy.
**M:** Well actually yes I've just met someone really nice. She started working in the office a fortnight ago and we liked each other straight away.
**D:** Well, well. That's why you're never home these days when I phone you. Are you actually going out with her then?
**M:** Yes I am.
**A:** So how many times have you been out?
**M:** Erm, quite a few.
**D:** Why are you so embarrassed?
**M:** Well actually, we've been out nearly every evening since that first day.
**D/A:** Every evening!
**M:** Anyway, enough of my personal life. What about you Dave? How's Sue?
**D:** Oh she's fine. We're trying to decide where to go on holiday this summer.
**A:** Maybe on honeymoon?
**D:** No way! I'm far too young to think about wedding bells yet.
**M:** But you've been together for years.
**D:** I know. I'm not saying we won't get married but not yet.
**A:** Well I'm going on a girls' night out this Saturday. We thought we'd go to that new disco in town.
**M:** I've been there, it's okay but very crowded and smoky and I had to leave early because the smoke was making my asthma bad. I could hardly breathe and felt terrible the next day.
**D:** You should really try alternative medicine for that Mark. Homeopathy really helped my cousin with his asthma.
**A:** Talking of cousins Mark, is your handsome cousin still young, free and single?
**M:** Yes he is actually, but I thought you were still suffering from a broken heart.
**A:** Well, the best cure for a broken heart is a new romance!
**M:** I'll see if I can arrange for him to be at the Christmas party and then you can casually chat him up.
**A:** Oh, thanks, Mark.

PAUSE 10 SECONDS

*You will hear the piece again.*

— *** —

REPEAT INSERT
PAUSE 5 SECONDS

*That is the end of Part Four.*
*There will now be a pause of five minutes for you to copy your answers onto the separate answer sheet. Be sure to follow the numbering of all the questions. I shall remind you when there is one minute left, so that you are sure to finish in time.*

PAUSE 4 MINUTES

You have one more minute left.

PAUSE 1 MINUTE

That is the end of the test. Please stop now. Your supervisor will now collect all the question papers and answer sheets.

# TEST 3

*I am going to give you the instructions for this test.*

*I shall introduce each part of the test and give you time to look at the questions.*

*At the start of each piece you will hear this sound:*

— *** —

*You will hear each piece twice.*

*Remember, while you are listening, write your answers on the question paper. You will have **five** minutes at the end of the test to copy your answers onto the separate answer sheet.*

*There will now be a pause. Please ask any questions now, because you must not speak during the test.*

PAUSE 5 SECONDS

*Now open your question paper and look at **Part One**.*

PAUSE 5 SECONDS

*You will hear people talking in eight different situations. For Questions **1–8**, choose the best answer (**A**, **B** or **C**).*

***Question 1***
*You are in a supermarket when you hear this announcement about a lost child.*

PAUSE 2 SECONDS

— *** —

Ladies and gentlemen. If I could just have your attention, please. We have with us a small boy by the name of Roland. He has red hair and is wearing a green and purple shell-suit. He is carrying a blue fluffy rabbit and says that he is four. When he last saw his mummy, he says, she was choosing some pears. If you are his mummy, please come to the customer service desk at the front of the store where he will be waiting for you.

PAUSE 2 SECONDS

— *** —

TAPE REPEAT
PAUSE 2 SECONDS

***Question 2***
*You are in an electrical shop when you overhear this woman speaking to the shop assistant.*

PAUSE 2 SECONDS

— *** —

***W** = Woman* ***M** = Man*

**W:** Er, is these curling tongs I bought here last Saturday?
**M:** What's the problem, madam? Is the item not functioning?
**W:** No, it works perfectly. That's not the problem at all.
**M:** Well, then let me guess. It's damaged?
**W:** No, it's your price-beater guarantee. You clearly said that if I found them at a cheaper price in any other shop, you would refund the difference and, well, imagine my surprise when I went into Lunthams and saw them there for only nine ninety-nine. I mean I know they were on special offer but that's not the point.

PAUSE 2 SECONDS

— *** —

TAPE REPEAT
PAUSE 2 SECONDS

***Question 3***
*You overhear a woman talking on the telephone.*

PAUSE 2 SECONDS

— *** —

... Yes, Paris ... Yes, Paris, France ... You still have some tickets? ... Yes, next Thursday ... 'No-smoking' please, and an aisle seat if possible. Which terminal is that leaving from? ... I see. And the flight number ... BA 893. And take-off time?

PAUSE 2 SECONDS

— *** —

TAPE REPEAT
PAUSE 2 SECONDS

***Question 4***
*Listen to a policeman talking to a householder.*

PAUSE 2 SECONDS

— *** —

***P*** *= Policeman* ***M*** *= Man*

**P:** Good morning, sir. Sorry to disturb you. This is just part of a routine inquiry. You are the owner of the house.
**M:** Er, yes.
**P:** Then I assume that you are familiar with a Mr Winston of number 43 just across the street there.
**M:** Er, yes.
**P:** Well, if you or any other member of your household happen to know of his whereabouts, we would like to speak to him on a rather urgent matter.

PAUSE 2 SECONDS

— *** —

TAPE REPEAT
PAUSE 2 SECONDS

***Question 5***
*You are listening to the host of a radio phone-in programme speaking.*

PAUSE 2 SECONDS

— *** —

Well, the subject of our phone-in this morning is a rather thorny issue that has been in the news a lot recently. We have heard many opinions from government ministers, church leaders and social workers on this delicate matter but little has been said by the people themselves. So, today, we want to hear from any single parents out there who are listening and, in fact, we have one on the line right now. Hello, Mary ...

PAUSE 2 SECONDS

— *** —

TAPE REPEAT
PAUSE 2 SECONDS

***Question 6***
*You have joined a four-day sailing course in Britain. Listen to your instructor giving some important information.*

PAUSE 2 SECONDS

— *** —

...and now I want to move on to the subject of water. When you're at sea, you're surrounded by salt water and this, of course, you cannot drink. Nor can you wash with it. Tap water these days is also not suitable for drinking, but you can wash with it. So we recommend that you carry at least ten gallons of bottled water, which you can buy from any nautical supply station. When you are buying it, however, you must check the label on the bottle to make sure you're buying the right sort of water.

PAUSE 2 SECONDS

— *** —

TAPE REPEAT
PAUSE 2 SECONDS

***Question 7***
*You overhear two people talking at a bus stop.*

PAUSE 2 SECONDS

— *** —

***W1*** *= Woman 1* ***W2*** *= Woman 2*

**W1:** So, when you get to the top of the hill, the bus will stop at the lights and you get out there in front of the war memorial. You can't miss it.
**W2:** Oh, thank you so much. I don't know what I'd have done without you.
**W1:** Oh, look, here's your bus coming now. Now, don't forget what I said.
**W2:** Thanks again. And I hope you don't have to wait too long for yours. Bye.

PAUSE 2 SECONDS

— *** —

TAPE REPEAT
PAUSE 2 SECONDS

***Question 8***
*You overhear a man chatting on the telephone about a form he has to fill in.*

PAUSE 2 SECONDS

— *** —

... Yes, just like I said ... They want to know everything about you. I mean it's an intrusion upon your privacy. Still, they say that the information is treated as confidential. But why would they want to know mother's maiden name? And Sophie's grown up now. She's left home. It's not really any of my business whether she has a boyfriend or whether she has any insurance of her own. Anyway, fortunately, they were both willing for me to include those details.

PAUSE 2 SECONDS

— *** —

TAPE REPEAT
PAUSE 2 SECONDS

*That is the end of Part One.*
*Now turn to* ***Part Two****.*

PAUSE 5 SECONDS

*You will hear part of a radio talk for young people about animals communicating with each other. For questions* ***9-18****, complete the sentences with a word or short phrase.*

*You now have 45 seconds in which to look at Part 2.*

PAUSE 45 SECONDS

— *** —

**Presenter:** If I asked you what the difference is between animals and human beings, you might think for a bit and then suggest something about the fact that humans can speak to each other using a language - or in some cases more than one language - and in a way you would be right. But that is not the whole story by any means. Many animals can communicate in surprisingly complicated ways, but they never quite achieve the range and depth of human languages. At the simplest level, several kinds of insect, including bees, have been observed performing a special dance to tell each other where they can find nectar and pollen, which is their food. This, of course, does not mean that they are using a 'language' but they are, all the same, communicating something. Many people think that certain birds like parrots can speak, but this is in fact not true. Such animals are only capable of copying the sounds of human speech but have no understanding of these sounds and generally use them at the wrong time. There is also no apparent logic in the way they select what to copy either. On the other hand, monkeys, apes and other primates are capable of communicating a small number of basic ideas using a range of simple sounds that are recognised by other members of their social group. Unfortunately though, none of the groups of monkeys observed so far have developed any form of grammar and so we cannot call this a language. However, some apes, chimpanzees in particular, can be trained to understand and respond to certain spoken commands by humans, but so far none have attempted to copy our speech. Now there is one kind of animal that does just this, although not many people can understand what they are saying. Dolphins have different shaped mouths to humans and as a result they are unable to make all the sounds that we can make. They can manage the vowel sounds 'a', 'e', 'i', 'o', 'u', ... and so on, but lack the necessary voice equipment to reproduce our consonants. Thus, a simple phrase like 'Hello, how are you?' becomes 'e - o - ah - u'. But what makes these noises more amazing is that dolphins do show an awareness of when to use such phrases and in this sense, are actually trying to communicate with humans.

But by far, the most remarkable form of animal communication are the 'songs' of whales. These are fast clicking and squeaking noises that whales make underwater and the sounds themselves actually contain more information than human speech. Scientists have noticed that some whales repeat certain long phrases of sounds, and this is in fact why they are called songs. Of particular interest is a species called the 'bottle-nosed' whale whose songs have many of the characteristics of human speech. But at the end of the day, we are the only species that have developed proper grammatical languages and most experts now agree that this is because of the large communities that we live in - where a child growing up can hear hundreds of different examples of his or her language being spoken every day. If, for any reason, a young child does not get enough contact with other people between the ages of one and four, he or she may never fully develop the power of speech. One can imagine that if whales or dolphins did start living in large communities then well ... FADE

PAUSE 10 SECONDS

*You will hear the piece again.*

— *** —

REPEAT INSERT

PAUSE 5 SECONDS

*That is the end of Part Two.*
*Now turn to* ***Part Three****.*

PAUSE 5 SECONDS

*You are going to hear five different people talking about their relationship with somebody. For questions* ***19-23,*** *match the speakers 1-5, with the letters* ***A-H****. Use the letters only once. There are three extra letters which you do not need to use.*

*You now have 30 seconds in which to look through Part 3.*

PAUSE 30 SECONDS

— *** —

**Speaker 1**
PAUSE 2 SECONDS

Generally I like living at home with my family. There are five of us. I've got a brother and a sister and we fight a lot but I love them really. My parents give us everything we need, in fact they buy us lots of things, especially clothes. My social life suffers a bit though as I have to babysit for my little brother and sister quite often and I have many jobs to do around the house apart from my work for university. It's difficult to get any spare time to go out and have fun. Sometimes I resent the fact that I have so many responsibilities for someone of my age.

**Speaker 2**
PAUSE 2 SECONDS

He takes up all of our time as there's so much that he needs; feeding, changing, bathing and sometimes just a cuddle or some attention. He really has changed our lives completely. I don't resent losing my free time though as he's worth it. When he smiles at me and looks contented I feel wonderful. We're both very proud of him of course. He's not very entertaining yet as he can't do much. He just sort of lies there and makes funny noises. The house is messier than it used to be too. His things are everywhere but on the other hand we try to keep everything really clean even if it is untidy.

**Speaker 3**
PAUSE 2 SECONDS

They were always fighting and I think we must have been known as the noisiest house in the street. I was never one for arguing so I used to try and keep out of the way as much as I could. She often used to cry after a fight and he'd go out, probably to the pub. Now it's much better. They are almost friends again. He comes to visit sometimes, especially on special occasions like a birthday or for Christmas. I think they stayed together for our sake but really it was the worst thing they could have done as we witnessed all the fights and that was very upsetting.

**Speaker 4**
PAUSE 2 SECONDS

I guess we have quite a large family for such a small house. Everyone helps out though and we all have our own chores to do. Both mum and dad work during the day and we are all at school so it's good to have someone at home to do the cooking and keep the house in order. They are both wonderful company anyway and sometimes when I have a problem and mum and dad aren't home or are very busy, they are there for me to talk to. They aren't as strict as my parents either and often stick up for me if my father doesn't want me to do something. I like having three generations living under one roof. It's taught us all to be more tolerant and not to be selfish.

**Speaker 5**
PAUSE 2 SECONDS

We do tend to get under each other's feet a lot and I wish I could have my own bedroom, but I think the advantages outweigh the disadvantages. For a start, there's always someone to talk to and someone to help me if I have a problem. There are enough of us to make a basketball team so we play as a family against our friends. Mum says that we have exhausted her but really she's very proud of us all. Dad always says he has to work overtime to feed and clothe us but really he just loves his job and is a workaholic. I think two children would be enough for me though.

PAUSE 10 SECONDS

*You will hear the piece again.*

— *** —

TAPE REPEAT
PAUSE 5 SECONDS

*That is the end of Part Three.*
*Now turn to* ***Part Four****.*

PAUSE 5 SECONDS

*Listen to these two friends discussing the British national lottery. For questions* ***24-30****, choose the best answer* ***A****,* ***B*** *or* ***C****.*

*There will now be a pause of 1 minute for you to look through Part 4.*

PAUSE 1 MINUTE

— *** —

***B*** *= Barry* ***T*** *= Tina*

**B:** Hey, Tina, what's up with you? You look like you've been to a funeral.
**T:** Oh, nothing really. I guess I've just had a bad week and then only one of my numbers came up last night.
**B:** You still doing that stupid old lottery? It's enough to make anyone depressed. I haven't got a good word to say about it myself. All the fuss they make on that silly programme on Saturday night.
**T:** But everyone's doing it. The paper says it's the biggest lottery in the world. Over twenty million people entered last week, which is a lot if you consider that it's only open to people over eighteen.
**B:** Well, that's a good thing, otherwise all the kids would be spending all their pocket money on it. How much are you spending on it these days?
**T:** Well, this week, I spent ten pounds.
**B:**Ten pounds! No wonder you're fed up, Tina.
**T:** I got five entries and the other five pounds went on scratch cards.
**B:** And you've been doing this every week since it started?
**T:** No, this week was special. I just thought I was going to be lucky but I've had at least 1 entry a week. It seems silly not to.
**B:** But you've lost all that money. And it's all gone to Camelot.
**T:** They don't keep the money, they give it all to charity and the 'arts'.
**B:** They don't give it all away. They keep a lot of the money and then they get rich while you get poor.
**T:** But I might win. Then we'd be millionaires.

**B:** When are you going to realise, you're not going to win? Not with twenty million other people playing. Look, how many people do you know who have won anything?
**T:** Well, er ... oh, yes. The man at the paper shop said that there's another customer who has won a hundred pounds, and I believe him.
**B:** Well, that's useless. You've probably spent more than a hundred pounds already.
**T:** I suppose you've never even played once.
**B:** No. Oh well, just the once. The lads and I at work did have a go when it started.
**T:** You mean you were a syndicate.
**B:** Oh yes, that's the new word for it now. Anyway, after that first week, I just decided I wasn't going to waste any more of my precious money on it. Besides, I don't think it's right. Somebody getting all that money - twenty million or more - for doing nothing. My dad always says: 'God help those who help themselves'.
**T:** But that's not going to help me win next week's jackpot.
**B:** Don't do it, Tina.
**T:** But I want the money.
**B:** And so do we all, but, if I needed extra cash, I'd go and do the overtime; earn the money in an honest way. You could get a better job instead of going down to the lottery shop.
**T:** Well, I was thinking of giving it a miss that week, anyway. Maybe that's what I'll do. An extra ten pounds would come in handy.
**B:** Yeah. Er, treat yourself to something nice. You need a bit of cheering up.
**T:** I know, we could go on a day-trip to Boulogne, stock up on duty-frees on the way back. I fancy something a bit cultural, especially with Christmas just around the corner.

PAUSE 10 SECONDS

*You will hear the piece again.*

— *** —

REPEAT INSERT
PAUSE 5 SECONDS

*That is the end of Part Four.*
*There will now be a pause of five minutes for you to copy your answers onto the separate answer sheet. Be sure to follow the numbering of all the questions. I shall remind you when there is one minute left, so that you are sure to finish in time.*

PAUSE 4 MINUTES

You have one more minute left.

PAUSE 1 MINUTE

That is the end of the test. Please stop now. Your supervisor will now collect all the question papers and answer sheets.

# TEST 4

*I am going to give you the instructions for this test.*

*I shall introduce each part of the test and give you time to look at the questions.*

*At the start of each piece you will hear this sound:*

— *** —

*You will hear each piece twice.*
*Remember, while you are listening, write your answers on the question paper. You will have **five** minutes at the end of the test to copy your answers onto the separate answer sheet.*

*There will now be a pause. Please ask any questions now, because you must not speak during the test.*

PAUSE 5 SECONDS

*Now open your question paper and look at **Part One**.*

PAUSE 5 SECONDS

*You will hear people talking in eight different situations. For Questions **1–8**, choose the best answer (**A**, **B** or **C**).*

***Question 1***
*You are visiting a friend when you hear him answer the telephone.*

PAUSE 2 SECONDS

— *** —

Hello, 776651 ... Yes, speaking.. Yes, that's right ... It's a Wattari 76C Gamemaster Deluxe and it's never been used ... erm, it was a present from an aunt in the States who doesn't realise how old I am ... Well, seeing as it's totally new, I had intended to stick with the original price but let's say 75 pounds.

PAUSE 2 SECONDS

— *** —

TAPE REPEAT
PAUSE 2 SECONDS

***Question 2***
You are sitting in an aeroplane when you hear this announcement.

PAUSE 2 SECONDS

— *** —

Ladies and gentlemen, we will shortly be crossing the Pyrenees mountain range where we have been warned to expect some quite severe turbulence. The seat-belt sign above your head is now on. Please return to your seats and remain there until the sign goes off. We will be altering our course to avoid the worst of the turbulence. However, we are fortunate in having a tail wind so we should still be arriving in Malaga five minutes ahead of schedule.

PAUSE 2 SECONDS

— *** —

TAPE REPEAT
PAUSE 2 SECONDS

***Question 3***
*You have visited an English doctor because of a skin problem.*

PAUSE 2 SECONDS

— *** —

Well, there's nothing really to worry about. I'm writing a prescription for a betadine ointment that you can get at any chemist. You can read English? ... Oh, good. Anyway, the only other thing is ... if you do decide to go out at all - I mean, out of the house - in the open air, especially in the daytime, just ... er ... take good care, and I'm sure you'll be back to normal in a week or so.

PAUSE 2 SECONDS

— *** —

TAPE REPEAT
PAUSE 2 SECONDS

***Question 4***
*While waiting to check in your luggage at an airport, you hear this conversation.*
PAUSE 2 SECONDS

— *** —

***W*** *= Woman* ***M*** *= Man*

**W:** I'm terribly sorry, sir, these bags weigh 32 kilograms. That's more than twice the normal baggage allowance for this flight.
**M:** Ah, but I packed them very carefully. I put all the shampoo and things into smaller bottles, but ... er ... maybe it's the golf clubs ... they weigh quite a bit. Could I possibly take them as hand luggage?
**W:** I'm sorry, sir, but I don't think they'll fit in the overhead lockers.
**M:** Well, I guess I'll just have to pay excess baggage then. How much is it please? ... FADE

PAUSE 2 SECONDS

— *** —

TAPE REPEAT

PAUSE 2 SECONDS

***Question 5***
*You are watching the weather forecast for Britain on TV.*

PAUSE 2 SECONDS

— *** —

... and moving on from the satellite picture we can see that tomorrow there will be a fair bit of rain in the whole of the south of England. Pretty much the same story in the west Midlands but the east Midlands should be getting some much brighter weather by mid-afternoon and indeed this may spread westwards by early evening. But I'm afraid there will be no improvement in north-eastern England and Scotland for a day or so.

PAUSE 2 SECONDS

— *** —

TAPE REPEAT
PAUSE 2 SECONDS

***Question 6***
*Listen to this answer phone message for a business.*

PAUSE 2 SECONDS

— *** —

This is T.J. Smith and Sons. Our offices are currently closed but if you wish to place an order, please state clearly the item, the quantity and the catalogue number and we will deliver it within the next thirty-six hours. We regret that we have been forced to delete all office cleaning supplies from our catalogue as we are no longer able to supply them at the price advertised. If you do wish to make an order, please leave your message after the tone.

PAUSE 2 SECONDS

— *** —

TAPE REPEAT
PAUSE 2 SECONDS

***Question 7***
*You overhear two people talking in an office.*

PAUSE 2 SECONDS

— *** —

***M*** *= Man* ***W*** *= Woman*

**M:** And, have you heard about Jack?
**W:** Yes, he's had it this time.
**M:** It does seem a bit much you know, getting the sack, just for...
**W:** He had a whole roll of fax paper in his car.
**M:** Well, I think Colin's being too hard on him. Couldn't you have a word? I mean, he listens to you.
**W:** He doesn't listen to anyone - least of all me. But I'll try speaking to him about it.
**M:** You're just siding with the boss, aren't you? I mean, come on, you're as guilty as the rest of us. I saw you with that ... FADE
PAUSE 2 SECONDS

— *** —

TAPE REPEAT
PAUSE 2 SECONDS
***Question 8***
*You hear a parent asking a child to go to the newsagent's and buy a newspaper.*

PAUSE 2 SECONDS

— *** —

Ah, Jason, are you going down the road to the newsagent's? Oh, good. Then you can get a copy of today's 'Andover Gazette'. Oh, and if they haven't got one, get us a copy of 'Today', but I'm sure they will because it's only half past five. So, you'll be needing forty-three p. and don't forget to look both ways when you cross the road.

PAUSE 2 SECONDS

— *** —

TAPE REPEAT
PAUSE 2 SECONDS

*That is the end of Part One.*
*Now turn to* ***Part Two****.*

PAUSE 5 SECONDS

*You will hear part of an international radio broadcast on the subject of Guy Fawkes Night, an annual public celebration in Great Britain. For questions* ***9-18****, complete the sentences with a word or short phrase.*

*You now have 45 seconds in which to look at Part 2.*

PAUSE 45 SECONDS

— *** —

**Presenter:** Every year in Britain, at the beginning of November, schools have a one week holiday and on the fifth of November, many people celebrate Guy Fawkes Night. The celebration centres around the burning of a life-sized model of a man, with a black hat and beard, called 'Guy'. The model has been specially made for this purpose. It's a wonderful time for kids of all ages but not so much fun for cats and dogs, which are usually terrified by sounds of exploding fireworks and skyrockets. To understand the reasons for this tradition, we have to go back almost 400 years to a time when there were two important religious groups in Britain - the Catholics and the Protestants. For many years, there had been fighting between them. In 1605, the king, James I, and his government, were Protestants and they made life rather difficult for the country's Catholics, of which there were many. According to the popular story, a group of prominent Catholics met secretly and decided that the king and his government must die. They came up with the idea of destroying the Houses of Parliament with explosives. The leader of this gang of conspirators was a man called Robert Catesby. Of course, being well-known Catholics, the group were not trusted by the government and so they needed the help of a professional soldier, who the government officers would not recognise. The man they eventually found for the job, was Guy Fawkes. After an unsuccessful attempt to dig a tunnel, the conspirators bought a house beside the parliament building, which already had a tunnel going into the Houses of Parliament from its cellar. For many weeks, Catesby and his companions moved huge barrels of highly explosive gunpowder along the tunnel and placed them in exactly the right places under the government building. When the king and his parliament had their first meeting of the year in November, the conspirators planned to explode the gunpowder and so kill everybody in the building. Guy Fawkes had the important job of watching the street outside the conspirators' house and warning the others of any approaching danger. Well, the king found out about the plot and he sent soldiers to arrest them. However, they found only Guy Fawkes on duty outside the house. The other conspirators had escaped. Eventually, all the plotters were caught and executed but Guy Fawkes has remained the most famous, probably on account of his being caught first. There was also another result of the discovery of the plot. Afterwards, all Catholics in England were blamed for the attempted attack, and this gave the Protestant government the excuse it wanted to persecute the Catholics even more. Although these events are still celebrated throughout Britain today, Catholics and Protestants have learned to live together in peace and so the celebration itself is mostly harmless fun. Besides, the story is no longer believed by most serious historians.

PAUSE 10 SECONDS

*You will hear the piece again.*

— *** —

REPEAT INSERT

PAUSE 5 SECONDS

*That is the end of Part Two.*
*Now turn to* ***Part Three****.*

PAUSE 5 SECONDS

*You will hear five different people describing five different recipes for desserts. For questions **19-23**, choose from the list **A-H** which speaker's recipe fits the description given. Use the letters only once. There are three extra letters which you do not need to use.*

*You now have 30 seconds in which to look through Part 3.*

PAUSE 30 SECONDS

— *** —

**Speaker 1**
PAUSE 2 SECONDS

This is one of my favourite desserts and it isn't too difficult if you've got a bit of time on your hands. The traditional recipe uses brown sugar but I have always preferred honey. You drip the honey over a thick layer of yoghurt to form a thin covering. This can be quite tricky and you need a steady hand. Then press the fruit into the honey and scatter chopped nuts over the top. Finally, to add that extra special something, put a few pinches of ground cinnamon over it shortly before serving.

**Speaker 2**
PAUSE 2 SECONDS

Once you've assembled all your chopped fruit pieces in a bowl, you need to make the blancmange mixture to pour over them. This is made by beating together cream, apple juice, honey and two tablespoons of rum, and then heating the mixture before dissolving the gelatin. I must just mention that gelatin is made from the hooves of cows so, unfortunately, some people won't be too keen on this. Anyway, once the mixture has cooled sufficiently, it can be poured over the fruit and left to set in the refrigerator.

**Speaker 3**
PAUSE 2 SECONDS

Take the sponge cake base out of the oven and then turn it out to cool on a wire rack. Now, you can turn your attention to the topping. The strawberries need to be fresh so you will only really be able to make this recipe from May to early July; after that, raspberries can be used instead, up to late August. The fruit should be halved and have the tough cores removed. You may need a good sharp knife for this. After that, arrange the halves in a symmetrical pattern around the top of the sponge and finally spread fresh yoghurt over this and garnish with grated chocolate.

**Speaker 4**
PAUSE 2 SECONDS

Now, this one is always popular with youngsters. There is really no point nowadays in making your own vanilla ice-cream since the quality in the shops is so good. But home-made chocolate sauce is another matter and quite inexpensive to make. You just heat some cooking chocolate in a pan with a little water and brown sugar and bring to the boil for a few minutes. When it has cooled, you'll have a thick, dark, sticky sauce that the kids will love ... and indeed it's such a simple method that they could even make it themselves.

**Speaker 5**
PAUSE 2 SECONDS

Once again you leave the sponge cake to cool after baking and turn your attention to the marzipan. You will need 250 grams of ground almonds. Now, these are about one pound fifty for a fifty gram packet, so you'll not want to waste any. Mix the ground almonds with 250 grams of castor sugar and, add a whole egg that's been thoroughly beaten and laced with dark rum and almond flavouring, knead the mixture into a thick paste and then roll flat on a work-surface sprinkled with icing sugar. Brush the sponge cake with a mixture of rum and almond flavouring before placing the marzipan around it.

PAUSE 10 SECONDS

*You will hear the piece again.*

— *** —

TAPE REPEAT

PAUSE 5 SECONDS

*That is the end of Part Three.*
*Now turn to **Part Four**.*

PAUSE 5 SECONDS

*You will hear a woman and a man speaking together on a train. For questions **24-30**, choose the best answer **A**, **B** or **C**.*

*There will now be a pause of 1 minute for you to look through Part 4.*

PAUSE 1 MINUTE

— *** —

***W*** *= Woman* ***M*** *= Man*

**W:** It's me again ... no ... no, look, this is no good. I'm talking to you on my mobile and the train keeps going into tunnels and we get cut off. Yes, I know this is important ... Look, I'll phone you again when I get off to change trains at Haywards Heath ... Okay then ...
**M:** Er, ... excuse me, did I just hear you say 'Haywards Heath'?
**W:** Well, er ... yes ... that's where...
**M:** But isn't this the train for Salisbury - I mean, that's what it said on the board?
**W:** Oh, I think you should have been in the front four coaches. You see, the train divided at Redhill and this is one of the rear four coaches, which goes on to Brighton.
**M:** Oh, oh ... but that's impossible, it didn't say anything on the announcement board. How ... how did you know?
**W:** They made an announcement, didn't you hear it?
**M:** Er ... no. I can't believe this is happening.
**W:** Well, if you don't believe me, go and ask the guard.
**M:** Oh ... hang on ... If this is the Brighton train, I haven't got the right ticket. I could end up having to pay extra and I've only got plastic, which he won't accept.
**W:** Well, what you could do is get off at the next station and get the next train going back to Redhill. Let's see, the last one was Three Bridges, so we should be arriving in Balcombe in just a minute.
**M:** And I can just get on another train without showing my ticket?
**W:** Ah, now that's a point. That'll be a bit difficult at a small station like Balcombe. No, what you need to do is get off at Haywards Heath and cross to platform 3 where the northbound trains depart from.
**M:** Is that what you're doing?
**W:** Not exactly, I'll be taking the connecting service to Lewes but I can show you where to go.
**M:** Er ... look ... thanks very much. I really appreciate this. Er ... you don't happen to know if there actually is a northbound train to Redhill at this time of night?
**W:** Mmm ... I think they run trains all night because of Gatwick airport. But if you like, I could phone through to central enquiries and make sure.
**M:** If it wouldn't be too much trouble. Look, um, I really appreciate this.
**W:** No, don't mention it. Now, let's see if I can get this thing to work this time.

PAUSE 10 SECONDS

*You will hear the piece again.*

— *** —

REPEAT INSERT
PAUSE 5 SECONDS

*That is the end of Part Four.*
*There will now be a pause of five minutes for you to copy your answers onto the separate answer sheet. Be sure to follow the numbering of all the questions. I shall remind you when there is one minute left, so that you are sure to finish in time.*

PAUSE 4 MINUTES

You have one more minute left.

PAUSE 1 MINUTE

That is the end of the test. Please stop now. Your supervisor will now collect all the question papers and answer sheets.

# TEST 5

*I am going to give you the instructions for this test.*

*I shall introduce each part of the test and give you time to look at the questions.*

*At the start of each piece you will hear this sound:*

— *** —

*You will hear each piece twice.*

*Remember, while you are listening, write your answers on the question paper. You will have **five** minutes at the end of the test to copy your answers onto the separate answer sheet.*

*There will now be a pause. Please ask any questions now, because you must not speak during the test.*

PAUSE 5 SECONDS

*Now open your question paper and look at **Part One**.*

PAUSE 5 SECONDS

*You will hear people talking in eight different situations. For Questions **1–8**, choose the best answer (**A**, **B** or **C**).*

***Question 1***
*You are watching TV and you hear this advertisement.*

PAUSE 2 SECONDS

— *** —

Every thirty seconds, somewhere in the UK, this happens, ... Sometimes this happens, too ... It is certain that if you drive a car, sooner or later you will have to make an emergency stop. Even if you always drive carefully; even if you never touch a drop of alcohol, something will happen. Whether it be another vehicle, a child crossing, or an unexpected bend in the road, a good set of tyres with at least five millimetres of tread can and will save your life.

PAUSE 2 SECONDS

— *** —

TAPE REPEAT
PAUSE 2 SECONDS

***Question 2***
*You overhear these two people discussing a football match.*

PAUSE 2 SECONDS

— *** —

***M1*** *= Man 1* ***M2*** *= Man 2*

**M1:** I just don't know what the referee was going on about. There was never an off-side just before the end of the first half!
**M2:** Well, you couldn't exactly see from where we were standing.
**M1:** But we were the better team; we should have won. I mean the Liverpool defence are rubbish. Man. United are far better than that, but last night, we couldn't even get near the goal.
**M2:** Look, I've been supporting this team longer than you have. I've seen this before. They were just having an 'off day'.
**M1:** That was no 'off day', the match was fixed.

PAUSE 2 SECONDS

— *** —

TAPE REPEAT
PAUSE 2 SECONDS

***Question 3***
*You are out shopping when you pass a man in the street selling something.*

PAUSE 2 SECONDS

— *** —

... with a tarnish resistant, rotating, aluminium, serrated cutting edge. And, of course, you've all seen it before on TV anyway, haven't you ladies? ... and here it is before your very eyes, exactly the same quality as all the others with one important difference, ladies and gentlemen ... because you won't find it anywhere at this superb knock-down, bargain-basement price of only £9.99.

PAUSE 2 SECONDS

— *** —

TAPE REPEAT
PAUSE 2 SECONDS

***Question 4***
*You are at a wedding reception when a man starts to make a speech.*

PAUSE 2 SECONDS

— *** —

When George told me somebody had agreed to marry him, well, frankly, I was amazed. Then he told me it was to be Samantha, and this is what happened ... I regained consciousness in the hospital with a big bump on my head ... And that was when I realised the true enormity of the problem that Samantha will be taking on. You see, ever since we were at school together, George has had the most hideously smelly feet ... and that is why I have bought him one of these ...

PAUSE 2 SECONDS

— *** —

TAPE REPEAT
PAUSE 2 SECONDS

***Question 5***
*Listen to this person speaking about a recent holiday.*

PAUSE 2 SECONDS

— *** —

Well, I suppose it wasn't a total disaster, I mean the scenery was nice and some of the local people were friendly but they should have told us we'd be staying in the city centre ... and they should have told us how hot it was going to be ... and they should certainly have printed the right departure time on the ticket ... and that hotel manager should be sacked right away. In fact, I've got a mind to write to Tomlinson's right now and tell them just what I think of them.

PAUSE 2 SECONDS

— *** —

TAPE REPEAT
PAUSE 2 SECONDS

***Question 6***
*You are in an office when you hear a woman making this telephone call.*

PAUSE 2 SECONDS

— *** —

Hi. Is that Crown Paper Company? ... Yes, I'd like to ask about an order that you delivered to our offices this morning ... No, no everything was supplied as ordered ... No, it was for this morning, so that's fine ... Well it's just that the amount stated on the invoice for the six items mentioned is $35, so you have overcharged us by $14. What I want to know is why on earth you have done this? FADE

PAUSE 2 SECONDS

— *** —

TAPE REPEAT
PAUSE 2 SECONDS

***Question 7***
*You hear a friend telephoning a sandwich delivery company.*

PAUSE 2 SECONDS

— *** —

Yes, hello, is that 'Well-Bred Sandwiches and Confections'? ... I'd like to order some filled rolls ... Yes ... it's for the offices of T.J. Smith and Sons ... OK then. We'll have cheese, ham, sausage, mayonnaise and crispy lettuce on brown and cheddar cheese, chicken and chutney, and roast beef, horse radish and cucumber, both on white. Have you got that?

PAUSE 2 SECONDS

— *** —

TAPE REPEAT
PAUSE 2 SECONDS

***Question 8***
*You are watching the evening news on TV when you hear this item about Dino the dog.*

PAUSE 2 SECONDS

— *** —

And finally, on a happier note, the Paganucci family were reunited today with their exceptionally streetwise pet dog, Dino. When the Paganuccis moved from Naples in southern Italy to Hamburg in Germany, naturally, they took Dino with them. But after two days in Hamburg, Dino went missing. Two weeks later, the family had all but given up hope of ever seeing Dino again when a letter arrived from a former neighbour in Naples where Dino had turned up looking for them. Apparently, Dino had decided that Germany was not for him.

PAUSE 2 SECONDS

— *** —

TAPE REPEAT
PAUSE 2 SECONDS

*That is the end of Part One.*
*Now turn to **Part Two**.*

PAUSE 5 SECONDS

*You will hear a psychologist speaking on British radio on the subject of astrology. For questions **9-18**, complete the sentences with a word or short phrase.*

*You now have 45 seconds in which to look at Part 2.*

PAUSE 45 SECONDS

— *** —

**Introducer:** We have with us today the psychologist Simon Calvin who has recently created quite a stir with some rather unlikely claims about Astrology. Simon, are you indeed claiming that our lives are ruled by the stars?
**Simon:** No, not at all. I would not for one minute say that all of our lives are affected by the movements of stars in the heavens. My research really concerns things that are far more down to earth. But, before I start, I should just say that by no means do the majority of people in general totally disbelieve the value of astrology. An incredible 62% of British adults say that their stars are of some interest to them although only 3.5% would use them to choose a husband or wife, and only 2.9% of people would refer to them in making business decisions. But anyway, coming back to what I said before, I'm not so interested in the stars themselves, as I am in the time of year somebody is born. Psychologists now widely agree that both early life experiences and time of birth are a great influence on the development of a person's character. Of course, this does not make the whole of a person's character, but rather the foundation or base on which later changes are made. However, these later changes in character are not connected with the person's time of birth. So the question is, then, after all these personality changes have happened, can we look at an adult and see any of this foundation or base as part of their psychological make-up? The technique I have been using to do just this is a very simple one, but I believe, very effective. I have simply made a statistical comparison between people's choice of career and their zodiac sign. Where somebody has made a strong choice in favour of a particular kind of career, I believe that this indicates something very important in their character. If you look at a particular profession, say entertainers for example, and find that more than 15% of them were born in a certain short period of the year, it suggests that their choice of that profession is in some way connected with their birth at that particular time of the year. And this is, in fact, the case. An astonishing 20% of artists and entertainers were born in the period between the 12th of July and the 20th of August. This, in fact, is the most positive connection we have found so far. But there have been others although they have been less obvious. We looked at keen sports players participating more than five times a week and found a sizable number were born in the winter months of January and February. Another group of people we looked at were frequent travellers, who we discovered were more likely to have been born in early spring while accountants, bankers, executives and people generally in financial professions more frequently have birthdays in the late spring. Now, so far, we haven't found any professions containing large percentages of one particular star sign, which is a little disappointing, but this is, no doubt, because our modern technological world has removed us further and further from the effects of nature. If, as was the case in the past, many people lived closer to nature, we could be seeing percentages as high as 40 or 50 or even more. This of course would mean that we would have ... FADE

PAUSE 10 SECONDS

*You will hear the piece again.*

— *** —

REPEAT INSERT

PAUSE 5 SECONDS

*That is the end of Part Two.*
*Now turn to **Part Three**.*

PAUSE 5 SECONDS

*You will hear five different people talking about pets. For questions **19-23**, choose from the list **A-H** which pet each one has at home. Use the letters only once. There are three extra letters which you do not need to use.*

*You now have 30 seconds in which to look through Part 3.*

PAUSE 30 SECONDS

— *** —

**Speaker 1**
PAUSE 2 SECONDS

You'd be surprised how affectionate they can be, especially at night when you see them all cuddled up together. Makes me wonder how some people can hate them so much. And they're really playful too sometimes. Of course, you can't have them running around the house all the time but we try to give them as much freedom as possible although we do have to keep them out of sight when Trevor's mother comes round. If she catches sight of just one of them, she starts yelling and screaming.

**Speaker 2**
PAUSE 2 SECONDS

We'd been trying for years to get the stupid thing to talk. You know, tempting him with biscuits and saying his name over and over again. But he didn't utter a word. He squawked every so often so in the end we kind of gave up hope of ever hearing him speak. And then he goes and comes out with a rude word right in front of the vicar, who was having tea in our living room at the time. I don't know where he could have heard that word before. It certainly wasn't from me. Mind you, the vicar did take it very well, but I suppose he must have heard language like that in the past from other parishioners.

**Speaker 3**

PAUSE 2 SECONDS

Maurice is so intelligent. I'm certain he recognises his name, which I'm told is quite unusual when you get them after they've grown up. He certainly knows he's onto a good thing with us, but I guess it couldn't really be much worse than what he was used to before. I mean, the people at the shelter for stray animals must have their hearts in the right place, but putting an animal like that in such a small cage - it's inhuman. You should have heard the yapping and barking coming from those cages. My Tony's more soft-hearted than I am. He wanted to take them all home.

**Speaker 4**
PAUSE 2 SECONDS

Well, at first, I wouldn't have it in the house but Matthew pleaded with me for a whole afternoon and in the end I gave in. And now I've grown to be quite fond of Ferdinand. He's not a bit like you'd imagine. I mean he's ever so clean and doesn't take that much looking after and if you are brave enough to hold him, he's actually quite soft and furry and really quite warm. Anyway, he's Matthew's responsibility and that's what matters. The only thing I don't like so much is this horrible clicking noise he makes with his mouth while he's eating.

**Speaker 5**
PAUSE 2 SECONDS

I really don't think I'd ever be interested in any other kind of pet. After all, we've had a dog and a cat in the past but it wasn't the same thing at all. I suppose it's the variety that interests me. I mean there are so many different colours and patterns and shapes and sizes and they all move in different ways as well. I can spend hours in front of the tank watching them going up and down and from side to side and this next week's going to be really interesting because one of them has laid some eggs and according to my reference book, they should be hatching any day now.

PAUSE 10 SECONDS

*You will hear the piece again.*

— *** —

TAPE REPEAT
PAUSE 5 SECONDS

*That is the end of Part Three.*
*Now turn to* ***Part Four****.*

PAUSE 5 SECONDS

*You will hear a conversation which takes place in a busy restaurant between a couple, Ivan and Hannah Smythe, and a young waiter, Joel. For questions* ***24-30****, choose the best answer* ***A****,* ***B*** *or* ***C****.*

*There will now be a pause of 1 minute for you to look through Part 4.*

PAUSE 1 MINUTE

— *** —

***I*** *= Ivan* ***H*** *= Hannah* ***J*** *= Joel*

**I:** I say, waiter. We're ready to order.
**H:** Not so loud, darling - people are looking.
**I:** Ah, there you are. What kept you? er ... Jo-elle.
**J:** Just a little mix-up with one of the other orders, sir.
**I:** I'm not surprised. I don't know who wrote this load of nonsense but it's all Greek to me ...
**H:** Darling, it's perfectly plain and obvious. I've just explained it. You choose a starter from list A, a main course from list B and dessert from list C and the prices are all colour-coded.
**I:** Well, what if I wanted two starters.
**J:** I'd have to ask the manager about that, sir and I don't think he'd be too happy.
**I:** No, no, there's no need for that Jo-elle, we'll just order one of everything as my wife said.
**J:** Well, do you know what you'd like, sir?
**I:** Well, my wife will have the garlic mushrooms and a T-bone steak well-done on both sides and ...
**J:** Sorry, sir. You have to give me the numbers. You see the garlic mushrooms are A36 up here.
**I:** Oh, I see. Well, you could try writing the numbers a bit more clearly. Er, can you deal with this, dear? I've left my reading glasses in the car.
**H:** Uh, uh. Now, where were we? ... Oh yes. We'll have one A36, one B7 and one C15 and my husband will have A12, B3, oh hang on, did you want to ask about the quiche, dear?
**I:** Ah, oh yes. Does the quiche contain animal fat, Jo-elle?
**J:** I've never really thought about that - I used to be a vegetarian but I eat almost everything now.
**H:** I'm sure the quiche is fine, dear. We'll have one B3, Jo-elle.
**J:** It's Joel actually, you don't pronounce the 'E'.
**I:** I could go for something else. Can you see anything, dear?
**H:** Oh, sorry. Er, yes. There's a nut roast - number B33 and it's with lemon sauce - sounds nice.
**I:** Lemon sauce? That's a bit odd. Is it any good er ... 'Jole'?
**J:** I don't know, sir. I don't eat nuts myself - they don't agree with my digestion.
**I:** I wasn't asking about you Jo-elle, I just wanted to know if it's popular.
**J:** Ah, it's one of our most popular dishes, sir.
**I:** Okay then, nut roast and lemon B33 and one banana split.
**H:** That's C11.
**I:** Thank you, dear - and don't forget the extra cream.
**J:** I'm sorry, sir, but all our meals are assembled in advance and nothing extra can be added - or removed.
**I:** What kind of restaurant is this?
**H:** Ivan, calm down. He's doing his best.
**J:** Will that be all then?
**I:** Suppose it'll have to be.
**J:** Well, if you'll wait just one and a half minutes, I'll bring you your food.
**I:** My word, that's very efficient. Even the officer's canteen in Stanbroke isn't that fast. Just shows what a bit of organisation and ...
FADE

PAUSE 10 SECONDS

*You will hear the piece again.*

— *** —

REPEAT INSERT
PAUSE 5 SECONDS

*That is the end of Part Four.*
*There will now be a pause of five minutes for you to copy your answers onto the separate answer sheet. Be sure to follow the numbering of all the questions. I shall remind you when there is one minute left, so that you are sure to finish in time.*

PAUSE 4 MINUTES

You have one more minute left.

PAUSE 1 MINUTE

That is the end of the test. Please stop now. Your supervisor will now collect all the question papers and answer sheets.

# TEST 6

*I am going to give you the instructions for this test.*

*I shall introduce each part of the test and give you time to look at the questions.*

*At the start of each piece you will hear this sound:*

— *** —

*You will hear each piece twice.*

*Remember, while you are listening, write your answers on the question paper. You will have* ***five*** *minutes at the end of the test to copy your answers onto the separate answer sheet.*

*There will now be a pause. Please ask any questions now, because you must not speak during the test.*

PAUSE 5 SECONDS

*Now open your question paper and look at* ***Part One****.*

PAUSE 5 SECONDS

*You will hear people talking in eight different situations. For Questions* ***1–8****, choose the best answer (****A****,* ***B*** *or* ***C****).*

***Question 1***
*You are at a college lecture when you hear this student interrupting the lecturer.*

PAUSE 2 SECONDS

— *** —

**L** = *Lecturer* **S** = *Student*

**L:** ... which was highly controversial anyway and of course if you consider the implications of this new law ... uh ... yes?
**S:** Excuse me. I'm sorry to interrupt. You said something very important about the core laws and I was just wondering ...
**L:** Actually, they were the corn laws - you know the agricultural plant.
**S:** Oh, sorry ... I missed some of what you said, it was very fast. Could you possibly go back over this?
**L:** Well, no. You'll find all of that in my book. Price fifteen ninety-nine at the college book shop. Now, where was I?

PAUSE 2 SECONDS

— *** —

TAPE REPEAT
PAUSE 2 SECONDS

***Question 2***
*You hear this politician being interviewed on TV.*

PAUSE 2 SECONDS

— *** —

No doubt, all of you listening are worried about taxes and so you should be. The Christian Democratic Alliance have said nothing about their plans to alter the tax brackets and these are changes that will go straight to the pockets of hardworking people like yourselves, and we all know where the Social Liberal Democrats stand on this issue. They'll be taxing everything in sight. However, we in the L.D.P. believe in a fairer approach to administering the national economy.

PAUSE 2 SECONDS

— *** —

TAPE REPEAT
PAUSE 2 SECONDS

***Question 3***
*You overhear a hotel receptionist speaking on the telephone with a customer.*
PAUSE 2 SECONDS

— *** —

Hello, Half-Way Hotel. Can I help you? ... Yes, we take bookings ... um ... er ... well, actually, I'm very sorry, but I don't think we'll be able to manage that. I suggest you try ringing the Spa Hotel in Tunbridge Wells. They have over twice the number of rooms we have and offer very much the same facilities and standards, although you will end up paying rather more.

PAUSE 2 SECONDS

— *** —

TAPE REPEAT
PAUSE 2 SECONDS

***Question 4***
*You overhear this woman talking to her child in a shop.*

PAUSE 2 SECONDS

— *** —

... and now we're just dying to see the next episode to see if they really ... Kylie! Put that down! It doesn't belong to you. I said, put it down! How many times have I told you not to touch things that don't belong to you? Now, where were we?

PAUSE 2 SECONDS

— *** —

TAPE REPEAT
PAUSE 2 SECONDS

***Question 5***
*You overhear this woman talking about a problem she had with a cd player.*

PAUSE 2 SECONDS

— *** —

Anyway, the cd was in the machine. I couldn't get it out, I couldn't play it and I was worried because I wasn't sure if it was still under guarantee. I was also furious because it was Angie's favourite album. So, I took the whole machine along to Luntham's service counter expecting to hear the worst, and they were wonderful. Said they'd been getting quite a lot of the same complaint about that model, and he fixed it right there in front of me, and I didn't have to pay a penny. Not like some shops I could mention.

PAUSE 2 SECONDS

— *** —

TAPE REPEAT
PAUSE 2 SECONDS

***Question 6***
*You are at a pay phone in a hotel when you hear this man ordering a taxi to take him home.*

PAUSE 2 SECONDS

— *** —

Yes, hello ... I'd like a taxi ... Yes, just one taxi ... The name is Carter ... Yes, I'm at the Half-Way Hotel ... I'd like to go to Radleigh Road number two-six-nine ... How soon can you send a cab? ... OK then, that's fine. I'll be waiting outside the main entrance. Thank you.

PAUSE 2 SECONDS

— *** —

TAPE REPEAT
PAUSE 2 SECONDS

***Question 7***
*You are on a train when you overhear this man talking about the prices of railway tickets.*
PAUSE 2 SECONDS

— *** —

That station-master was really helpful, wasn't he? I mean, he didn't have to tell me about the young person's travel card. I've just saved three pounds off the full price. This ticket would have cost me nine pounds fifty but with the card it's only six fifty, which is, in fact, a lot less than I paid last year and that was before the fares increased. It was seven fifty then. Mind you, I did also have to pay ten pounds to buy the card, but it's going to be very useful over the next few months what with travelling to Scotland ... FA DE

PAUSE 2 SECONDS

— *** —

TAPE REPEAT
PAUSE 2 SECONDS

***Question 8***
*You hear this man on the radio introducing a song.*

PAUSE 2 SECONDS

— *** —

And that, of course, was the latest single from the Vegetables and that is currently at number nine in the charts after six weeks in the top 10. And still at number one for the seventh successive week, the song that everyone loved when they first heard it, but I think we're all ready for a new number one, aren't we? Well, if you're not, here it is again, 'Husky Lady' from Rap It Up.

PAUSE 2 SECONDS

— *** —

TAPE REPEAT
PAUSE 2 SECONDS

*That is the end of Part One.*
*Now turn to **Part Two**.*

PAUSE 5 SECONDS

*You will hear a programme about roller-coasters. For questions **9-18**, complete the sentences with a word or short phrase.*

*You now have 45 seconds in which to look at Part 2.*

PAUSE 45 SECONDS

— *** —

A roller-coaster is a self-inflicted, techno, primal jab at frail human courage with fierce names and perilous heights and no brakes on board. Yep you pay your money to get shaken and stirred. And the amusement parks wouldn't have it any other way. Absolutely, they want bragging rights. In fact there's been law suits over who has had the tallest coaster in the world and who's had the fastest and that kind of thing.

So where do you go to meet the twisted minds that come up with all this twisted metal? You go to a place where there isn't even a roller-coaster in sight. The shores of Utah's Great Salt Lake.

"What's the G-Forces right here?" Aerodynamics in Clear Field, Utah. These loop artists can make you sick but they won't. There are certain things that do that, our experience and knowledge of what forces and geometries do to people that we won't do that we refuse to do. It's in the shop at Aero that the need for speed is satisfied. The cars are easy, fibreglass frames over a steel chassis. The real art comes in designing the track.

The roller-coaster uses gravity, energy from having been carried up a lift. The science is making sure that once that potential energy is released, there's enough to get the car back to the station. The art is spending that energy in new and interesting ways. And that means engineering maximum height, maximum drops and maximum "Gs" or no "Gs" at all.

The Dragonfire at Bush Gardens in Wallensbury Virginia; in that first hill we put a parabolic curve in there and what that does is give you about 4 seconds of zero Gs.

But, above all, coasters are about maximum speed. The current record is 85 m.p.h.

There's even a psychological element to coaster design. How much to you want your riders to be aware of their predicament? The coaster that doesn't look an especially very large one, speeds are very high and you're able to comprehend everything that's going on and there's a lot more kind of fear factor, it's, it's they're scarier, they really are.

And if you think these guys don't know more about throwing your body around than a pro wrestler, listen to the next step in coaster design called a "Pipeline". Our current coasters when you bank into a corner, you kinda rock back and forth. But the Pipeline puts the point of rotation right in the centre of your chest so that we can just flip you over really quick. And it allows you to do barrel rolls, snap rolls, aeroplane acrobatic type manoeuvres.

So that's coaster science; make it fast, make it safe and give it a vicious name. After that build it and they will come.

Oh. What's the next step in roller-coaster? The tallest, the fastest, the biggest, indoors. Well anyway you got the point. Here it is, the biggest indoor coaster in the world. Grand Slam Canyon at Circus, Circus in Las Vegas. A two loop with corkscrew, 24 hundred foot, 40 plus mile an hour screamer. And the next step beyond this?

I think the next generation of coasters is gonna have elements of ride and technology that is employed currently in simulators thinking. I see a combining of those two kind of things. A coaster with digital displays or maybe a coaster with a virtual reality helmet attached to it so you get the G. Forces and you get maybe some different visual sensations, things like that.

The most expensive technology in a roller-coaster is in the wheels. The tyres cost five times what they do on your car, the same goes for the brakes and finally a physics lesson. Any roller-coaster will go faster when the air is warm but dry and when it's heavier, so if you're gonna do it right, get a bunch of friends together, pack that car and ride on a warm Autumn day.

PAUSE 10 SECONDS

*You will hear the piece again.*

— *** —

REPEAT INSERT

PAUSE 5 SECONDS

*That is the end of Part Two.*
*Now turn to **Part Three**.*

PAUSE 5 SECONDS

*You will hear five different people being interviewed on the radio about Christmas. For questions **19-23**, choose from the list **A-H** which words best describe their feelings about this celebration. Use the letters only once. There are three extra letters which you do not need to use.*

*You now have 30 seconds in which to look through Part 3.*

PAUSE 30 SECONDS

— *** —

**Speaker 1**
PAUSE 2 SECONDS

Well, I suppose some of it was quite nice but it really could have been so much better. After all, I went to a lot of effort this year to make it something special, but somehow it didn't quite work. I mean everybody had masses to eat, there were eight of us sitting down to dinner, and we must have spent a fortune on presents this year, but looking around the room, you couldn't see it in people's faces. And then there was all the quarrelling over what we were going to watch on TV, and I don't seem to remember a single person actually saying thank you and really meaning it.

**Speaker 2**
PAUSE 2 SECONDS

I was all set to have another unexciting Christmas in the bedsitter where I'm living now. Of course, I'd sent my kids Christmas presents but I knew I wouldn't be hearing from them. My ex-wife doesn't allow it. So I'd bought myself a two pound chicken from Dewhursts and a four-pack of Lion Brand Extra and I got a stack of pound coins for the electric meter so that at least I could be warm and watch some telly. And then, just as I was just putting the chicken into the oven, there was a knock at the door and it was the father of the family just across the road saying they'd noticed that I was going to be alone that day and would I like to join them. And of course, I had a wonderful time.

**Speaker 3**
PAUSE 2 SECONDS

It isn't over yet. I mean, we've had the actual festivities on the 25th, but there's so much more to Christmas than that. Our parish church is putting on a festival of 9 lessons and carols on Sunday evening. And if that's not your cup of tea then there's the Charitable Associa-tion Santa Claus pram-race on Monday, although I won't be taking part in that this year. And this Christmas it's even been snowing so I'll be taking my grandchildren up to Connerston Hill for some tobogganing or they can build a snowman if the snow's good enough. That's on Tuesday and then ... FADE

**Speaker 4**
PAUSE 2 SECONDS

It wasn't as good as it's been in the past. For a start the telly was pretty disappointing, especially after last year's. I mean we had 'Terminator' last Christmas Eve, but all we got this year was 'Robocop' again. And the weather, huh, the weather's been really bad, so most of the football was cancelled and then to top it all, our video machine broke down on Christmas day so there's been nothing to watch all Christmas. And then, just to finish off any last chance of a decent holiday, someone suggested we all played Monopoly. Well, I went out to walk the dog in the snow.

**Speaker 5**
PAUSE 2 SECONDS

Well, I wouldn't say I enjoyed it. I spent the three days before the twenty-fifth standing outside Fielding's pet shop with a placard trying to stop people buying pets as presents. And did they listen? People were going in and out of the pet shop all day and you should have seen the number of baby cats, dogs and rabbits that people were buying as presents. And you know what's going to happen to them. The same as every year. A week after Christmas they'll be out on the streets fending for themselves in temperatures well below zero. But what's most distressing is the tropical birds. These beautiful animals can die in a matter of hours if left outside.

PAUSE 10 SECONDS

*You will hear the piece again.*

— *** —

TAPE REPEAT
PAUSE 5 SECONDS

*That is the end of Part Three.*
*Now turn to **Part Four**.*

PAUSE 5 SECONDS

*You will hear an extract from a radio programme. For questions **24-30**, decide which of the choices **A**, **B** or **C** is the correct answer.*

*There will now be a pause of 1 minute for you to look through Part 4.*

PAUSE 1 MINUTE

— *** —

***JA** = Jim Adams* ***R** = Reader* ***PS** = Paul Spenser*

**JA:** Hi, this is "Say it like it is", the programme in which your comments about what's been on Radio One for the last week are read. And for today ... Well, we had many listeners writing in about last Tuesday's science programme which is based on weather this time. John Holmes from Oxford says:
**R:** Your "Climate changes" turned out to be quite an interesting programme. Professor Jones' theory that we're slowly going towards another Ice Age was quite astounding. I was taught that the earth was moving nearer the sun!
**JA:** You could be right. But I don't think that it will happen in our lifetime. Mrs Kent from Brighton talks about weather problems which could affect us in the near future.
**R:** Some experts may tell us what the weather may be like in the next century but I'm more concerned about the present day situation. I think that tax money and scientific studies should try to focus on short-term weather forecasts and try to make them more precise and accurate.
**JA:** Many listeners have the same point of view. On the other hand, Tom Sheridan from Manchester has a different opinion.
**R:** I hear that experiments are being made to change the weather in Britain. But, who wants it? Nobody would like a set weather pattern. All those conversations about the weather would disappear.
**JA:** We'd find something else to talk about. I'm sure. Food, for example. It seems to be a favourite of our readers judging from the letters we receive ...
**R:** Dear Jim, I'm writing in objection to the Cookery Series on Wednesdays.
**JA:** Tim Saunders, from Coventry writes;
**R:** Most men already know how to do things like making toast so our time shouldn't be wasted by such programmes.
**JA:** Tim would like more challenging cooking tips. We've got the producer of our cookery show here today, Mr. Paul Spenser. What about more difficult cookery on your show?
**PS:** I can relate to what Mr. Saunders is saying. Up to now we've been doing basic things to help beginners but we'll be moving on to more difficult recipes in the next few weeks. I hope that the programme will be more interesting for Mr. Saunders in the future.
**JA:** I hope so! To finish off we have a few letters referring to the rumours that lending libraries won't be free to the public anymore. Jane from Bournemouth has a few things to say about this.
**R:** For students like me, books are too expensive to buy and we depend on libraries for our books! 20p is too much to pay for every book we take out.
**JA:** Don't worry Jane. It's only a rumour so far. And our last letter comes from one of the elderly in our community.
**R:** The elderly have to pay for their needs so why shouldn't others pay for theirs? They pay in pubs and discos, why not at libraries.
**JA:** Well, that's all for today. More for you to think about. If there's something you'd like to comment on write to Jim Adams, "Say It Like It Is" Radio One.

PAUSE 10 SECONDS

*You will hear the piece again.*

— *** —

REPEAT INSERT
PAUSE 5 SECONDS

*That is the end of Part Four.*
*There will now be a pause of five minutes for you to copy your answers onto the separate answer sheet. Be sure to follow the numbering of all the questions. I shall remind you when there is one minute left, so that you are sure to finish in time.*

PAUSE 4 MINUTES

You have one more minute left.

PAUSE 1 MINUTE

That is the end of the test. Please stop now. Your supervisor will now collect all the question papers and answer sheets.

# TEST 7

*I am going to give you the instructions for this test.*

*I shall introduce each part of the test and give you time to look at the questions.*

*At the start of each piece you will hear this sound:*

— *** —

*You will hear each piece twice.*
*Remember, while you are listening, write your answers on the question paper. You will have **five** minutes at the end of the test to copy your answers onto the separate answer sheet.*

*There will now be a pause. Please ask any questions now, because you must not speak during the test.*

PAUSE 5 SECONDS

*Now open your question paper and look at **Part One**.*

PAUSE 5 SECONDS

*You will hear people talking in eight different situations. For Questions **1–8**, choose the best answer (**A**, **B** or **C**).*

***Question 1***
*You are in a large electrical shop when you overhear this man describing a washing machine.*

PAUSE 2 SECONDS

— *** —

... which, of course, comes with a three-year guarantee. And finally, there's the 'Amitron Eco'. You'll notice right away that it's a more expensive model but, in the long run, it'll cut a substantial slice off your family's electricity and water bills. This particular model has been specially designed to be economical with both water and energy making running costs a third less, although it has the same features as all our other models and does the job just as well. Would you care to have a look at the technical profile ... ? FADE

PAUSE 2 SECONDS

— *** —

TAPE REPEAT
PAUSE 2 SECONDS

***Question 2***
*You hear a man on TV talking about a programme on Tuesday night.*

PAUSE 2 SECONDS

— *** —

... and Alvin Major's guests tonight include the singer 'Lolita', the ghost writer Peter Miller and Bobby Antonio, then after the 9 o'clock news, Penelope Parchment has a particularly difficult case to solve when one of her house guests goes missing ... and can Penelope take time out to patch up her shaky marriage? That's 'Just Penelope' at 9:45 ... and then to round off the evening on Channel 9, Robert Mulholland presents another another ... FADE

PAUSE 2 SECONDS

— *** —

TAPE REPEAT
PAUSE 2 SECONDS

***Question 3***
*You are in a supermarket when you hear this couple arguing.*

PAUSE 2 SECONDS

— *** —

***M*** = *Man* ***W*** = *Woman*

**M:** No, don't get that one. That's the one that had a bitter taste.
**W:** But that one's the best value. It says here that it makes more than fifty cups.
**M:** And have you ever counted them? ... Look, every jar's got the same amount ... see! It says on the label 450 grams.
**W:** Well, what's wrong with this one then?
**M:** It's the flavour. You didn't like it either. Look, this one's only 9 pence extra. Couldn't we just try it once and see ... ? FADE

PAUSE 2 SECONDS

— *** —

TAPE REPEAT
PAUSE 2 SECONDS

***Question 4***
*You dial a number to find out about night classes. You hear this recorded message.*

PAUSE 2 SECONDS

— *** —

You have reached the Piddleton Technical College freephone information service. Courses starting next month include Norwegian clog-dancing and traditional English floral dancing - both classes taking place on Mondays and Wednesdays. Cookery courses for the new year are in Chinese, South American and Indian cuisine and will take place at the centre on weekday evenings apart from the Indian cookery course on Mondays, Wednesdays and Saturdays, which will consequently last an extra 2 weeks beyond the usual 5-week duration.

PAUSE 2 SECONDS

— *** —

TAPE REPEAT
PAUSE 2 SECONDS

***Question 5***
*You overhear this man talking about a book.*

PAUSE 2 SECONDS

— *** —

Well, when I first started, I bought a copy of 'How to Get the Most Out of your Trumpet'; but I think it made a lot of things unnecessarily difficult. I mean, it helps anyway having a teacher to show you what to do because no book can really explain what you have to do with your mouth when you're blowing. Mind you, it does have some useful diagrams that helped me pick up the fingering ... but if I were you, I'd spend my money on having some actual lessons with a proper instructor.

PAUSE 2 SECONDS

— *** —

TAPE REPEAT
PAUSE 2 SECONDS

***Question 6***
*You overhear a woman on the telephone inviting a friend to dinner.*

PAUSE 2 SECONDS

— *** —

Hello, is that George? ... Yes, very well thank you ... and you? ... Yes, I was wondering if you'd like to come to dinner on Thursday night ... it'll just be a small gathering ... Oh, what a pity. Still, you deserve a break with all that work you do. You've been quite run down recently - and we don't want you getting ill. Will you be going abroad? FADE

PAUSE 2 SECONDS

— *** —

TAPE REPEAT
PAUSE 2 SECONDS

***Question 7***
*You ask a policeman for directions to the bus station.*

PAUSE 2 SECONDS

— *** —

Well, the bus station is not too far. You'll be able to get there on foot quite easily. You keep going along this road until there's a bend and you follow it all the way round and then there's a big hill in front of you. That's called St Mark's Hill. So, you go all the way up St Mark's Hill, over the top and right down to the traffic lights ... and the bus station is just after the lights ... on your left ... and if you get to the river, you know that you've gone too far.

PAUSE 2 SECONDS

— *** —

TAPE REPEAT
PAUSE 2 SECONDS

***Question 8***
*You are watching a repeat of a British TV sitcom called Teacher's Always Right.*

PAUSE 2 SECONDS

— *** —

**T** = Teacher **L** = Lucy

**T:** Er ... Lucy can I have a word?
**L:** 'Imbecile' ... that's a word, sir.
**T:** No, no, I want to talk to you.
**L:** Look, sir, I promise I'll try to pay more attention and bring the right books next time, I just thought that everyone would find it interesting - my Dad does.

**T:** Look, that's not the problem ... haven't you been missing your classes quite a lot recently?
**L:** Oh, no sir. I didn't miss them at all. We had a great time.
**T:** Lucy, this has got to stop. It's high time you changed your attitude, young lady.

PAUSE 2 SECONDS

— *** —

TAPE REPEAT
PAUSE 2 SECONDS

*That is the end of Part One.*
*Now turn to* ***Part Two****.*

PAUSE 5 SECONDS

*You will hear part of a talk from a television programme about dealing with broken bones. For questions* ***9-18****, complete the sentences with a word or short phrase.*

*You now have 45 seconds in which to look at Part 2.*

PAUSE 45 SECONDS

— *** —

**Presenter:** In this programme, we will deal with another common result of violent injuries, that of fractures - or to put it more simply - broken bones. It is worth first mentioning a few facts about the bones themselves. Bones form an essential framework around which our bodies are shaped, performing the two vital functions of support for the body and protection for the internal parts of the body (such as the heart and the brain), which could easily be damaged otherwise. Bones are not dead tissue as many people think but are made up of a hardened outer layer of cells around a soft material in the centre, known as the bone marrow. The bone marrow, incidentally, performs the equally vital function of producing new blood cells. Bones do not break easily. When a small amount of force is applied, the bones - particularly of young people - can actually bend to a surprising degree, but, of course, there is a limit to this and beyond that limit the bones break. Because of the large forces and sudden movement involved, it is unlikely that somebody would break a bone and not be aware of it. There is also usually an unmistakable audible crack that can be heard by other people as well. So, what can we do in terms of first aid for people with fractures - beyond making the victim as comfortable as possible and calling an ambulance? In general, the answer is not much - but this is important to note; because the vital function of support has been lost in the damaged part of the body, any attempt to move the victim could result in further damage to that area. In any instance, where it is necessary to move such a victim, it is vital to provide another means of support for a damaged limb. For this reason, you should locate any fractures before attempting to move the victim. If this is not done, further movement of the damaged area will result in 'multiple fractures'; in other words, many small breaks, which are much harder to repair. If the victim is conscious, it is likely that he or she will be able to tell you the position of any fractures that may have occurred. But, in the case of an unconscious victim, a different procedure should be followed. After checking the victim's breathing, circulation, eyes and face as described in previous programmes, the next step in checking the victim's condition is to methodically feel each major bone in the body noting any change in shape that would indicate the presence of a break. For this reason, it is important to be aware of the correct healthy shape of all the major bone structures in the human body. For example, the shape of the shoulders, backbone, arms and legs. You should practise feeling other members of your family or members of your FIRST AID training group. Otherwise, you may end up treating a person who has no fracture at all.

PAUSE 10 SECONDS

*You will hear the piece again.*

— *** —

REPEAT INSERT

PAUSE 5 SECONDS

*That is the end of Part Two.*
*Now turn to* ***Part Three****.*

PAUSE 5 SECONDS

*You will hear five different people talking about jobs they have done around the house. For questions* ***19-23****, choose from the list A-H which job each speaker is describing. Use the letters only once. There are three extra letters which you do not need to use.*

*You now have 30 seconds in which to look through Part 3.*

PAUSE 30 SECONDS

— *** —

**Speaker 1**
PAUSE 2 SECONDS

These days it isn't a problem. I just set everything up, switch on the radio and get into the rhythm and it's all finished in no time. But I remember the first time I tried it. I hadn't got a clue. The fabric was too wet and I just couldn't get things to come out without creases ... and then the telephone rang ... I suppose it's a good thing it was only a wrong number because when I came back it was already starting to smoke and there was a big black mark on the back of my favourite shirt. So, I poured water all over it and then, of course, I had to start all over again.

**Speaker 2**
PAUSE 2 SECONDS

Well, you see my wife just can't do it because of her skin condition. So, in the end, we decided that rather than send everything to the laundry ... I would do the whole lot myself. It doesn't bother me. Joanne does the shopping and cuts the grass. The only thing that I don't like is hanging everything out afterwards. You know ... you get all the looks from the neighbours and one of the kids next door even has the cheek to call me 'Mrs' Simpson. I'll tell you one thing though; if I ever get hold of that boy, I'll show him a thing or two.

**Speaker 3**
PAUSE 2 SECONDS

I'd read a DIY manual that gave full instructions with pictures. It made it look so easy that I thought I'd save us a hefty bill and do it myself. What the manual didn't say was anything about turning off the stopcock before you start ... Well, I'm sure you can imagine what happened. Suddenly, there was a huge fountain coming out of the top of the thing and I just couldn't get the top back on. In the end, we did end up having to call a professional plumber out and paid a fortune because it was a Sunday morning. And then, I had to clean up the kitchen floor. It was like a swimming pool.

**Speaker 4**
PAUSE 2 SECONDS

Well, in the old days you used to use vinegar and paper towels. But nowadays there are so many different cleaning products on the market that you can hardly remember which one is which. Luckily, there's usually a picture on the front of the bottle that shows you just exactly which part of the house you're supposed to clean with it. The containers even have little levers on so you can point the bottle and spray the liquid wherever you want it. But then the difficult part is taking it off again. You rub and rub until you think you've finished and then ten minutes later, when you go outside, you see a bit you've missed.

**Speaker 5**
PAUSE 2 SECONDS

There's loads of things I wouldn't touch around the house but this is one thing that doesn't take any special talent or know-how at all. Even wallpapering is so much easier than it looks; you just put plenty of paste on the wall and then you just slide the paper into place. And, if you do get any wrinkles, you can iron them out with a brush. Plus, it's easy to do a straight line if you steady your hand on something and there's nobody there to distract you. You just have to watch out for the mess, that's all. Put plenty of newspaper on the floor or a couple of old sheets.

PAUSE 10 SECONDS

*You will hear the piece again.*

— *** —

TAPE REPEAT
PAUSE 5 SECONDS

*That is the end of Part Three.*
*Now turn to* ***Part Four****.*

PAUSE 5 SECONDS

*You will hear a conversation which takes place in an open market between three people, Bob and Andrea Jones, and Bob's friend Carl. For questions* ***24-30****, choose the best answer* ***A****,* ***B*** *or* ***C****.*

*There will now be a pause of 1 minute for you to look through Part 4.*

PAUSE 1 MINUTE

— *** —

***A*** *= Andrea* ***B*** *= Bob* ***C*** *= Carl*

**A:** Look Bob! That's a new stall we haven't seen before.
**B:** You mean the one with all those CD's and cassettes ... hang on ... hey! That's Carl.
**A:** You mean Carl who used to work with you at 'Acres'? What's he doing here?
**B:** Must have started up a new business - though he's the last person I'd have expected to ...
**C:** Hey, Bob!
**B:** Quick, pretend we haven't seen him.
**A:** Oh, come on! He's your friend, you can't ignore him like that.
**C:** Bob, what a great surprise ... haven't seen you for ... must be years.
**B:** Carl. Good to see you mate. Er ... This is my fiancee, Andrea.
**C:** Oh, pleased to meet you. Are you interested in country music? I know Bob's not too keen.
**A:** Is that what all this is? All country music? Have you got any Irish Folk music?
**B:** Oh, God.
**C:** I did have, but it didn't seem to sell too well.
**B:** I'm not surprised.
**C:** So I got rid of it all - pity really.
**B:** Good thing if you ask me ... And, how long have you been doing this?
**C:** You mean the stall? Oh, about two months. After 'Acres' closed down, I was out of work for about a year and then one day, I got talking to my claims officer ... er ... about my collection ... and he suggested that I did this ... and so far it's been quite profitable.
**A:** Do you make a profit?
**C:** Last week I took a bit over 3,000 pounds.
**B:** Three thousand quid!
**C:** Well, some of it has to pay for overheads and VAT but I should get to keep at least half of it.
**A:** Was it difficult to get started? What did you have to do?
**C:** No, no, it was quite easy really. I just talked to a 'small business adviser' at the bank and luckily, I still had some redundancy money left so there was no need for a loan or anything ... anyway what about you?
**B:** Oh, I spent my redundancy money on a holiday.
**A:** And the car!
**B:** Well, yeah, yeah, it didn't quite cover the car so I had to take out a loan, which I'm still paying off - you see the new job pays even less than 'Acres' did. I guess I should have done something like you have.
**A:** You still could. I'm sure the bank could extend you a loan if you asked. Have you seen Bob's silverware? ... It's really quite unique.
**C:** Er yeah, yes, he did show me some pictures once. Come to think of it, there's a man who sells similar stuff at a car boot sale in Blackpool, where I do a stall on Sundays.
**A:** There, you see. You could do a stall on Sundays and keep on your job at the bakery.
**B:** Oh, er ... I don't know about that. I'm not sure all that standing around in the cold would be good for my circulation. The doctor said I need to stay in a warm environment and keep moving.
**A:** You're just making excuses now. This is a fantastic chance to make some money ... FADE

PAUSE 10 SECONDS

*You will hear the piece again.*

— *** —

REPEAT INSERT
PAUSE 5 SECONDS

*That is the end of Part Four.*
*There will now be a pause of five minutes for you to copy your answers onto the separate answer sheet. Be sure to follow the numbering of all the questions. I shall remind you when there is one minute left, so that you are sure to finish in time.*

PAUSE 4 MINUTES

You have one more minute left.

PAUSE 1 MINUTE

That is the end of the test. Please stop now. Your supervisor will now collect all the question papers and answer sheets.

# TEST 8

*I am going to give you the instructions for this test.*

*I shall introduce each part of the test and give you time to look at the questions.*

*At the start of each piece you will hear this sound:*

— *** —

*You will hear each piece twice.*
*Remember, while you are listening, write your answers on the question paper. You will have* ***five*** *minutes at the end of the test to copy your answers onto the separate answer sheet.*

*There will now be a pause. Please ask any questions now, because you must not speak during the test.*

PAUSE 5 SECONDS

*Now open your question paper and look at* ***Part One****.*

PAUSE 5 SECONDS

*You will hear people talking in eight different situations. For Questions* ***1–8****, choose the best answer (****A****,* ***B*** *or* ***C****).*
***Question 1***
*You switch on the radio and hear this exchange in progress.*

PAUSE 2 SECONDS

— *** —

***P*** *= Presenter* ***R*** *= Roger*

**P:** Okay Roger, ... Now, this man was born in South Western Australia in 1946. He came to London in the sixties and made a name for himself in the West End before moving into film and television. His stage appearances include 'Prospero' in Shakespeare's 'Tempest' and 'Clive' in 'Where did you last see your trousers?' His first film appearance ...
**R:** Is it Oliver Fulcher?
**P:** Sorry Roger, I can't give you a point for that. It was in fact Barney Fulcher. Now Muriel, this man ...

PAUSE 2 SECONDS

— *** —

TAPE REPEAT
PAUSE 2 SECONDS

***Question 2***
*You overhear this man talking about a restaurant.*

PAUSE 2 SECONDS

— *** —

Well, I hadn't been to Willard's for about four years and it came as something of a shock to find the place under new management. It really isn't the same any more but I suppose you could say it's changed with the times. After all, it's still good value ... but you do have to wait longer for everything and there isn't the same selection as before - especially the desserts - but I'd imagine it will remain quite competitive, especially in this part of town.

PAUSE 2 SECONDS

— *** —

TAPE REPEAT
PAUSE 2 SECONDS

***Question 3***
*Listen to this woman interviewing a man on a TV chat show.*

PAUSE 2 SECONDS

— *** —

***L** = Lucy* ***R** = Roddy*

**L:** So Roddy ... How are you shaping up to life on the outside?
**R:** Well, Lucy not all the guys are as lucky as me - I mean, being a celebrity ... I get a different deal.
**L:** Do you mean with the film they're making about your life?
**R:** Well, yeah, ... you see, the day I got out, Sam Beesly, the famous detective writer came up to see me with this contract ... yeah for my story ... Well, yeah, I suppose if I'd actually killed somebody ... they wouldn't have been so keen to make a movie about my exploits and the bank of England.

PAUSE 2 SECONDS

— *** —

TAPE REPEAT
PAUSE 2 SECONDS

***Question 4***
*You are travelling by train when you overhear this exchange.*

PAUSE 2 SECONDS

— *** —

***W** = Woman* ***M** = Man*

**M:** That really is the most incredible coincidence. I mean it must have been ... oh ... fifty years now. Let's see. Ah yes, it was the winter of '47. I distinctly remember your good father playing in the school yard.
**W:** So you were his form master that year?
**M:** No, no, no arithmetic and geometry ... we taught proper subjects in those days ...
**W:** So, how did you know that I was his daughter?
**M:** It's the shape of your ears ... *(turning to his friend)* his father had them, too ... very distinctive ears ...

PAUSE 2 SECONDS

— *** —

TAPE REPEAT
PAUSE 2 SECONDS

***Question 5***
*Listen to this teacher giving a lesson.*

PAUSE 2 SECONDS

— *** —

If you open your books to page 62, you will see two contrasting maps of the region. The first one dates back to the 1950's when this part of the world was underdeveloped and mainly agricultural, but if you now look at the second one, there has been a marked shift in population from the countryside to the cities, accompanied by rapid industrialisation and centralisation of services. So, what effect do you think this has had on the agriculture of this region? Yes, Jaswinda?

PAUSE 2 SECONDS

— *** —

TAPE REPEAT
PAUSE 2 SECONDS

***Question 6***
*You hear this announcement being made in a railway station.*

PAUSE 2 SECONDS

— *** —

Ladies and gentlemen, this is an announcement for all passengers awaiting the arrival of the 7:15 train for London, Victoria. This service is now running about 7 minutes late and will now depart at 7:22 from platform 3 as advertised. We apologise for any inconvenience this may cause. The late departure from Three Bridges Central was due to the cancellation of a connecting service.

PAUSE 2 SECONDS

— *** —

TAPE REPEAT
PAUSE 2 SECONDS

***Question 7***
*You overhear this man answering a telephone in a record shop.*

PAUSE 2 SECONDS

— *** —

Good morning, Spinster Records ... Yes, we do have some discs of 'Valhalla' ... Ah, but ... no, that's a very new release and it hasn't reached us yet ... but we should be getting it in the next fortnight ... Would you like me to reserve a copy for you? ... Yes, I know it was advertised on television but the distributor ... Well, I'm sorry, too ... Well, you'll just have to do that, won't you ... Goodbye.

PAUSE 2 SECONDS

— *** —

TAPE REPEAT
PAUSE 2 SECONDS

***Question 8***
*You are staying in the home of a British family when you hear this exchange between the husband and wife.*

PAUSE 2 SECONDS

— *** —

***M** = Man* ***W** = Woman*

**M:** Morning dear. Did you sleep well?
**W:** No, I didn't, and you know very well why not.
**M:** Well, there's nothing more I can do about it. I've already fitted new windows in our room.
**W:** Well, you'll just have to go straight to the source of the trouble.
**M:** Look dear, they're students, they wouldn't understand.
**W:** Well, if you don't go round there and talk to them, ... I will. They're sending me to an early grave, that's what they're doing. And if they think they can have another...

PAUSE 2 SECONDS

— *** —

TAPE REPEAT
PAUSE 2 SECONDS

*That is the end of Part One.*
*Now turn to* ***Part Two****.*

PAUSE 5 SECONDS

*You will hear part of a scientific television programme for young people in which the speaker explains what 'meteors' are. For questions **9-18**, complete the sentences with a word or short phrase.*

*You now have 45 seconds in which to look at Part 2.*

PAUSE 45 SECONDS

— *** —

**Presenter:** Even if you have never watched the sky at night, you probably know what you would see if you did. The view is best on a night with no moon. You stare upwards into the inky blackness over which are scattered millions of tiny points of light. These, of course, are the stars. Then just as you're beginning to get bored with this unchanging scene, a tiny white streak of light shoots across the sky. It's going too fast to be a plane. Then two seconds later you see another one. What you are witnessing is the beginning of a shower of meteors or shooting stars.

To understand what is happening, it helps us to imagine a car driving fast along the road. In a way, our planet Earth is like that car. As it is racing along, it comes towards a large group of insects all flying together just above the road.

Now, not all the insects are hit by the car, but several of them crash into the car's windscreen with an unpleasant noise. In many ways, the meteors are similar to the swarm of insects, although they aren't really animals. In fact, meteors are mostly tiny pieces of iron that look like little stones.

In a similar way, the Earth is not really moving along a road. But it does follow the same circular route around the sun once every year. This enormous circular path is called the Earth's 'orbit'. All the other planets are in orbits like this as well. Now, there are small groups of those stones waiting in certain places along the Earth's route around the sun. Some of them are fixed in one orbit while others are moving around the sun in their own orbits. Once every year, the Earth's circular path around the sun takes us through some of these groups of little rocks.

Now, when the earth approaches one of these stones, it is pulled downwards towards our planet by a strong force called gravity. And when the meteor starts to rush towards the ground, a shooting star is born. Normally, as shooting stars fall, they are travelling at speeds of 10 kilometres every second. This is about a hundred times faster than a jet plane. However, before the meteor can reach the Earth, it must go through the air around it - the atmosphere. Now, because it is going through the air so fast, the shooting star starts to become hotter and hotter and the air around it gets very hot too. This is a bit like the head of a match rubbing along the side of a matchbox. Now, very soon the outside of this piece of iron gets very hot indeed and, as a result, it gets soft and melts and then starts to burn. So, as this hot little rock rushes through the atmosphere, it leaves a tail of hot burning metal and flames behind it. This is the bright streak we can see from the ground - 100 kilometres below. Yes, you see, fortunately for us, most meteors are so small that they have completely burned up long before they could ever reach the ground - which is just as well because, otherwise, we would need to carry rather stronger umbrellas!

PAUSE 10 SECONDS

*You will hear the piece again.*

— *** —

REPEAT INSERT

PAUSE 5 SECONDS

*That is the end of Part Two.*
*Now turn to **Part Three**.*

PAUSE 5 SECONDS

*You will hear five different people talking about journeys they have made. For questions **19-23**, choose from the list **A-H** the correct word or phrase that describes how each person completed their journey. Use the letters only once. There are three extra letters which you do not need to use.*

*You now have 30 seconds in which to look through Part 3.*

PAUSE 30 SECONDS

— *** —

**Speaker 1**
PAUSE 2 SECONDS

We were going up to York to see her relatives ... it was quite early in the morning, as I recall. There wasn't too much traffic on the roads so we were doing a good ninety up the central lane of the M1 - and there were still plenty of other vehicles passing us in the fast lane ... and then suddenly, out of nowhere, there was a car in front of us, doing about fifty - it must have moved out from the slow lane to overtake something really slow. Anyway, Jessica saw it first and shouted 'Look out' and Sally braked but we still went into the back of it. Luckily, nobody was hurt. But the front of the car was completely smashed in ... FADE

**Speaker 2**
PAUSE 2 SECONDS

... so I locked my bike and told the guard to keep a good eye on it ... it's still worth quite a lot of money, even now ... and then I went to find a seat. We'd started moving by then, which made it more difficult going from carriage to carriage. I went all the way up to the front and then all the way back again and the only seat I could find was in a first class compartment. So, I was just making myself comfortable when the guard appeared. I suppose he could have made much more trouble if he'd wanted to. You see, he'd seen my ticket so he knew it was only for second class ... but he was a decent bloke and he just gave me a warning.

**Speaker 3**
PAUSE 2 SECONDS

I was already running late when I came out of the door, I got in the car, turned the ignition key and nothing happened. I didn't have time to look under the bonnet, so I set off on foot to get a train. What I had forgotten was that the trains were on strike. So anyway, after that, I tried for about half an hour to get a number eight bus. Four came past but they were all totally packed, of course. Then I saw Jack going past in his red Capri ... but he was in too much of a hurry to see me. So, after that, I tried phoning three different taxi companies, but I was out of luck there - and in the end, I had no choice but to set off on a four-mile march to the office. I arrived two hours late.

**Speaker 4**
PAUSE 2 SECONDS

I'd just reached the bottom of Furze Hill and I was really going quite fast when I must have accidentally touched my brakes or something because the next thing ... the chain had come off. So, I pulled over and stopped and then tried to put it back on without getting oil all over my hands and my clothes - that wouldn't go down too well in the office. So, I found this piece of paper, lying beside the road, and used it to hold the chain with and it was only when I'd finished that I noticed that this piece of paper had been a hot-dog wrapper and so I had mustard and ketchup and disgusting greasy stuff all over my hands.

**Speaker 5**
PAUSE 2 SECONDS

So there I was sitting looking out of the window and we'd been sitting there for over an hour by then. We'd taxied to the end of the runway and just waited and waited for something to happen. I was getting a bit bored with the few buildings we could see from where we were. I could just make out the road in the distance, with the occasional car or bus. And, it was about then that I suddenly remembered that I'd left the back door unlocked. Of course, I told Bill but we both agreed there was nothing we could do until we got to our destination ... and, of course, by then, it was too late.

PAUSE 10 SECONDS

*You will hear the piece again.*

— *** —

TAPE REPEAT
PAUSE 5 SECONDS

*That is the end of Part Three.*

*Now turn to* ***Part Four****.*

PAUSE 5 SECONDS

*You will hear a scene from a radio soap opera called Willowdale Green, in which a couple, Charles Miller and Daphne Jameson, are speaking with the barman Bill Dexter in a village pub. For questions* ***24-30****, choose the best answer* ***A****,* ***B*** *or* ***C****.*

*There will now be a pause of 1 minute for you to look through Part 4.*

PAUSE 1 MINUTE

— *** —

***B*** *= Bill* ***C*** *= Charles* ***D*** *= Daphne*

**B:** I'm afraid I can't serve you another pint if you're driving home tonight, sir.
**C:** I'm not driving, actually. I live just up the road at Draycott farm - you must know it.
**B:** The Farm - I know very well ... but you, I don't.
**C:** The name's Charles Miller, and this is my partner Daphne.
**B:** What can I get you then, Mrs Miller?
**D:** I'll just have a tonic water - you see we came in my car tonight - oh, and the name's Jameson, actually.
**B:** Oh, so we're not married. And I suppose you're living up at the farm, as well. Old Arnie Draycott would've liked that.
**D:** Well, yes, we moved in last week.
**B:** I suppose you know what happened there.
**D:** About the suicide you mean? Yes. What a terrible tragedy.
**B:** Oh yeah ... but I don't suppose that fancy estate agent of yours told you why he did it.
**C:** He did mention something but that's not really any of our business. Of course, I did actually meet the poor man once - worked there one summer picking strawberries. Mind you, in those days things must have been going quite well.
**B:** Well, over the years, I got to know him quite well and what with his money problems and his son getting sick and so many other things ... it all got too much for him.
**D:** Oh, how ghastly! Poor fellow! What an awful thing to happen.
**B:** Yeah, it is ... and he would have wanted the farm to go to someone from Willowdale ... which you are not. Pardon me for being so frank - but there it is.
**C:** So that's a problem, is it? I suppose you all think that this is just a weekend cottage for us ... and that we'll be disappearing to the city all week and that Draycott farm won't be a farm any more and ...
**B:** Steady on. That is what people have been saying ... and they're not very happy.
**C:** Well, if that's what they've been saying, they're all wrong ... And, I suppose that explains the broken window.
**D:** Look, we've just both decided to move to the country ... and we really want to live here. Charles is a technical writer and he'll be working at home from now on ... and we have every intention of using the shops and the local services.
**C:** That is, of course, if we are welcome.
**D:** Charles has a heart condition. He even had an operation last month. So we wanted to get away from the city and make a healthier life.
**B:** Like running a farm you mean. It won't be very easy with a heart condition.
**C:** Well, that's where we thought you might be able to help. You see, we were hoping to find somebody who could manage the farm for us, ... we'd be willing to pay of course.
**B:** How much were you thinking you might pay this ... er ... somebody?
**C:** Well, we haven't decided exactly but I should think somewhere in the region of fifteen hundred a month.
**B:** Well, that is rather generous. I can think of one or two people who would drop everything to work for that sort of money. If I wasn't working here, I would consider it. You are serious?
**C:** Absolutely! ... It's what we've always wanted.

PAUSE 10 SECONDS

*You will hear the piece again.*

— *** —

REPEAT INSERT

PAUSE 5 SECONDS

*That is the end of Part Four.*
*There will now be a pause of five minutes for you to copy your answers onto the separate answer sheet. Be sure to follow the numbering of all the questions. I shall remind you when there is one minute left, so that you are sure to finish in time.*

PAUSE 4 MINUTES

You have one more minute left.

PAUSE 1 MINUTE

That is the end of the test. Please stop now. Your supervisor will now collect all the question papers and answer sheets.

# TEST 9

*I am going to give you the instructions for this test.*

*I shall introduce each part of the test and give you time to look at the questions.*

*At the start of each piece you will hear this sound:*

— *** —

*You will hear each piece twice.*
*Remember, while you are listening, write your answers on the question paper. You will have* ***five*** *minutes at the end of the test to copy your answers onto the separate answer sheet.*

*There will now be a pause. Please ask any questions now, because you must not speak during the test.*

PAUSE 5 SECONDS

*Now open your question paper and look at* ***Part One****.*

PAUSE 5 SECONDS

*You will hear people talking in eight different situations. For Questions* ***1–8****, choose the best answer (****A****,* ***B*** *or* ***C****).*

***Question 1***
*You are at a public celebration when you hear this announcement.*

PAUSE 2 SECONDS

— *** —

Er ... Excuse me everybody ... this will only take a minute. We have an announcement and the announcement is: Could the owner of the grey Skoda, registration CRA 179P please remove his car from its parking space at the far end of the street? Sorry, we appreciate this is your legal parking space, but if your car remains there, the floats won't be able to get past and then everybody will be complaining.

PAUSE 2 SECONDS

— *** —

TAPE REPEAT
PAUSE 2 SECONDS

***Question 2***
*You have taken your camera to a shop where the assistant explains why it is not working.*

PAUSE 2 SECONDS

— *** —

Ah well ... there doesn't appear to be anything the matter with the camera itself. But I don't think you paid much attention to the instruction manual. And don't worry about the film, I wound it back into its container. Now, if you look here into the battery compartment, this should be put in this way round with the little metal bit pointing down towards the base of the camera ... and then if you depress the shutter just a bit, you'll see this little light comes on - so now we have power.

PAUSE 2 SECONDS

— *** —

TAPE REPEAT
PAUSE 2 SECONDS

***Question 3***
*You switch on the radio to find a phone-in programme in progress.*

PAUSE 2 SECONDS

— *** —

***G*** *= Gerald* ***C*** *= Cecilia*

**G:** And our first caller today is Cecilia. Cecilia, what is your question for Gerald?
**C:** Well, I've been having quite a lot of trouble with my Swiss Cheese plant. I just can't get it to do what I want. It's in quite a large pot now, I transplanted it last spring, but the leaves and stems haven't spread out at all. I've been wondering if it could be root-bound.
**G:** Well, Cecilia, this is more common than you might think. What you've got to do is ... FADE

PAUSE 2 SECONDS

— *** —

TAPE REPEAT
PAUSE 2 SECONDS

***Question 4***
*You are in the lounge of an expensive hotel when you hear this exchange.*

PAUSE 2 SECONDS

— *** —

***W*** *= Woman* ***M*** *= Man*

**W:** I'm terribly sorry sir, but we can't allow you to do that here.
**M:** But why ever not? I've paid my money, now just leave me alone.
**W:** I'm awfully sorry, but we simply can't allow it. You see the flash disturbs other visitors and damages the colouring in our priceless antique paintings.
**M:** Well, what about that man over there with the dog?
**W:** I think you will find, sir, that he is not using a flash.
**M:** Well, I'm going to talk to the manager.
PAUSE 2 SECONDS

— *** —

TAPE REPEAT
PAUSE 2 SECONDS

***Question 5***
*You are in the office of a major trading company when you hear this woman talking on the phone.*

PAUSE 2 SECONDS

— *** —

Well, Peter, I do have rather a tight schedule on Friday ... let's see ... at 3:30 I've a meeting with my agent. That goes on till 3:45 and then I have to drive to the office for the departmental heads meeting at 4:15 and that won't be finished till quarter to six at the earliest ... No, I know what. I'll cancel my agent. After all, I'm the one who's paying his fee. He'll just have to lump it ... and then we can meet at quarter to four and I'll still get to the meeting for 4:15.

PAUSE 2 SECONDS

— *** —

TAPE REPEAT
PAUSE 2 SECONDS

***Question 6***
*Listen to this woman speaking on a TV travel programme.*

PAUSE 2 SECONDS

— *** —

***W*** *= Woman* ***M*** *= Man*

**W:** ... and now turning to a subject that we discussed last week. We have had a number of phone calls from other customers who also suffered the same inconvenience as a result of booking 'Horden Sun and Save' package deals last summer. We have also been informed that the Office of Fair Trading have in fact carried out an investigation and issued the following statement:
**M:** While not directly responsible, Horden's Limited should provide compensation of no less than sixty pounds for each individual ...

PAUSE 2 SECONDS

— *** —

TAPE REPEAT
PAUSE 2 SECONDS

***Question 7***
*You overhear this man talking in a fast food restaurant.*

PAUSE 2 SECONDS

— *** —

Well, Samantha's really calmed down in the last month or so. In fact, she's been a lot better behaved since she had her last little adventure. You did hear about that, didn't you? It is really quite incredible. I mean, she actually survived a whole wash cycle in the washing machine. It's a good thing I came back before it started to spin ... and her fur did come out such a beautiful, snowy white colour afterwards. Mind you she won't go near the washing machine again.

PAUSE 2 SECONDS

— *** —

TAPE REPEAT
PAUSE 2 SECONDS

***Question 8***
*You telephone a number in order to hear a freephone message about a new product.*

PAUSE 2 SECONDS

— *** —

Thank you for phoning the Positronic Information Service regarding the new Brain-Booster Theta-Wave Expander. You have already read our newspaper advertisement and will know that over a six-month period the Brain-Booster is capable of raising your intelligence level by as much as 40 I.Q. points without affecting other brain functions such as memory. If you wish to hear an example of the Brain-Booster's unique Theta-Wave Stimulator, please listen after the tone.

PAUSE 2 SECONDS

— *** —

TAPE REPEAT
PAUSE 2 SECONDS

*That is the end of Part One.*
*Now turn to* ***Part Two****.*

PAUSE 5 SECONDS

*You will hear a woman called Yvonne on a TV programme giving her opinion about children being punished at school. For questions 9-18, complete the sentences with a word or short phrase.*

*You now have 45 seconds in which to look at Part 2.*

PAUSE 45 SECONDS

— *** —

**Yvonne**: Any of you who are of my generation or older will no doubt remember ... the strap. But for those youngsters listening, I'd better explain because I'm saying this for your benefit. The strap, as they called it, was a thick piece of leather about an inch wide and half as long as a belt and it was especially designed for hitting small children, on the palms of their hands. Nowadays, if you do something wrong at

school, you're unlucky if you even get a telling off. And even the most serious offences get little more than a concerned phone call from the head teacher to your mum and dad. Now, when I was at St Anne's School for Girls in the fifties, we didn't have things quite so easy. It didn't take much to get a strapping. I'll never forget the first time it happened to me. One morning, I came to school in the wrong shoes - brown ones instead of black - and that was enough for the principal to call me up in front of the whole class of children and beat my hand until it bled. I saw this and many other examples of our school's discipline system as very cruel and unfair.
Now, unlike many people of that time, I didn't just forget about it when my school days were over. Soon I had children of my own and the thought that they would one day get the same treatment, really made my blood boil ... and that's when I heard about P.O.P.P.I. ... er ... Parents Opposed to Physical Punishment of Infants. All the other members were like me. They had young children and didn't want some unfeeling teachers filling their lives with misery. So we started writing letters. First, to the schools, then to the education department and eventually, to our local politicians, and in 1979, the government put an end to the strap ... and to the cane ... and to the paddle and we thought that we had guaranteed our children the chance to grow up into fine young people. And that, I'm afraid, did not happen. My own son and daughter have turned into lazy, irresponsible young adults who really have no idea how lucky they are. I'm sure you all know people like them ... and they're not the worst by far. But it's only recently that I've begun to think - to wish - that they'd never changed the law. Cruel it may have been, unfair it often was, but it taught us our place in society. And that's something that few young people today seem to know or want to respect. For example, we wouldn't have all the teenage crime that goes on nowadays if those teenagers concerned had, when they'd been younger, been given the strap.

PAUSE 10 SECONDS

*You will hear the piece again.*

— *** —

REPEAT INSERT

PAUSE 5 SECONDS

*That is the end of Part Two.*
*Now turn to **Part Three**.*

PAUSE 5 SECONDS

*You will hear five different people describing different unusual musical instruments from around the world. For questions **19-23**, choose from the list **A-H** which speaker's instrument best fits the description given. Use the letters only once. There are three extra letters which you do not need to use.*

*You now have 30 seconds in which to look through Part 3.*

PAUSE 30 SECONDS

— *** —

**Speaker 1**
PAUSE 2 SECONDS

There are only two examples of this instrument in the world, one in a museum in Japan and one recently unearthed in southern China. Many experts do not consider it to be one instrument as it is made up of 46 silver alloy bells each suspended from its own supporting wooden frame. I must mention that some of these bells weigh as much as 40 kilograms. What makes this assembly one instrument, in my opinion, is the fact that each one of the forty six bells plays a separate note and that the wooden supporting structure has been designed so that they fit together in an ascending scale rather like the strings inside a piano or the frets on a guitar.

**Speaker 2**
PAUSE 2 SECONDS

What gives this drum its unique mellow tone is the fact that the bowl around which the skin has been stretched is made from a single piece of white ivory. The outer surface of the bowl has been carved with special places for the fingers. In each of these there is a hole that the player can cover with one of the fingers of his left hand to slightly alter the tone as he beats the skin with his right hand. The finger movements of the left hand are not dissimilar to those used with a guitar. It is, perhaps, rather sad that since international trade in ivory has been made illegal, few of these instruments have been made. There is a risk that the tradition behind its production will soon be lost forever.

**Speaker 3**
PAUSE 2 SECONDS

What is particularly interesting about this traditional hand drum are the unique red and gold patterns painted on its wooden underside. This, of course, does not affect the sound but reflects the social importance of this instrument for the Sachawaya tribe who produce it. They believe that as a result of its use in pubic celebrations, it is filled with the good spirits of the community. Then, later in the year, when the autumn winds begin to blow, the drum can be displayed outside a building of importance to drive away the evil spirits that may cause destruction in the winter ahead.

**Speaker 4**
PAUSE 2 SECONDS

The stem and sound-box of this instrument are made from the wood of the eucalyptus tree. This is quite a soft wood which means that the instrument goes out of tune very rapidly. The craftsmen who construct them still use stretched snake-gut to make the five strings. This, of course, makes the instrument very expensive and it was traditionally only played by tribal chiefs and their families. Surprisingly, not only its appearance but the tuning as well are similar to that of a classical guitar, suggesting that this tribe must have had some contact with the outside world long before the twentieth century.

**Speaker 5**
PAUSE 2 SECONDS

The curved base and supporting structure of this instrument are made of matured rose-wood while the nails that hold the blocks are traditionally made of ebony, which was the hardest wood available until recently. Four different trees are used to make the blocks themselves which are matured in different ways, to give each one its own individual note. The special hammers are fashioned by hand from willow, a wood still widely used in the manufacture of guitars. As a result of its construction, the instrument is surprisingly light, making it easy for the Nabungda tribe to use it at its various social functions and annual celebrations.
PAUSE 10 SECONDS

*You will hear the piece again.*

— *** —

TAPE REPEAT
PAUSE 5 SECONDS

*That is the end of Part Three.*
*Now turn to **Part Four**.*

PAUSE 5 SECONDS
*As you are leaving an aeroplane at the end of a flight, you overhear this conversation between a passenger and a flight attendant. For questions **24-30**, choose the best answer **A**, **B** or **C**.*

*There will now be a pause of 1 minute for you to look through Part 4.*

PAUSE 1 MINUTE

— *** —

***FA** = Flight Attendant* ***P** = Passenger*

**FA:** Sorry, you'll have to leave by the door at the front, sir.
**P:** OK, and thanks for everything.
**FA:** Have a good holiday, sir.
**P:** Well, actually I'm not exactly on holiday.
**FA:** Oh? Do you live here?
**P:** Well, that's what I'm planning to do. I'm visiting a friend who says he can get me a job. So, I'm going to be around this area for a bit. Is

this your last flight today?
**FA:** I wish it was. I've already been 'on' for five hours and I've got the return flight to come.
**P:** So, have you got another five hours ahead of you?
**FA:** More like five and a half and that's if there are no delays!
**P:** So, the return flight is longer?
**FA:** Well, it's the same distance but from London to Athens we have a tail wind which makes it quicker ... but on the way back that becomes a head wind which slows us down.
**P:** That's a long day. Do you work any longer days?
**FA:** Well, the longest working day is about twelve hours ... but if there are delays at either end, it can soon mount up.
**P:** Is that twelve hours - actually in the air?
**FA:** No, it's not actually flying time. There's a one-hour pre-flight and post-flight routine that we have to go through.
**P:** Oh, I don't envy you. Mind you, I used to work nights in a hotel and that was often twelve hours or more. But at least it was on the ground. I hope you don't mind me asking ... what do you do on longer flights?
**FA:** Well, actually they're better ... um ... anything over four and a half hours is rostered as a stop over ... so you do the outflight on one day and we fly back on the next. And sometimes, if you're lucky, you even get a two-night stop-over.
**P:** Does that happen often?
**FA:** About once a week usually. I'm doing Moscow tomorrow, that's one ... and it's a nice place ... but it's a bit chilly around this time of year.
**P:** The weather there must be very cold. Do you stay there often?
**FA:** Not very often. But you are right; it's not the best place to be in in the winter!
**P:** I like warm weather. Spain, Greece and Italy are my favourite countries.

PAUSE 10 SECONDS

*You will hear the piece again.*

— *** —

REPEAT INSERT
PAUSE 5 SECONDS

*That is the end of Part Four.*
*There will now be a pause of five minutes for you to copy your answers onto the separate answer sheet. Be sure to follow the numbering of all the questions. I shall remind you when there is one minute left, so that you are sure to finish in time.*
PAUSE 4 MINUTES

You have one more minute left.

PAUSE 1 MINUTE

That is the end of the test. Please stop now. Your supervisor will now collect all the question papers and answer sheets.

# TEST 10

*I am going to give you the instructions for this test.*

*I shall introduce each part of the test and give you time to look at the questions.*

*At the start of each piece you will hear this sound:*

— *** —

*You will hear each piece twice.*
*Remember, while you are listening, write your answers on the question paper. You will have* ***five*** *minutes at the end of the test to copy your answers onto the separate answer sheet.*

*There will now be a pause. Please ask any questions now, because you must not speak during the test.*

PAUSE 5 SECONDS

*Now open your question paper and look at* ***Part One****.*

PAUSE 5 SECONDS

*You will hear people talking in eight different situations. For Questions* ***1–8****, choose the best answer (****A****,* ***B*** *or* ***C****).*

***Question 1***
*You are in the service department of an electrical store when you overhear this technician speaking on the telephone.*

PAUSE 2 SECONDS

— *** —

Hello, Lunthan's service department ... Yes, we can repair a colour TV set ... what seems to be the problem? .,. Yes ... yes ... uh, uh ... and the picture is permanently like this? ... and the sound? ... No, no, is the sound clear? ... Ok ... well, if you can just try changing the contrast and brightness controls, they're on the back of that model, and try repositioning the aerial ... and if there's no improvement, ring us again and we'll send a service engineer.

PAUSE 2 SECONDS

— *** —

TAPE REPEAT
PAUSE 2 SECONDS

***Question 2***
*You are in a railway waiting room when you overhear this man speaking.*

PAUSE 2 SECONDS

— *** —

Well, touch wood, I'm completely over it now. I must have been away from my desk for almost a fortnight. Still, they seem to have got by all right without me. After all, I simply couldn't have gone into the office in my condition. I mean, I had a shocking temperature, feeling hot and cold all the time and shivering - and a couple of days I felt so dizzy I couldn't even stand up ... but I'm back on my feet now. Mind you, apparently, there's quite a pile of papers for me waiting when I get back to work.

PAUSE 2 SECONDS

— *** —

TAPE REPEAT
PAUSE 2 SECONDS

***Question 3***
*You are standing at the bar of an English pub when you overhear this exchange.*

PAUSE 2 SECONDS

— *** —

***W*** *= Woman* ***M*** *= Man*

**W:** Can I help you, love?
**M:** Yes, we'd like something to eat ... er, does it all cost the same?
**W:** Yes, all meals are five-fifty including side-salad and a bap.
**M:** That sounds all right. Can I take this over there to show my friends?
**W:** Well, there is only one of them. Couldn't they come over here to have a look?
**M:** Oh, go on. It'll only take a second.
**W:** Oh, right. There you are.

PAUSE 2 SECONDS

— *** —

TAPE REPEAT
PAUSE 2 SECONDS

***Question 4***
*You are visiting the offices of a construction company when you overhear a woman answering the phone.*

PAUSE 2 SECONDS

— *** —

Yes ... Yes ... We're very sorry about that if indeed ... Yes? And your property is next door to the construction site? ... Well, sir, it is our company policy that no work begins before 7 a.m. but we can check with the foreman to see if this rule has in fact been broken ... Well, I can't say anything about that but I think you'll find that if there's been no damage to your actual property, we are not legally required to pay compensation.

PAUSE 2 SECONDS

— *** —

TAPE REPEAT
PAUSE 2 SECONDS

***Question 5***
*You overhear this exchange in an office.*

PAUSE 2 SECONDS

— *** —

***D*** *= David* ***A*** *= Amanda*

**D:** Oh, hi Amanda.
**A:** Hello, David. I've just finished typing this letter ... you know, with the shipping inventory for Uni-Parcel Express Limited.
**D:** And you want my opinion?
**A:** Well, not really. I do know how to write a letter.
**D:** Well, what's the problem then?
**A:** I just wondered if you could read through it and see if I've made any spelling mistakes.
**D:** Well, it's a bit late if you have.
**A:** Well, if there are any, I can just type it up again.

PAUSE 2 SECONDS

— *** —

TAPE REPEAT
PAUSE 2 SECONDS

***Question 6***
*You are listening to the results of football matches on a Saturday sports programme.*

PAUSE 2 SECONDS

— *** —

And now for some late results. Watford 3, Carlisle 0. Bolton Wanderers 1, Cardiff City 3. The Fulham Brighton and Hove Albion match was postponed due to rain and we're still waiting for a score from the West Bromwich Albion - Wolverhampton game which has been delayed by flooding of the pitch ... and ... Sheffield Wednesday 1, Coventry 0, Oxford United 2, Lyme Regis 9 ... FADE

PAUSE 2 SECONDS

— *** —

TAPE REPEAT
PAUSE 2 SECONDS

***Question 7***
*You are at a rock concert where the lead singer makes this announcement.*

PAUSE 2 SECONDS

— *** —

... Thank you, thank you very much. I just want to tell you about one of our fans who can't be here tonight. His name is Simon and right now he's in Southcliff Memorial hospital not far from here. I just want to tell you that he's a brave little guy because he's also very sick, but he's promised to come to our next gig in the UK when he's better and can walk again. This song is for Simon and anyone else with cerebrospinal arthritis.

PAUSE 2 SECONDS

— *** —

TAPE REPEAT
PAUSE 2 SECONDS

***Question 8***
*You are a passenger travelling in a car when you are stopped by a policeman.*

PAUSE 2 SECONDS

— *** —

***P*** *= Policeman* ***M*** *= Man*

**P:** Excuse me, sir. Can I see your licence, please? ... and the insurance documents? ... This is your car I presume.
**M:** Yes, it is my car.
**P:** It's just I did happen to notice while you were stationary at the traffic lights back there, that your tail-lights are not functioning. Were you aware of that?
**M:** Um, yes, the garage is waiting for the part.
**P:** Well then, could I ask you to refrain from using the vehicle in the meantime? Otherwise, there'll be an accident.

PAUSE 2 SECONDS

— *** —

TAPE REPEAT
PAUSE 2 SECONDS

*That is the end of Part One.*
*Now turn to* ***Part Two****.*

PAUSE 5 SECONDS
*You are going to hear somebody giving an introductory talk about a course of lessons at a summer school. For questions* ***9-18****, complete the sentences with a word or short phrase.*

*You now have 45 seconds in which to look at Part 2.*

PAUSE 45 SECONDS

— *** —

Good morning, I'd like to welcome you to Trinity college. It's good to see so many new faces here today although I'm sure most of you are feeling a little lost at the moment. I'm here to give you plenty of information about the college generally and about the course and I'll be more than happy to answer any questions at the end.

At this campus we teach English Literature, history, archaeology, art history and music. For you, the history students, most of your seminars will be held from 9-12.30 in rooms 201 and 95. There is always a coffee break at 10.30 for 20 minutes though.

Many of your lecturers teach here at the college all year round although we also have some very talented visiting lecturers who will just be here for the eight week course that you are following. In the afternoons there will be many field trips which will include castles, museums and stately homes. The highlight of this is always the trip to the British Museum on Saturday 5th July. This museum is particularly famous for the Parthenon Marbles and the Egyptian Mummies which are an important part of our course and so must be seen.

The canteen is open daily from 12.-2.30 p.m. and again from 5-8 p.m. although on Fridays it closes at 7 p.m. There are also recreational facilities in the leisure centre. These are available every day and all are free with the exception of the aerobic classes. I recommend that you take advantage of the excellent sports facilities here, particularly the Olympic size swimming pool.

If any of you have any problems with your accommodation, which I think is highly unlikely, you can find the accommodation officer in Room 16 in Western House. Her name is Mrs. Grosvenor and she will be pleased to help you. Now if there are any questions, now is the time to ask them.

PAUSE 10 SECONDS

*You will hear the piece again.*

— *** —

REPEAT INSERT

PAUSE 5 SECONDS

*That is the end of Part Two.*
*Now turn to* ***Part Three****.*

PAUSE 5 SECONDS

*You will hear five different people talking about incidents at work involving children. For questions* ***19-23****, choose from the list* ***A-H*** *which occupation each speaker has. Use the letters only once. There are three extra letters which you do not need to use.*

*You now have 30 seconds in which to look through Part 3.*

PAUSE 30 SECONDS

— *** —

**Speaker 1**
PAUSE 2 SECONDS

It was an unusually slow Saturday morning, just after the New Year sales, as I recall. I didn't have much to pay attention to at the time and that's how I came to be looking at a youngster in a green and purple shell-suit as he picked up a crystal decanter, looked at it and then put it back on the shelf. But he didn't quite get it right because the next thing I knew, there was an almighty crash. Well, of course, he immediately went running off back to his mum. So, I was more than a little put out when his mum insisted that he'd been right there by her side all the time, so how could he have done it? A very proper lady she was too.

**Speaker 2**
PAUSE 2 SECONDS

It was some time mid-morning after second break when a little four-year-old called Josh came up to me and said his tummy was hurting. Now, we get this all the time, so, at first, I didn't pay too much attention but then a few minutes later, I noticed the same kid sitting on his own away from the others - crying and holding his tummy. He was also sweating and looking really pale. So, after quickly phoning his mum, I asked Sam to take care of my group, bundled Josh into the car and whisked him round to the children's clinic on Preston Road, and it's just as well I did, but it turned out to be appendicitis.

**Speaker 3**
PAUSE 2 SECONDS

Well, I'd only got about half a mile from the school when I noticed this commotion going on in the back. So, I pulled over and stopped and then went down there to see what all the fuss was about. Anyway, there was this really little lad lying on the floor crying his eyes out and all his books and pens and pencils were all over the floor and there were three or four pieces of chewing gum pressed into his hair. Anyway, I knew straight away who'd done it because they were making for the door at the front. But I'd shut it when I'd stopped. Not that I could do very much. If I'd laid a finger on any of them, I'd have lost my licence.

**Speaker 4**
PAUSE 2 SECONDS

Toys aren't at all like other products when it comes to market research. I mean, you can't go out in the street with a clip-board and a questionnaire to assess the response of 5-year-olds to a new inflatable dinosaur. You have to get twenty of them together in a room with a child psychologist present to get some idea of the market potential of anything new. I do remember one occasion when a certain four-year-old managed to break everything we presented him with in a matter of seconds. Needless to say he wasn't invited back again.

**Speaker 5**
PAUSE 2 SECONDS

In legal terms there really should have been no contest at all. The mother had remarried to a very respectable gentleman and she was being very reasonable about things. After all, it was the husband who had divorced her and she still let him keep the house in Watford. All she wanted was to have custody of the child. And according to her rights, she should have ... if it weren't for the child herself. Jenny, she's called, just won't see sense. She's remarkably grown up for a six-year-old and we've talked it over at length. But she just insists on staying with her dad in that run-down maisonette. And until she comes round to our point of view, I won't be collecting my fee.

PAUSE 10 SECONDS

*You will hear the piece again.*

— *** —

TAPE REPEAT
PAUSE 5 SECONDS

*That is the end of Part Three.*
*Now turn to* ***Part Four****.*

PAUSE 5 SECONDS

*You will hear three people, Norman and Linda Hunter, and Linda's friend Patty, talking in a shopping centre about their children. For questions* ***24-30****, choose the best answer* ***A****,* ***B*** *or* ***C****.*

*There will now be a pause of 1 minute for you to look through Part 4.*

PAUSE 1 MINUTE

— *** —

***N*** *= Norman* ***L*** *= Linda* ***P*** *= Patty*

**N:** And then have we finished after 'Smith's'?
**L:** Er ... we've just got to pick up the dry-cleaning and then we'll still get back in time for the match.
**P:** Linda!
**L:** Patty! You've met Norman, haven't you?
**P:** Oh, yes. We met at the Thomson's Christmas party last year.
**N:** Yes, you were telling me all about your young rocket scientist!
**L:** Oh, yes. How is Stewart getting on?
**P:** Oh fine, fine. You know the usual.
**N:** Didn't sound very usual to me.
**L:** Norman! He doesn't mean it. You'll never guess what! Our Matthew's started French lessons; he's only seven and he already knows all the numbers and how to tell the time.
**P:** Yes, Stewart does French and German - after all, languages are so important these days. And you know, the younger you start ...
**N:** Oh, yes, just what every seven-year-old needs. It never caused me any trouble not knowing three languages.
**P:** But this is the nineties. In ten years, everyone will need these things and if you don't invest in his education now, Matthew won't be thanking you in years to come.
**L:** And he can teach us about these things at the same time. He was showing me how to play chess on the computer the other night - he's already got to level three.
**P:** Oh Linda, you ought to find out about these things. He expects to learn from you, not be your teacher. I did a course at night school just so I could show Stewart the important things - and he's progressing so fast now that I've had to start the night classes again.
**L:** I could never manage that - what with the hours I work.
**P:** So you're still doing six nights a week?
**L:** I'm afraid so. Still, tomorrow night's my night off.
**P:** Poor you! I don't know how you put up with it.
**N:** Is your husband still sending you the maintenance cheques every month then?
**L:** Norman!
**P:** Actually, he's my ex-husband now, but he does still send the cheques and he's even agreed to cover Stewart's school fees when he goes to Hanborough in six year's time.
**L:** Oh, how wonderful!

**P:** Well, they do have one of the best computer departments which will be so important in his later life.
**N:** Does Stewart ever have time to play?
**P:** What do you mean? He's got all the latest computer games if that ...
**N:** No, I mean play with other kids, kick a ball around, get in fights ...
**P:** Well, he goes to junior school and he probably does those things ...
**L:** Norman, it's not the same as when we were at school.
**N:** Isn't it? Matthew's a kid isn't he? He likes to laugh sometimes and all he seems to do is one lesson after another. What a way to spend a childhood.
**L:** So, this is about ... *FADE*

PAUSE 10 SECONDS

*You will hear the piece again.*

— *** —

REPEAT INSERT
PAUSE 5 SECONDS

*That is the end of Part Four.*
*There will now be a pause of five minutes for you to copy your answers onto the separate answer sheet. Be sure to follow the numbering of all the questions. I shall remind you when there is one minute left, so that you are sure to finish in time.*

PAUSE 4 MINUTES

You have one more minute left.

PAUSE 1 MINUTE

That is the end of the test. Please stop now. Your supervisor will now collect all the question papers and answer sheets.

# SUCCESSFUL FCE - ANSWER KEY

## TEST 1

### Reading & Use of English

**Part 1**
1B 2D 3B 4D
5B 6D 7C 8C

**Part 2**
9. still 10. myself 11. not
12. take 13. died
14. something 15. though/when
16. draw/work/sketch

**Part 3**
17. observant 18. irrefutable
19. decoration 20. foolish
21. necessarily 22. alternative
23. appreciation 24. adaptable

**Part 4**
25. haven't heard from
26. looked up to
27. in the mood to
28. didn't deserve to be
29. too expensive for him to
30. the exception of Joy

**Part 5**
31C 32A 33A
34B 35C 36B

**Part 6**
37B 38G 39D
40C 41F 42E

**Part 7**
43C 44B 45A 46B 47A
48C 49D 50D 51C 52D

### Listening

**Part 1**
1A 2C 3C 4B
5C 6 A 7B 8B

**Part 2**
9. Bristol 10. alcohol
11. tobacco 12. ten-day course
13. want no more
14. physically sick
15. give up early
16. most unlikely
17. trained personnel
18. great embarrassment

**Part 3**
19H 20E 21D 22F 23C

**Part 4**
24A 25C 26C 27B
28A 29B 30C

## TEST 2

### Reading & Use of English

**Part 1**
1D 2D 3B 4A
5D 6B 7A 8A

**Part 2**
9. for/during 10. few
11. from 12. its/the
13. during/on 14. who/that
15. him 16. together

**Part 3**
17. managerial/management
18. bearable 19. temptation
20. absolutely 21. conference
22. arrival 23. receptionist
24. intentions

**Part 4**
25. isn't used to getting
26. wish you had come
27. didn't succeed in entering
28. must have/get my hair cut
29. wondered why he hadn't
30. is believed to be

**Part 5**
31A 32C 33B
34D 35B 36C

**Part 6**
37F 38A 39E
40D 41G 42C

**Part 7**
43A 44E 45A 46D 47A
48B 49B 50D 51E 52C

### Listening

**Part 1**
1B 2B 3C 4A
5B 6C 7C 8A

**Part 2**
9. newspapers 10. campaigns
11. public eye 12. 4%
13. TV 14. images/pictures
15. fiction/lies 16. £1,000,000
17. apology 18. tabloids

**Part 3**
19G 20B 21F 22C 23E

**Part 4**
24A 25B 26A 27C
28C 29B 30B

## TEST 3

### Reading & Use of English

**Part 1**
1A 2B 3A 4C
5D 6A 7B 8B

**Part 2**
9. was 10. them 11. over
12. country/region 13. looked
14. charge/control/possession
15. What 16. went

**Part 3**
17. modernising 18. delightful
19. invitation 20. employee
21. extensively 22. possessions
23. arrangements 24. transformation

**Part 4**
25. had her hair done
26. is responsible for supervising
27. is a faster reader than
28. denied stealing/having stolen
29. first time we had travelled/been
30. does this car belong to

**Part 5**
31B 32A 33B
34B 35C 36C

**Part 6**
37B 38A 39E
40G 41F 42C

**Part 7**
43A 44A 45D 46C 47B
48D 49B 50B 51D 52C

### Listening

**Part 1**
1C 2B 3B 4C
5B 6A 7B 8A

**Part 2**
9. special dance 10. copying
11. basic ideas 12. grammar
13. consonants 14. awareness
15. more information 16. characteristics 17. large communities 18. contact

**Part 3**
19A 20D 21C 22F 23E

**Part 4**
24B 25A 26A 27C
28B 29A 30C

## TEST 4

### Reading & Use of English

**Part 1**
1A 2D 3C 4B
5A 6D 7A 8A

**Part 2**
9. at/around/over 10. Where
11. year 12. be 13. this/that
14. of 15. had 16. out

**Part 3**
17. criminals 18. prevention
19. careless 20. precautions
21. householders 22. protection
23. opportunist(ic) 24. signature

**Part 4**
25. train gets/takes you to the
26. are not supposed to write
27. was caused by
28. cannot tell the difference
29. may have left early
30. wish our teammate had not

**Part 5**
31D 32C 33D
34B 35B 36D

**Part 6**
37F 38A 39B
40D 41G 42E

**Part 7**
43B 44A 45D 46B 47A
48A 49D 50C 51C 52D

### Listening

**Part 1**
1B 2C 3C 4A
5A 6B 7C 8A

**Part 2**
9. life-sized model 10. purpose
11. terrified 12. Catholics
13. must die 14. a tunnel
15. explosive gunpowder
16. approaching danger
17. caught first 18. harmless fun

**Part 3**
19D 20A 21B 22E 23F

**Part 4**
24C 25A 26A 27B
28A 29C 30B

## TEST 5

### Reading & Use of English

**Part 1**
1D 2B 3D 4B
5A 6C 7B 8C

**Part 2**
9. It 10. play 11. have
12. there 13. was 14. did
15. mine 16. call

**Part 3**
17. competitors 18. provincial
19. peacefully 20. specialise
21. obsession 22. dreadful
23. thunderous 24. innocence

**Part 4**
25. cost us 26. did the expert know 27. Mary nor her mother like 28. the most beautiful houses Helen 29. must have lied 30. looked after her cat

**Part 5**
31C 32B 33B
34A 35C 36A

**Part 6**
37D 38B 39E
40G 41A 42C

**Part 7**
43A 44B 45D 46B 47D
48B 49C 50C 51D 52A

### Listening

**Part 1**
1A 2B 3B 4A
5A 6C 7B 8B

**Part 2**
9. British adults 10. business decisions 11. character
12. foundation/base 13. choice of career 14. artists and entertainers 15. less obvious
16. winter 17. disappointing
18. effects of nature

**Part 3**
19H 20C 21B 22F 23D

**Part 4**
24A 25A 26C 27C
28B 29A 30C

# TEST 6

## Reading & Use of English

**Part 1**
1C 2A 3C 4B
5C 6B 7C 8D

**Part 2**
9. she 10. given
11. say/wave 12. reached
13. somewhere 14. possible
15. girl 16. was

**Part 3**
17. (un)predictable
18. frustration(s)
19. anticipation 20. wonderful
21. unspoilt/unspoiled
22. confident(ly)
23. accommodation
24. homesickness

**Part 4**
25. were made to wash
26. suggested playing
27. can't/couldn't have shown up
28. object to her smoking
29. hasn't been to France
30. will be built by

**Part 5**
31C 32C 33A
34C 35A 36D

**Part 6**
37F 38G 39A
40C 41D 42B

**Part 7**
43B 44A 45B 46D 47C
48C 49B 50C 51D 52A

## Listening

**Part 1**
1C 2B 3A 4C
5C 6A 7B 8C

**Part 2**
9. brakes 10. Great Salt Lake
11. sick 12. track 13. gravity
14. 85 mph 15. scared/fear
16. 40 mph 17. virtual reality
18. warm but dry

**Part 3**
19D 20F 21A 22B 23C

**Part 4**
24C 25B 26B 27A
28A 29C 30A

# TEST 7

## Reading & Use of English

**Part 1**
1A 2D 3C 4D
5B 6C 7D 8A

**Part 2**
9. time 10. hit
11. last/final 12. of/for
13. there 14. with
15. then/so 16. raised/waved

**Part 3**
17. retirement 18. optional
19. formalities 20. maintenance
21. enthusiasm 22. performance
23. eagerness 24. expertise

**Part 4**
25. cause for alarm
26. all (mis)took that man for
27. had his pet dog examined
28. accused her parents of lying
29. village in which we were
30. to take part in

**Part 5**
31A 32A 33C
34B 35C 36D

**Part 6**
37A 38D 39C
40E 41B 42F

**Part 7**
43B 44B 45D 46C 47D
48C 49A 50B 51A 52A

## Listening

**Part 1**
1C 2C 3A 4B
5A 6A 7C 8B

**Part 2**
9. broken bones 10. support
11. hardened 12. (new) blood
13. bend 14. move
15. multiple 16. position
17. previous programmes
18. change in shape

**Part 3**
19F 20B 21A 22C 23E

**Part 4**
24B 25A 26C 27A
28A 29B 30A

# TEST 8

## Reading & Use of English

**Part 1**
1B 2D 3A 4B
5B 6C 7D 8A

**Part 2**
9. course 10. one/punishment
11. whom 12. treat 13. not
14. whole 15. one 16. of

**Part 3**
17. primarily 18. reputation
19. tendency 20. Disturbances
21. implications 22. unpredictable 23. variations
24. distraction

**Part 4**
25. told us not to park
26. to get over his
27. high time we made
28. is said to be leaving
29. was little we could do
30. we didn't eat was

**Part 5**
31B 32D 33D
34A 35C 36C

**Part 6**
37E 38G 39D
40A 41B 42F

**Part 7**
43A 44C 45A 46B 47A
48D 49D 50B 51B 52C

## Listening

**Part 1**
1C 2B 3A 4A
5C 6C 7B 8B

**Part 2**
9. shooting stars 10. car
11. insects 12. iron 13. orbit
14. downwards 15. a jet plane
16. hotter and hotter 17. melts
18. reach the ground

**Part 3**
19G 20B 21E 22F 23A

**Part 4**
24B 25C 26A 27A
28B 29A 30C

# TEST 9

## Reading & Use of English

**Part 1**
1B 2D 3D 4A
5B 6C 7D 8D

**Part 2**
9. it 10. not 11. part/area
12. thought 13. there 14. as
15. end 16. looked/were

**Part 3**
17. treatment 18. illness
19. suspicious 20. inflammation(s) 21. untreated
22. severity 23. assistance
24. disruption

**Part 4**
25. last time I wrote to
26. to cut down on
27. not like Michael to be
28. as / so long as you do
29. is the same age as
30. may not have seen you

**Part 5**
31C 32D 33D
34A 35B 36C

**Part 6**
37C 38B 39A
40F 41G 42E

**Part 7**
43B 44A 45D 46C 47A
48B 49D 50C 51B 52D

## Listening

**Part 1**
1A 2B 3A 4A
5A 6C 7A 8B

**Part 2**
9. hitting 10. telling off
11. the wrong shoes 12. (very) cruel 13. young children
14. the government 15. lazy
16. how lucky 17. changed the law 18. (teenage) crime

**Part 3**
19D 20E 21F 22B 23A

**Part 4**
24B 25B 26A 27C
28A 29C 30B

# TEST 10

## Reading & Use of English

**Part 1**
1C 2D 3D 4B
5A 6D 7C 8C

**Part 2**
9. had 10. going
11. made 12. been
13. it 14. whether/if
15. leave 16. already

**Part 3**
17. stylish 18. assistants
19. imagineable 20. instalments
21. fondness 22. tasteful
23. inspiration 24. excellent

**Part 4**
25. faster we walk the sooner
26. has been learning
27. is his intention to visit
28. must have been
29. would have passed the test
30. had her purse stolen

**Part 5**
31A 32D 33B
34B 35D 36A

**Part 6**
37E 38B 39G
40C 41F 42A

**Part 7**
43B 44B 45C 46B 47A
48A 49A 50A 51B 52C

## Listening

**Part 1**
1B 2C 3A 4C
5B 6A 7B 8A

**Part 2**
9. Trinity 10. History
11. 9 - 12.30 12. 95 and 201
13. 8 weeks 14. The British Museum 15. Egyptian Mummies
16. 2.30, 5 17. Aerobic classes/Aerobics 18. Western House

**Part 3**
19A 20D 21E 22C 23F

**Part 4**
24C 25A 26C 27B
28B 29A 30C

**Published by**
**GLOBAL ELT LTD**
Brighton & Hove
East Sussex, BN2 9YN
www.globalelt.co.uk